The
VOCA⁺
BULARY

완전 개정판

6

The VOCA⊕BULARY 완전 개정판 ⑥

지은이 넥서스영어교육연구소
펴낸이 임상진
펴낸곳 (주)넥서스

출판신고 1992년 4월 3일 제311-2002-2호 [2-4]
10880 경기도 파주시 지목로 5
Tel (02)330-5500 Fax (02)330-5555

ISBN 978-89-98454-39-5 54740
      978-89-98454-33-3 (SET)

www.nexusEDU.kr

The VOCA⁺ BULARY

완전 개정판

6

넥서스영어교육연구소 지음

NEXUS Edu

1 Essential words for the school test

수능, 토플, 텝스 기본 어휘 625개를 선별하여 수록했을 뿐 아니라 영영 풀이, 유의어 및 반의어, 파생어, 접두사를 추가하여 다양한 어휘를 폭넓게 학습할 수 있도록 구성했습니다.

2 Sentence-based recognition

각 표제어마다 예문을 제시하여 단어를 보다 효율적으로 암기할 수 있도록 구성했습니다.

3 Synonym / Antonym / Derivative를 통한 어휘 확장

연계 학습을 통해 각 단어와 관련된 유의어 및 반의어, 파생어를 학습할 수 있도록 구성했습니다.

4 A variety of question types

Exercise → Review Test → Accumulative Test로 이어지는 단계적 테스트를 통해 반복 학습 효과를 높일 수 있도록 구성했습니다.

5 Sound-based recognition

학습한 단어를 음성으로 복습할 수 있도록 음성 파일을 제공하여 청취 실력 향상에 도움이 되도록 구성했습니다.

6 학습 리뷰 테스트 온라인 제공

온라인(www.nexusEDU.kr)을 통해 학습 어휘를 테스트해 보면서 다른 학습자들과 결과를 비교할 수 있어 자신의 학습 성취도를 모니터링할 수 있습니다.

구성과 특징

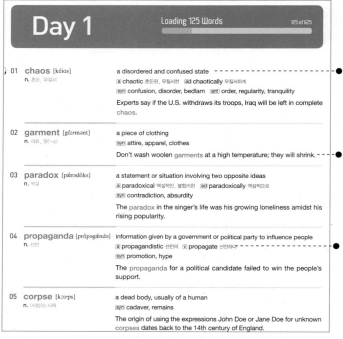

Day Lesson

각 25개씩 단어 목표를 제시하였습니다.

표제어마다 정확한 의미 파악을 위해 영영 풀이를 소개하여 영영 사전으로 학습하는 효과를 얻을 수 있도록 구성했습니다.

Sentence

각 표제어마다 예문을 제시하여 효과적으로 단어를 외울 수 있도록 구성했습니다.

Synonym/Antonym/Derivative

각 단어와 관련된 유의어 및 반의어, 파생어를 학습할 수 있도록 구성했습니다.

Day 1 내용 (이미지 내)

Day 1 Loading 125 Words 125 of 625

01 **chaos** [kéias]
n. 혼돈, 무질서
a disordered and confused state
ⓐ chaotic 혼돈된, 무질서한 ⓐⓓ chaotically 무질서하게
ⓢⓨⓝ confusion, disorder, bedlam ⓐⓝⓣ order, regularity, tranquility
Experts say if the U.S. withdraws its troops, Iraq will be left in complete chaos.

02 **garment** [gá:rmənt]
n. 의류, 옷(~s)
a piece of clothing
ⓢⓨⓝ attire, apparel, clothes
Don't wash woolen garments at a high temperature; they will shrink.

03 **paradox** [pérədàks]
n. 역설
a statement or situation involving two opposite ideas
ⓐ paradoxical 역설적인, 불합리한 ⓐⓓ paradoxically 역설적으로
ⓢⓨⓝ contradiction, absurdity
The paradox in the singer's life was his growing loneliness amidst his rising popularity.

04 **propaganda** [prɑ̀pəgǽndə]
n. 선전
information given by a government or political party to influence people
ⓐ propagandistic 선전의 ⓥ propagate 선전하다
ⓢⓨⓝ promotion, hype
The propaganda for a political candidate failed to win the people's support.

05 **corpse** [kɔːrps]
n. (사람의) 시체
a dead body, usually of a human
ⓢⓨⓝ cadaver, remains
The origin of using the expressions John Doe or Jane Doe for unknown corpses dates back to the 14th century of England.

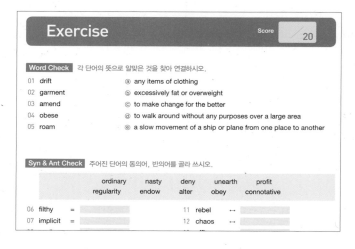

Exercise

Exercise를 통해 학습 단어를 다시 한 번 확인할 수 있습니다.

Exercise 내용 (이미지 내)

Exercise Score 20

Word Check 각 단어의 뜻으로 알맞은 것을 찾아 연결하시오.

01 drift ⓐ any items of clothing
02 garment ⓑ excessively fat or overweight
03 amend ⓒ to make change for the better
04 obese ⓓ to walk around without any purposes over a large area
05 roam ⓔ a slow movement of a ship or plane from one place to another

Syn & Ant Check 주어진 단어의 동의어, 반의어를 골라 쓰시오.

| | ordinary | nasty | deny | unearth | profit |
| | regularity | endow | alter | obey | connotative |

06 filthy =
07 implicit =
11 rebel ↔
12 chaos ↔

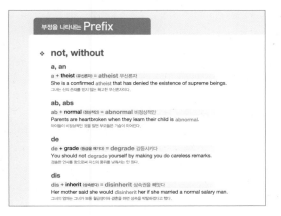

Prefix

알아두면 유용한 접두사를 선별하여 수록했습니다.

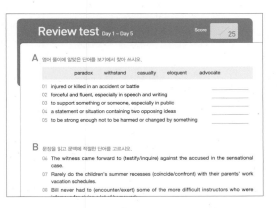

Review Test

5일마다 Review test를 실시하여 앞에서 배운 단어를 한 번 더 검토할 수 있도록 구성했습니다.

Accumulative Test

Accumulative test를 통해 누적된 단어를 다시 한 번 복습할 수 있습니다.

차례

Part 1

Part 2

Part 3

Part 1

---

01 chaos [kéiɑs]
n. 혼돈, 무질서

a disordered and confused state
ⓐ chaotic 혼돈된, 무질서한　ⓐⅾ chaotically 무질서하게
ⓢⓨⓝ confusion, disorder, bedlam　ⓐⓝⓣ order, regularity, tranquility

Experts say if the U.S. withdraws its troops, Iraq will be left in complete chaos.

---

02 garment [gáːrmənt]
n. 의류, 옷(~s)

a piece of clothing
ⓢⓨⓝ attire, apparel, clothes

Don't wash woolen garments at a high temperature; they will shrink.

---

03 paradox [pǽrədɑ̀ks]
n. 역설

a statement or situation involving two opposite ideas
ⓐ paradoxical 역설적인, 불합리한　ⓐⅾ paradoxically 역설적으로
ⓢⓨⓝ contradiction, absurdity

The paradox in the singer's life was his growing loneliness amidst his rising popularity.

---

04 propaganda [prɑ̀pəgǽndə]
n. 선전

information given by a government or political party to influence people
ⓐ propagandistic 선전의　ⓥ propagate 선전하다
ⓢⓨⓝ promotion, hype

The propaganda for a political candidate failed to win the people's support.

---

05 corpse [kɔːrps]
n. (사람의) 시체

a dead body, usually of a human
ⓢⓨⓝ cadaver, remains

The origin of using the expressions John Doe or Jane Doe for unknown corpses dates back to the 14th century of England.

---

06 abnormal [æbnɔ́ːrməl]
a. 비정상적인, 이상한

different from what usually happens or ought to be
ⓝ abnormality 이상, 변칙　ⓐⅾ abnormally 이상하게
ⓢⓨⓝ unnatural, peculiar, unusual　ⓐⓝⓣ normal, usual, ordinary

The abnormal climate change has caused serious problems such as rising sea levels, droughts and floods.

---

01 전문가들은 미국이 자국의 군대를 철수하면 이라크는 무질서 상태에 빠질 것이라고 말한다. 02 높은 온도에서 모직 의류를 세탁하지 마. 옷이 줄어들 거야.
03 인기를 얻을수록 외로움도 커져만갔다는 것이 그 가수의 삶의 역설적인 면이었다. 04 그 정치 입후보자의 선전은 사람들의 지지를 얻는 데 실패했다.
05 신원 미상의 시체를 일컫는 John Doe 또는 Jane Doe 표현의 기원은 14세기 영국으로 거슬러 올라간다. 06 이상 기후 변화는 해수면의 상승, 가뭄, 홍수와 같은 심각한 문제를 야기하고 있다.

07 filthy [fílθi]
a. 불결한, 더러운

extremely dirty

n filth 불결, 오물   ad filthily 불결하게, 더럽게

syn nasty, foul, squalid   ant clean

After the festival ended, the streets were absolutely filthy, covered in trash and dirt.

08 implicit [implísit]
a. 암시적인, 함축적인

suggested or understood, but not stated directly

v imply 함축하다, ~을 뜻하다   ad implicitly 함축적으로

syn implied, suggestive, connotative   ant explicit

The mayor's implicit message was understood by everyone in the room.

09 intimate [íntəmət]
a. 친밀한, 개인적인

having a very close relationship with someone

n intimacy 친밀, 친교   ad intimately 친밀하게

syn familiar, near, private   ant unfriendly, distant, public

Even the strongest and most intimate relationships can suffer under continual public scrutiny.

10 magnificent [mægnífəsnt]
a. 장대한, 훌륭한

very impressive because of being big, beautiful, etc.

n magnificence 장대, 훌륭함   ad magnificently 장대하게, 훌륭히

syn splendid, grand, imposing, excellent   ant ordinary

The scene spreading beyond the valley was magnificent.

11 obese [oubíːs]
a. 비만의

extremely or abnormally fat

n obesity 비만, 비대

syn corpulent, overweight   ant slender, skinny, underweight

Obese people are more likely to have suffered from heart disease, diabetes or high blood pressure.

12 affirm [əfə́ːrm]
v. 단언하다, 긍정하다

to state publicly that something is true

n affirmation 확언, 단언   a affirmative 확언적인, 긍정적인

syn confirm, assert, verify   ant deny, negate, contradict

The governor officially affirmed his position on illegal drugs.

13 amend [əménd]
v. 개정하다, 개선하다

to make small changes or improvements, especially in the law

n amendment 변경, 개선   a amendatory 개정의, 수정의

syn revise, improve   ant damage, impair, worsen

The state legislature voted not to amend the constitution.

---

07 축제가 끝나자 거리는 쓰레기와 오물로 뒤덮여 정말 지저분했다. 08 그 방 안의 모든 사람들은 시장이 암시하는 메시지를 이해했다. 09 가장 강하고 친밀한 관계라 해도 끊임없이 다른 사람들의 감시를 받으면 그 관계는 위태로워질 수 있다. 10 계곡 너머로 펼쳐진 광경은 장대했다. 11 비만인 사람들은 심장 질환, 당뇨병 또는 고혈압을 앓고 있을 가능성이 크다. 12 주지사는 공식적으로 불법 마약에 관한 그의 입장을 단언했다. 13 입법부는 헌법을 개정하지 않기로 했다.

14 avail [əvéil]

v. 도움이 되다, 쓸모가 있다

n. 이익, 효용

to be use of or take advantage of

n availability 이용도, 유효성   a available 쓸모 있는, 유효한

syn profit, benefit, utilize, usefulness   ant harm, hinder, hurt

You can avail of our exclusive services by registering your personal information.

It is of no avail to give him such advice now.

---

15 confide [kənfáid]

v. 털어놓다, 신용하다

to tell a secret to someone who one trusts

n confidence 신뢰   a confident 확신하는   a confidential 기밀의

syn unbosom, disclose, reveal, trust   ant conceal, hide, distrust

Having someone we can confide in has a positive effect on our mental health.

---

16 deprive [dipráiv]

v. 빼앗다, 박탈하다

to take something that someone needs away from him

n deprivation 박탈, 해임   a deprived 빈곤한, 풍족하지 못한

syn strip, divest, despoil   ant endow, present, provide, supply

In most third world countries poverty deprives children of the right of being educated.

---

17 dismay [disméi]

v. 당황케 하다, 낙담시키다

n. 당황, 실망

to make someone feel disappointed and unhappy

a dismaying 당황하게 하는   ad dismayingly 당황하게 하여

syn disappoint, depress, discouragement   ant encourage, stimulate

The bad grade dismayed Melissa because she'd studied so hard in class.

The man's face had a look of great dismay on it.

---

18 plead [pliːd]

v. 간청[탄원]하다

to ask for something that someone wants very much, in an earnest way

pleading n 변명, 탄원 a 탄원[간청]하는   n plea 간청, 변명

syn implore, solicit, appeal   ant command, order

After the accident, the injured people pleaded for help from a stranger.

---

19 excavate [ékskəvèit]

v. 파다, 발굴하다

to dig a hole in the ground

n excavation 발굴, 굴착

syn shovel, unearth   ant bury, embed

On their second survey, a large amount of dinosaur fossils were excavated.

---

14 개인 정보를 등록하시면 저희 최고의 서비스를 이용하실 수 있습니다. 이제 와서 그에게 그런 조언을 해봐야 아무 소용없다. 15 마음을 털어놓을 수 있는 사람이 있다는 것은 우리의 정신 건강에 긍정적인 효과를 가져온다. 16 대부분의 제3세계의 국가에서 가난은 아이들이 교육받을 권리를 박탈한다. 17 수업 시간에 정말 열심히 공부한 Melissa는 자신의 성적이 엉망인 것을 보자 낙담했다. 그 남자의 얼굴에 당황한 기색이 역력했다. 18 사고가 난 뒤, 부상자들은 낯선 사람에게 도움을 요청했다. 19 그들의 두 번째 답사에서 많은 공룡화석이 발굴되었다.

20 halt [hɔːlt]
v. 정지시키다
n. 정지, 멈춤

to make something stop
[syn] discontinue, cease, pause　[ant] start, commence, continue

Policemen rushed forward to halt the protest march at the venue of the conference.

The manager called a temporary halt to the project since there was lack of funds.

21 modify [mάdəfài]
v. 변경하다, 수정하다

to make small changes in something to improve it
[n] modification 변경, 수정　[a] modifying 변경[수정]하는
[syn] vary, alter, revise　[ant] maintain, preserve, retain

Marketing plans should be modified consistently to meet growing customer demands in the fast changing global market.

22 drift [drift]
v. 표류하다
n. 표류, 흐름

to move very slowly through air or on the surface of the water
[a] drifting 표류하는
[syn] float, blow, waft　[ant] lead, steer, guide

Sometimes it's wonderful to just lie still and watch the clouds drift through the sky.

The oil slick has continued to spread south affected by the drift of the current and the wind.

23 rebel [rébəl]
v. 반항하다
n. 반역자, 저항자

to oppose or fight against someone who is in authority
[n] rebellion 반란, 폭동　[a] rebellious 반역하는, 반역자의
[syn] defy, resist, revolt, riot　[ant] obey, comply

The teenager often tends to rebel against their parents and society.

People unused to change tend to think of those with fresh ideas as rebels.

24 restrain [ristréin]
v. 억제[제지]하다

to prevent someone from doing something
[n] restraint 억제, 제지　[a] restrained 자제하는, 억제된
[syn] confine, curb, restrict　[ant] encourage

Restraining your desire is one of the most difficult things to do.

25 roam [roum]
v. 배회하다

to walk or travel for a long time with no clear purpose
[n] roamer 배회자, 방랑자
[syn] wander, ramble, stroll　[ant] stay

Wild animals escaped from the zoo were roaming around the streets.

---

20 시위대의 행진을 진압하기 위해 경찰들이 서둘러 회담 장소로 향했다. 자금이 부족했기 때문에 매너저는 그 사업을 일시적으로 중지하라고 명했다. 21 급속히 변화하는 세계 시장에서 증가하는 소비자들의 욕구를 충족시키기 위해서 마케팅 계획은 끊임없이 수정되어야 한다. 22 가끔은 가만히 누워서 하늘 위의 떠다니는 구름을 보는 것이 정말 좋다. 기름띠는 해류의 흐름과 바람의 영향을 받아 계속해서 남쪽으로 확산되고 있다. 23 청소년들은 종종 그들의 부모와 사회에 반항하는 경향을 보인다. 변화에 익숙치 않은 사람들은 참신한 생각을 가진 사람들을 반항자로 여기는 경향이 있다. 24 당신의 욕망을 억제하는 것이 가장 하기 어려운 일 중 하나이다. 25 동물원에서 탈출한 야생 동물들이 거리를 배회하고 있었다.

Exercise

/ 20

Word Check 각 단어의 뜻으로 알맞은 것을 찾아 연결하시오.

01 drift   ⓐ any items of clothing
02 garment   ⓑ excessively fat or overweight
03 amend   ⓒ to make change for the better
04 obese   ⓓ to walk around without any purposes over a large area
05 roam   ⓔ a slow movement of a ship or plane from one place to another

Syn & Ant Check 주어진 단어의 동의어, 반의어를 골라 쓰시오.

ordinary	nasty	deny	unearth	profit
regularity	endow	alter	obey	connotative

06 filthy   = _____   11 rebel   ↔ _____

07 implicit   = _____   12 chaos   ↔ _____

08 avail   = _____   13 affirm   ↔ _____

09 excavate = _____   14 deprive   ↔ _____

10 modify   = _____   15 abnormal ↔ _____

Sentence Practice 문장을 읽고 빈칸에 알맞은 단어를 고르시오.

16 Celebrities are often in the _____ of being famous but lonely.
   ⓐ garment   ⓑ corpse   ⓒ propaganda   ⓓ paradox

17 At times of crisis we expect our _____ friends to rally around us.
   ⓐ filthy   ⓑ abnormal   ⓒ implicit   ⓓ intimate

18 She was filled with _____ at the thought of having to redo her assignment.
   ⓐ drift   ⓑ halt   ⓒ dismay   ⓓ rebel

19 The father went against all his principles to _____ to the judge on behalf of his erring son.
   ⓐ plead   ⓑ deprive   ⓒ avail   ⓓ roam

20 The four hefty policemen struggled to _____ the criminal from doing harm to himself.
   ⓐ modify   ⓑ restrain   ⓒ confide   ⓓ amend

Day 2

01 sake [seik]
n. 동기, 이유

a reason or purpose for doing something
[syn] motive, interest, benefit
For the sake of the future of our country, change in education policy is needed.

02 sanctuary [sǽŋktʃuèri]
n. 신성한 장소, 피난처

a holy place, especially a church or temple
[syn] altar, chancel, sanctum, shelter
The church had a beautiful sanctuary with many colorful windows.
This sanctuary for street kids was established in 2005.

03 spectator [spékteitər]
n. 구경꾼, 관객

someone who watches without taking an active part
[n] spectacle 광경, 장관 [a] spectacular 구경거리의, 장관의
[syn] bystander, onlooker, viewer [ant] participant, player
Many spectators left the game early because it was boring.

04 tremor [trémər]
n. 떨림, 전율

any tremulous or vibratory movement
[a] tremulous 떠는, 떨리는 [ad] tremulously 떨려서
[syn] vibration, trembling, shaking, quiver [ant] stillness
A few small tremors occurred before the large earthquake.

05 vacuum [vǽkjuəm]
n. 진공, 진공 상태
v. 진공 청소기로 청소하다

a space entirely without matter
[syn] void, vacuity, vacuum-clean
Beyond the life-giving oxygen of earth's atmosphere is an airless vacuum.
We vacuum our carpets every week to keep them free of dust.

06 apprehension [æ̀prihénʃən]
n. 이해, 불안

perception or understanding
[a] apprehensive 이해가 빠른 [v] apprehend 이해하다
[syn] comprehension, anxiety, worry [ant] misunderstanding, incomprehension
Last semester I took calculus, which was beyond my apprehension.
The author views the future of the earth with more apprehension than hope.

01 우리나라의 미래를 위해 교육 정책의 변화가 필요하다. 02 교회에는 화려한 창으로 꾸며진 성소가 있었다. 거리를 배회하는 아이들을 위한 이 안식처는 2005년에 설립되었습니다. 03 게임이 지루해서 많은 관객들은 자리에서 일찍 일어났다. 04 엄청난 지진이 발생하기 전에 몇 차례의 미진이 있었다. 05 생명을 주는 산소를 포함하고 있는 지구의 대기 너머에는 공기가 없는 진공 상태이다. 우리는 먼지를 없애기 위해 매주 진공청소기로 카펫을 청소한다. 06 지난 학기에 미적분 수업을 받았는데 도통 이해할 수가 없었어. 그 작가는 지구의 미래를 희망보다는 걱정스러운 시각으로 바라보고 있다.

07 **thesis** [θí:sis]
n. 논제, 논문

a proposition to be defended in argument
[syn] premise, treatise

A doctoral thesis in any discipline requires several years of careful research and study.

08 **profound** [prəfáund]
a. 조예가 깊은, 깊은

showing deep insight or understanding
[n] profundity 깊음, 심원 [ad] profoundly 깊이, 완전히
[syn] knowledgeable, informed, bottomless [ant] superficial, shallow

Something as simple as daily exercise is said to have a profound impact on one's mental well-being.

09 **secondary** [sékəndèri]
a. 제2위의, 부차적인

next after the first in order, place, time, etc.
[ad] secondarily 제2위로, 종속으로
[syn] subsequent, inessential, minor [ant] main, primary

The quality of life is of secondary importance to people dying of starvation.

10 **bleak** [bli:k]
a. (전망 등이) 어두운, 황량한

providing little or no hope
[n] bleakness 적막함, 음침함 [ad] bleakly 적막하게, 음침하게
[syn] gloomy, hopeless, bare, deserted [ant] hopeful, lush

The future of the Indian Tiger looks bleak unless something drastic is done to save its dwindling numbers.
A strong wind blew over the bleak and barren landscape of the desert.

11 **adequate** [ǽdikwət]
a. 적당한, 충분한

enough or suitable for what is required
[n] adequacy 적당함, 타당성 [ad] adequately 적당히, 충분히
[syn] sufficient, decent [ant] inadequate, insufficient, unsuitable

People with depression should receive adequate medical treatment since it can cause secondary disorders.

12 **slaughter** [slɔ́:tər]
v. 도살하다, 학살하다
n. 도살, 학살

to kill animals, especially for food
[a] slaughterous 살육을 좋아하는, 잔인한
[syn] butcher, killing, carnage, massacre

Nazis slaughtered about six million Jews during the Second World War.
The online video clip shows truly how cows are treated during the slaughter.

---

07 어떤 분야든지 박사학위 논문을 쓰기 위해서는 수년간의 면밀한 조사와 연구를 해야 한다. 08 매일 하는 운동처럼 간단한 것이 우리의 정신 건강에 깊은 영향을 준다고 한다. 09 삶의 질은 배고픔으로 죽어가는 사람들에게는 그리 중요하지 않다. 10 줄어드는 개체 수를 늘리기 위해 과감한 조치를 취하지 않으면 인디안 호랑이의 미래는 어두워질 것이다. 강풍이 사막의 황량하고 척박한 땅에 일었다. 11 우울증에 걸린 사람들은 우울증이 이차적인 장애를 유발할 수 있기 때문에 적절한 의학 치료를 받아야 한다. 12 나치는 2차 세계대전 당시 6백만여 명의 유대인을 학살했다. 그 온라인 동영상은 도살 과정에서 소들이 어떻게 처리되는지를 여실히 보여준다.

13 **surpass** [sərpǽs]

v. 능가하다, (한계를) 넘다

to be superior to someone or something

[a] surpassing 뛰어난, 빼어난　[ad] surpassingly 뛰어나게

[syn] exceed, excel, outdo　[ant] fail, lose, fall behind

The company has already surpassed the break even point in the last quarter.

14 **teem** [tiːm]

v. 충만하다, 가득 차다

to be full of moving people or animals

[a] teeming 가득 찬, 풍부한　[ad] teemingly 가득 차게

[syn] swarm, pullulate　[ant] lack, need, want

The weekly outdoor markets usually teem with buyers before the holiday season.

15 **wander** [wάndər]

v. 헤매다

to move or travel around an area without a clear direction or purpose

[a] wandering 헤매는, 방랑하는　[ad] wanderingly 헤매어, 방랑하여

[syn] amble, ramble, roam, stray　[ant] stay

She found herself wandering aimlessly barefoot around the park.

16 **abound** [əbáund]

v. 풍부하다, 많다

to exist in great numbers

[n] abundance 풍부, 충만　[a] abundant 풍부한

[syn] swarm, teem, pullulate　[ant] lack, want

Toronto is a global city that abounds with people of diverse cultural backgrounds.

17 **accelerate** [æksélərèit]

v. 가속하다

to increase the speed

[n] acceleration 촉진, 가속　[a] accelerative 가속적인, 촉진시키는

[syn] quicken, speed　[ant] slow, retard, decelerate

Cars should not accelerate from low speeds to high when going through dangerous mountain curves.

18 **immerse** [imə́ːrs]

v. 담그다, 몰두시키다

to be put completely in something

[n] immersion 담금, 투입

[syn] dip, plunge, engross, absorb

You can increase your blood circulation by immersing your feet in warm water.

Olga became immersed in English by having to speak it every day in Canada.

---

13 그 회사는 지난 분기 때 이미 손익분기점을 넘겼다. 14 야외에서 매주 열리는 장은 보통 휴가철 전엔 쇼핑객들로 발 디딜 틈이 없다. 15 그녀는 정처없이 맨발로 공원을 헤매고 있는 자신을 발견했다. 16 Toronto는 다양한 문화 배경을 가진 사람으로 가득 찬 세계적인 도시이다. 17 산에서 위험한 커브길을 돌 때에는 자동차의 속도가 낮은 상태에서 가속하면 안 된다. 18 따뜻한 물에 발을 담그면 혈액 순환을 촉진할 수 있습니다. 캐나다에서 Olga는 매일 영어로 말을 해 영어에 몰두할 수 있었다.

19 withstand [wiθstǽnd]
v. 견디다, 버티다

to remain unchanged or unharmed by something

[a] withstanding 견디어 내는

[syn] endure, bear [ant] surrender, yield

The explorers withstood the harsh weather conditions and survived.

---

20 classify [klǽsəfài]
v. 분류하다

to arrange in classes according to a system

[n] classification 분류, 구분 [a] classified 분류된

[syn] assort, sort, categorize [ant] disorganize, disorder, disarrange

Your project is classified Top Secret for another month.

---

21 fluctuate [flʌ́ktʃuèit]
v. 변동하다

to be continually varying in an irregular way

[n] fluctuation 변동 [a] fluctuating 변동이 있는

[syn] alter, vary, change [ant] steady

The train's schedule fluctuates because of the weather and the number of passengers.

---

22 coincide [kòuinsáid]
v. 동시에 일어나다, 일치하다

to coexist in the same time, space or position

[n] coincidence 일치, 부합 [a] coincidental 일치하는, 부합하는

[syn] co-occur, correspond, concur [ant] clash, differ, disagree

A change of plan will ensure that the advertisement campaign coincides with the product launch.

---

23 degrade [digréid]
v. 지위를 낮추다, 강등시키다

to treat someone without respect or make worse

[n] degradation 강등, 하락 [a] degraded 품위가 떨어진 [a] degrading 품위를 떨어뜨리는

[syn] demote, discredit, belittle [ant] admire, promote, upgrade

She left the party to avoid watching her colleagues degrade themselves by drinking too much at it.

---

24 elevate [éləvèit]
v. 올리다, 향상시키다

to move something or someone to the higher position

[n] elevation 높이, 고지 [a] elevated 높은

[syn] lift, raise [ant] decrease, drop, lower

Infection with a virus can elevate our body temperature.

---

25 confront [kənfrʌ́nt]
v. 직면하다

to face something or someone, especially boldly or defiantly

[n] confrontation 직면 [a] confrontational 대립의, 대치되는

[syn] front, encounter, meet [ant] avoid, evade

The new administration confronted serious issues of the country soon after taking office.

---

19 그 탐험가들은 혹독한 날씨를 견디어 살아 남았다. 20 당신의 프로젝트는 한 달 더 절대 보안 등급으로 분류될 것입니다. 21 열차 운행 시간표는 날씨와 승객 수에 따라 바뀐다. 22 계획이 바뀌어 제품 광고가 새 상품의 출시와 함께 시작될 것이다. 23 그녀는 동료가 술을 너무 마셔 자신들의 품위를 떨어뜨리는 것이 보기 싫어 파티에서 일찍 나왔다. 24 바이러스 감염이 우리 체온을 높일 수 있다. 25 새 행정부가 출범하고 나서 곧 국가 주요 문제에 직면했다.

Exercise

Word Check 각 단어의 뜻으로 알맞은 것을 찾아 연결하시오.

01	confront	ⓐ	hopeless and depressing
02	immerse	ⓑ	to dip something into in a liquid
03	vacuum	ⓒ	space which is entirely empty of matter
04	bleak	ⓓ	to contain something in large number or amount
05	abound	ⓔ	to bring face to face in a brave or defiant way

Syn & Ant Check 주어진 단어의 동의어, 반의어를 골라 쓰시오.

comprehension	stray	primary	sufficient	surrender
trembling	exceed	lack	promote	lower

06	adequate	=	11	elevate	↔
07	apprehension	=	12	degrade	↔
08	tremor	=	13	secondary	↔
09	wander	=	14	teem	↔
10	surpass	=	15	withstand	↔

Sentence Practice 문장을 읽고 빈칸에 알맞은 단어를 고르시오.

16 One lucky stadium _____ got to meet the winning team after the match.

 ⓐ sake   ⓑ spectator   ⓒ thesis   ⓓ tremor

17 Meditation often leads to a _____ sense of calm and inner peace.

 ⓐ profound   ⓑ bleak   ⓒ secondary   ⓓ adequate

18 The car spun out of control when the driver tried to _____ to high speeds.

 ⓐ teem   ⓑ accelerate   ⓒ wander   ⓓ surpass

19 The temperatures in this region are likely to _____ between 50 and 80 degrees Fahrenheit all this week.

 ⓐ confront   ⓑ degrade   ⓒ abound   ⓓ fluctuate

20 It took me several hours to _____ all the documents according to the manager's instructions.

 ⓐ immerse   ⓑ slaughter   ⓒ coincide   ⓓ classify

01 timber [tímbər]
n. 목재

trees and wood used for building houses, ships and making furniture, etc.
syn wood, lumber

As illegal logging has accelerated, Indonesia has become the world's largest timber producer.

---

02 glaze [gleiz]
n. 유약, 광택
v. 유약을 바르다, 광택[윤]이 나다

a thin liquid that produces a shiny surface on pottery or foods
a glazed 유약을 바른, 광택이 있는
syn gloss, enamel, polish

Ted watched in fascination as the master chef added the chocolate glaze to the pudding.
All of our pottery is glazed with a lead-free glaze.

---

03 compass [kʌ́mpəs]
n. 나침반, 컴퍼스
v. 일주하다, 둘러싸다

an instrument for showing directions
syn enclose, surround, encircle

The compass needle always points north because of the earth's north and south magnetic fields.
The soldiers completely compassed the city before they attacked.

---

04 casualty [kǽʒuəlti]
n. 사상자, 피해자

someone who is hurt or killed in an accident or battle
syn fatality, victim, injured

The total number of fire casualties has been increasing dramatically.

---

05 realm [relm]
n. 왕국, 범위, 영역

a country over which a king or queen rules
syn kingdom, domain, region, field

Freud explored the realm of unconsciousness in his book, *The Interpretation of Dreams*.

---

06 tyrant [táiərənt]
n. 폭군

a cruel and oppressive ruler or master
n tyranny 폭정, 압제   a tyrannical 전제적인   v tyrannize 폭정을 펴다
syn despot, autocrat, dictator   ant democrat

Macbeth is portrayed as a power hungry tyrant who lost his soul in the book.

---

01 불법 벌목이 가속화되면서, 인도네시아가 세계에서 가장 많은 목재를 생산하는 국가가 되었다. 02 Ted는 주방장이 푸딩에 초콜릿 액을 바르는 것을 넋을 잃고 바라보았다. 저희는 모든 도자기 제품에 납이 포함되지 않은 유약을 바릅니다. 03 지구의 북극과 남극의 자기력 때문에 나침반의 자침은 항상 북쪽을 가리킨다. 공격하기 전 군인들은 그 도시를 완전히 포위했다. 04 화재로 인한 총 사상자 수가 급격히 증가하고 있다. 05 Freud는 그의 책 '꿈의 해석'에서 무의식의 영역을 탐구했다. 06 그 책에서 Mecbeth는 영혼을 잃어버리고 권력에 굶주린 폭군으로 그려지고 있다.

07 outburst [áutbə̀:rst]

n. 폭발, 분출

a sudden release as of feeling or energy

[syn] eruption, blowup, outbreak, explosion

Donna's angry outburst during the executive committee meeting yesterday took us all by surprise.

08 recruit [rikrú:t]

n. 신병, 신참자, 모집 신고

v. 모집하다

a new member of a group or the military

[n] recruiter 신병[신인] 모집자

[syn] newcomer, levy, enlist   [ant] veteran, dismiss

The army recruits will take basic training such as physical training, weapon handling and shooting and first aid.

The teacher recruited some students to play baseball for his school.

09 dilemma [dilémə]

n. 딜레마, 진퇴 양난

a situation requiring a choice between unpleasant alternatives

[a] dilemmatic 딜레마의, 진퇴 양난의

[syn] perplexity, predicament, quandary

Matt's dilemma was between staying with his sick mother and attending his daughter's court hearing.

10 pat [pæt]

n. 가볍게 두드림

v. 가볍게 두드리다

a gentle tap or stroke with the hand or a flat object

[syn] tap, rap, chuck

Children enjoy it when their mothers give them pats on the back for doing well.

Maria watched the women at the exhibition pat the clay into beautiful shapes.

11 scope [skoup]

n. 범위, 영역

v. 자세히 보다

the area of action, things, activity, etc.

[a] scopeless (활동) 영역이 없는

[syn] range, extent

Your question lies beyond the scope of this report.

The surgeon scoped the soccer player's knee and repaired it.

12 laborious [ləbɔ́:riəs]

a. 힘든, 고된

requiring hard work, much time and effort

[n] labor 노동, 노력   [ad] laboriously 애써서, 고생하여

[syn] arduous, hard   [ant] easy, simple

The task of taking the census is laborious because workers must go to each home or apartment to ask questions.

---

07 어제 집행 위원회 회의에서 동안 Donna의 화가 폭발해 우리를 놀라게 했다. 08 신병들은 체력 단련, 무기를 다루고 쏘는 법, 응급 처지법과 같은 기본적인 훈련을 받게 될 것이다. 선생님은 학교 야구 팀에서 뛸 선수를 모집했다. 09 아픈 어머니의 옆을 지켜야 하는지 아니면 딸의 법원 심리를 참석을 해야 할 것인지를 선택하는 것이 Matt가 처한 딜레마였다. 10 아이들은 엄마가 잘했다고 등을 두드려 주는 것을 좋아한다. Maria는 전시회에서 여인들이 진흙을 두드려 아름다운 모양으로 만드는 것을 보았다. 11 당신의 질문은 이 보고에 관한 내용이 아닙니다. 의사는 그 축구선수의 무릎을 자세히 살펴본 후 치료를 시작했다. 12 조사자가 한 사람 한 사람의 집이나 아파트를 방문해 설문을 해야 하기 때문에 국세조사는 매우 힘든 업무이다.

13 partial [pάːrʃəl]

a. 부분적인, 불공평한, 불완전한

relating to only a part of something

n partiality 부분적임, 불공평   ad partially 부분적으로, 불공평하게

syn unfair, unjust, incomplete   ant whole, impartial, complete

Most students have only a partial understanding of the concept of chemical equilibrium because it is so complex.

The reporter was partial in his coverage of the political candidate.

14 prehistoric [prìːhistɔ́ːrik]

a. 선사의, 옛날의

of the period before recorded history

n prehistory 선사학

syn ancient, old, early

The discovery of prehistoric fossils in Africa throws new light upon the process of evolution.

15 extraterrestrial [èkstrətəréstriəl]

a. 지구 밖의
n. 외계인

being of or from outside the earth's limits

syn alien   ant earthly, worldly

There is still no apparent evidence for the existence of extraterrestrial life.

One of the Steven Spielberg's movies, E.T. is about friendship between a boy and an extraterrestrial.

16 implore [implɔ́ːr]

v. 간청하다

to ask for something in an emotional way

n imploration 간청, 애원   a imploring 탄원[애원]하는

syn beg, appeal, entreat

Community leaders came forward to implore the people to stay calm in the difficult circumstances.

17 entangle [intǽŋgl]

v. 얽히게 하다, 말려들게 하다

to involve in a difficulty or a tangle

n entanglement 얽힘, 함정

syn complicate, engage   ant disentangle, extricate, disengage

My brother became entangled with some bad friends and their problems.

18 depict [dipíkt]

v. 묘사하다, 표현하다

to describe something by drawing, painting, etc.

n depiction 묘사, 서술   a depictive 서술[묘사]적인

syn represent, portray, delineate

The main character was depicted in the movie as a good man.

---

13 대부분의 학생은 화학 평형 개념이 너무 복잡했기 때문에 그 개념을 완전히 이해할 수 없었다. 기자는 그 정치 입후보자에 대해 편파적으로 기사를 썼다. 14 아프리카에서 발견되는 선사시대의 화석은 진화 과정을 새롭게 조명해 준다. 15 외계 생명체가 존재한다는 확실한 증거는 아직 없다. Steven Spielberg의 영화 중 하나인 'E.T.'는 소년과 외계인의 우정을 그리고 있다. 16 그 지역 지도자는 사람들에게 어려운 상황에서도 침착함을 유지해 달라고 부탁하기 위해 앞으로 나섰다. 17 내 동생은 나쁜 친구들과 문제에 휘말리게 되었다. 18 주인공은 영화에서 선한 사람으로 그려졌다.

19 encounter [inkáuntər]

v. 만나다, 직면하다

to meet someone or something unexpectedly

syn confront, face   ant avoid, retreat, escape

I encountered an old friend that I hadn't seen for 10 years while walking to work.

20 grin [grin]

v. 방긋 웃다, (고통 등으로) 이를 드러내다
n. 싱긋 웃음

to show the teeth in a smile or pain

syn smile, beam   ant frown, scowl

The hockey player grinned and revealed a missing front tooth.

The children laughed at the circus clown's silly grin.

21 fling [fliŋ]

v. 내던지다

to throw, especially with force

syn hurl, sling, pitch   ant catch, seize

The boy flung off his coat as he ran inside the house.

22 exert [igzə́:rt]

v. (능력, 힘 등을) 쓰다, 발휘하다

to put into action with great effort

n exertion 힘을 내기, 발휘   a exertive 노력하는, 힘을 발휘하는

syn exercise, apply, utilize

Dylan had to exert great pressure to open the warped door of the shack.

23 oversee [òuvərsí:]

v. 감시[감독]하다

to be in charge of a job, person, activity, etc.

n overseer 감독관, 관리인

syn superintend, supervise, manage   ant overlook, mismanage

Greg will be appointed to oversee a new project team.

24 inquire [inkwáiər]

v. 묻다, 조사하다

to ask for information about something

n inquiry 질문, 문의, 조사   a inquiring 묻는, 알고 싶어하는

syn interrogate, question, investigate   ant answer, respond

If you would like to inquire further information, please contact our sales department.

The police will inquire into his other business agreements.

25 impair [impέər]

v. 손상시키다

to make worse or less

n impairment 감손, 손상   a impaired 약화된, 장애가 있는

syn damage, spoil, disfigure   ant enhance, improve

Too much TV can impair children's observational and imaginative capacities.

---

19 회사로 걸어가는데 10년 동안 만나지 못했던 오랜 친구를 만났다. 20 하키 선수가 웃자, 앞니가 빠진 게 드러났다. 아이들이 서커스 광대의 바보같은 미소에 웃음을 터뜨렸다. 21 소년은 집안으로 뛰어오면서 외투를 내던졌다. 22 Dylan은 판잣집의 찌그러진 문을 열려고 세게 밀어야만 했다. 23 새로운 사업팀을 감독하도록 Greg가 임명될 것이다. 24 보다 더 자세한 정보를 문의하시려면 저희 영업부로 연락해 주십시오. 경찰은 그의 다른 사업 계약을 조사할 것이다. 25 과도한 TV 시청은 아이들의 관찰력과 상상력을 저해할 수도 있다.

Exercise

Word Check 각 단어의 뜻으로 알맞은 것을 찾아 연결하시오.

01 dilemma   ⓐ to seek information by asking

02 encounter   ⓑ to look at or over someone or something carefully

03 scope   ⓒ the wood of a tree, cut and used as building materials, etc.

04 inquire   ⓓ to be faced with someone or something usually, without intention

05 timber   ⓔ a situation that requires a choice from two options, neither pleasant

Syn & Ant Check 주어진 단어의 동의어, 반의어를 골라 쓰시오.

eruption	catch	apply	enhance	arduous
victim	disengage	entreat	earthly	veteran

06 outburst = _____

07 exert = _____

08 laborious = _____

09 implore = _____

10 casualty = _____

11 fling ↔ _____

12 impair ↔ _____

13 entangle ↔ _____

14 extraterrestrial ↔ _____

15 recruit ↔ _____

Sentence Practice 문장을 읽고 빈칸에 알맞은 단어를 고르시오.

16 Elizabeth I successfully brought religious peace to her _____ after decades of strife.

     ⓐ realm   ⓑ outburst   ⓒ timber   ⓓ dilemma

17 The class felt that the teacher was being unduly _____ to the bright students.

     ⓐ prehistoric   ⓑ laborious   ⓒ partial   ⓓ extraterrestrial

18 The paintings in the old castle _____ some of the most compelling scenes of 16th Century Dutch life.

     ⓐ implore   ⓑ exert   ⓒ impair   ⓓ depict

19 The _____ arrested everyone who opposed his brutal regime and had them executed.

     ⓐ tyrant   ⓑ recruit   ⓒ glaze   ⓓ pat

20 An expert was called in from abroad to _____ preparations for the international event.

     ⓐ encounter   ⓑ impair   ⓒ entangle   ⓓ oversee

🎧 **01 agenda** [ədʒéndə]

n. 의제, 일정

a plan or list of matters to be acted upon or discussed

ⓐ agendaless 의제가 없는

syn schedule, program, docket

Economic stability could be the most important part of the agenda for the new administration.

---

02 throb [θrɑb]

n. 고동, 진동

v. 고동치다

a strong beat or vibration

ⓐ throbbing 고동치는, 두근거리는　ad throbbingly 고동치는

syn pulse, pulsation, pulsate

After mouth-to-mouth breathing, the rescuer could feel the dull throb of the boy's beating heart.

My head was throbbing with pain from a bad headache.

---

03 cowardice [káuərdis]

n. 겁, 비겁

lack of courage to face something

coward ⓝ 겁쟁이 ⓐ 겁 많은, 비겁한

syn timidity, fearfulness　ant bravery, valor, courage

Young children often lie out of cowardice rather than out of intention.

---

04 accord [əkɔ́ːrd]

n. 일치, 조화, 협정

v. 일치[조화]하다

a mutual agreement or harmony

ⓝ accordance 일치, 조화　ad according ~에 따라서, 일치하여

syn concord, concur　ant conflict, antagonism, discord

Talks between the two warring nations led to a peace accord after 12 years of fighting.

The statement of the witness did not accord with the evidence that was presented.

---

05 norm [nɔːrm]

n. 기준, 표준

a way of behaving regarded as typical for a particular group

ⓐ normal 표준의, 전형적인　ⓥ normalize 표준적으로 하다, 기준에 맞추다

syn criterion, standard, model, pattern　ant exception

Confucianism has been the most influential philosophy in shaping the social norm in Korea.

---

01 경제 안정이 새 행정부의 가장 중요한 안건이 될 것이다. 02 인공호흡 후, 구조대원은 소년의 약한 심장 박동을 느낄 수 있었다. 심한 두통 때문에 머리가 통증으로 욱신거렸다. 03 어린아이들은 종종 의도해서가 아니라 겁을 먹어 거짓말을 한다. 04 12년의 교전을 끝으로 두 적대 국가는 회담을 통해 평화 협정을 맺게 되었다. 그 증언의 진술은 제시된 증거와 일치하지 않았다. 05 유교는 한국의 사회 규범을 형성하는 데 가장 중대한 역할을 한 철학이다.

06 vain [vein]
a. 헛된, 허영심이 강한

having useless effect or result

n vainness 헛됨, 허영   ad vainly 헛되이, 자만하여

syn conceited, futile, fruitless   ant successful, modest

The teenage boy had a vain belief that he would not be punished.

07 eloquent [éləkwənt]
a. 설득력 있는, 웅변의

able to express one's ideas well in speech or writing

n eloquence 웅변, 말재주   ad eloquently 능변으로, 감동적으로

syn persuasive, fluent   ant ineloquent, inarticulate

Cherie's eloquent speech captured the hearts of the listeners at the seminar.

08 mischievous [místʃivəs]
a. 해를 끼치는, 장난이 심한

harmful or inclined to annoy with playful tricks

n mischief 해, 해악   ad mischievously 해롭게, 짓궂게

syn damaging, playful, naughty   ant harmless, well-behaved

My son is so mischievous that I have a hard time disciplining him.

09 impending [impéndiŋ]
a. 임박한, 절박한

about to happen

n impendence 절박(한 상태)   v impend (위험 등이) 임박하다, 절박하다

syn forthcoming, imminent   ant distant

The meteorologist had a sense of an impending hurricane when looking at the image of the cloud.

10 grind [graind]
v. 갈다, 빻다

to crush or cut into small pieces or powder

syn powder, mill   ant mold, solidify

I will tell you some tips to grind coffee beans and brew coffee.

11 shuffle [ʃʌfl]
v. 질질 끌며 걷다

to move the feet along the ground slowly

a shuffling 발을 끌며 걷는

syn drag, stumble

Brian shuffled his feet with the sprain on his left ankle.

12 hurl [həːrl]
v. 세게 던지다, 퍼붓다

to throw or speak with force or violence

n hurler 던지는 사람, 투수

syn cast, fling, dash   ant catch, hold

The boy hurled a baseball through the neighbor's window accidentally.

---

06 그 십대 소년은 처벌을 받지 않을 거라는 헛된 믿음을 가지고 있었다. 07 Cherie의 감동적인 연설은 세미나에서 청중들의 마음을 사로잡았다. 08 내 아들이 너무 장난꾸러기여서 그를 훈육하는 게 너무 힘들어요. 09 그 기상학자는 구름의 모습을 보고 허리케인이 곧 닥칠 것이라고 느꼈다. 10 제가 원두를 갈고 커피를 끓이는 비법을 알려 드리겠습니다. 11 Brian은 그의 왼쪽 발목이 삐었기 때문에 발을 끌며 걸었다. 12 소년은 뜻하지 않게 야구공을 이웃집 창문으로 던졌다.

13 nourish [nə́:riʃ]

v. 영양분을 주다, 기르다

to provide with substances necessary for life and growth

n nourishment 영양물, 양육 a nourishing 영양분이 많은, 영양이 되는

syn feed, nurture ant starve

The gardener is nourishing the new bushes with fertilizer.

14 flee [fli:]

v. 달아나다, 도망치다

to run away swiftly or escape, as from danger

syn escape

My ancestors fled from persecution for their religious beliefs.

15 replicate [réplikèit]

v. 모사하다, 복제하다

to produce an exact copy of something

syn duplicate, reproduce ant originate

On the second experiment, the scientist was not able to replicate the same results as the first one.

The replicated cells will grow for two weeks in the lab.

16 tumble [tʌ́mbl]

v. 넘어지다, 구르다

to fall or roll in a sudden uncontrolled way

syn topple, trip, flop

The large rocks tumbled into the water without any warning.

The young woman took a tumble down the stairs and her face turned red like a tomato.

17 assess [əsés]

v. 평가하다

to make a careful judgment about someone or something or its value

n assessment 평가 a assessable 평가할 수 있는

syn evaluate, appraise, valuate, value

Experts were called in to assess whether the land was truly worth $200 per square meter.

18 sneer [sniər]

v. 비웃다, 빈정대다

to show a lack of respect for a person by words or facial expressions

a sneering 조소하는, 비꼬아 말하는 ad sneeringly 냉소하여

syn mock, jeer, taunt ant compliment, praise, admire

The man sneered when he heard the news about his rival's victory.

19 penetrate [pénətrèit]

v. 관통하다

to pass through something

n penetration 관통, 간파 a penetrating 침투하는, 관통하는

syn pierce, perforate

The bullet penetrated her abdomen, leaving her in a coma.

---

13 정원사는 갓 심은 관목에 비료를 주고 있다. 14 내 선조는 종교의 박해를 피해 달아났다. 15 과학자는 두번째 실험에서 첫 실험과 똑같은 결과를 얻을 수 없었다. 복제된 세포는 2주 동안 실험실에서 배양될 것입니다. 16 큰 바위가 아무런 조짐도 없이 물로 굴러 떨어졌다. 젊은 여인은 계단에서 넘어져 얼굴이 토마토처럼 빨개졌다. 17 그 땅이 실제로 1평방 미터 당 200달러의 가치가 있는지를 평가하려고 전문가를 불렀다. 18 그 남자는 자신의 경쟁자가 승리했다는 뉴스를 듣고 빈정댔다. 19 총알이 그녀의 복부를 관통해 그녀는 혼수 상태에 빠졌다.

20 deplore [diplɔ́ːr]
v. 비탄[한탄]하다, 비난하다

to regret or disapprove of something or criticize

[n] deploration 개탄, 탄식   [a] deplorable 슬픈, 개탄스러운   [ad] deploringly 한탄하면서

[syn] lament, condemn   [ant] delight, praise

Many of my friends deplore the lack of job opportunities in their small, insular towns.

21 banish [bǽniʃ]
v. 추방시키다

to send someone away from a place or country as a punishment

[n] banishment 추방

[syn] exile, deport, expel   [ant] receive, welcome

The man was banished from his own country because of his political beliefs.

22 deduct [didʌ́kt]
v. 빼다, 공제하다

to take away an amount from a total

[n] deduction 빼기, 공제   [a] deductible 뺄 수 있는, 공제할 수 있는

[syn] subtract, reduce   [ant] add, sum

A monthly service charge of $10 will be deducted from your account balance.

23 accumulate [əkjúːmjulèit]
v. 쌓다, 모으다

to pile up or collect something

[n] accumulation 축적   [a] accumulative 축적하는

[syn] heap, gather, assemble   [ant] scatter, dissipate

The savings account will accumulate interest until you withdraw your money.

24 boost [buːst]
v. 밀어올리다, 증대시키다
n. 밀어올림, 상승

to increase something

[syn] lift, advance, raise   [ant] lower, decrease, reduce

The company made a concentrated effort to boost sales by following new marketing strategies.

The politician's image got a boost after his active participation in local projects.

25 tailor [téilər]
v. (목적, 용도에) 맞추다
n. 재단사, 재봉사

to form or change for a certain purpose

[syn] adjust, adapt, fit

Management consultants worked to tailor the business plan to the requirements of the board.

The old tailor is well-known to make wonderful business suits that fit.

---

20 많은 내 친구들은 그들이 사는 작은 섬마을에서는 직업을 얻을 기회가 적다고 한탄한다. 21 그 남자는 그의 정치적인 신념 때문에 고국에서 추방을 당했다. 22 10달러에 해당하는 월 서비스 수수료는 당신의 은행잔고에서 공제됩니다. 23 저축예금은 돈을 인출하기 전까지 이자가 적립된다. 24 회사는 새로운 마케팅 전략에 따라 매출을 올리는 데 집중하고 있다. 그 정치가는 지역 사업에 적극적으로 참여해 그의 이미지를 끌어올렸다. 25 경영 상담자는 위원회의 요구에 따라 사업 계획을 조정하는 일을 했다. 그 나이 든 재단사는 딱 떨어지는 정장을 만드는 것으로 잘 알려져 있어.

Exercise

Score [/20]

Word Check 각 단어의 뜻으로 알맞은 것을 찾아 연결하시오.

01 mischievous   ⓐ to repeat or duplicate
02 assess   ⓑ something to be done or discussed
03 agenda   ⓒ to enter by piercing or affect deeply
04 penetrate   ⓓ causing harm, annoyance or damage
05 replicate   ⓔ to estimate the value of something or someone

Syn & Ant Check 주어진 단어의 동의어, 반의어를 골라 쓰시오.

fling	well-behaved	starve	add	concur
imminent	lament	bravery	criterion	modest

06 hurl   = _____
07 impending   = _____
08 norm   = _____
09 accord   = _____
10 deplore   = _____

11 deduct   ↔ _____
12 mischievous ↔ _____
13 cowardice   ↔ _____
14 vain   ↔ _____
15 nourish   ↔ _____

Sentence Practice 문장을 읽고 빈칸에 알맞은 단어를 고르시오.

16 My heart _____ loudly in my chest whenever I gaze upon her beauty.
ⓐ tumbles   ⓑ hurls   ⓒ deplores   ⓓ throbs

17 A(n) _____ appeal by the prime minister ensured that aid poured in by the millions from all quarters.
ⓐ mischievous   ⓑ eloquent   ⓒ vain   ⓓ impending

18 Some citizens want to _____ taxes to pay for more welfare programs but others oppose the idea.
ⓐ accumulate   ⓑ assess   ⓒ replicate   ⓓ boost

19 Don't _____ at others who may be less fortunate than you are.
ⓐ sneer   ⓑ penetrate   ⓒ shuffle   ⓓ grinds

20 The new king's first move was to _____ the corrupt advisors to a distant island where they could do no harm.
ⓐ nourish   ⓑ deduct   ⓒ banish   ⓓ flee

THE VOCA **31**

Day 5

01 shortcoming [ʃɔ́ːrtkʌ̀miŋ]
n. 결점, 단점

a fault or weakness that someone or something has
[syn] defect, disadvantage, flaw   [ant] strength, advantage

Clive's greatest shortcoming is his inability to stand up for himself when others bother him.

---

02 merchandise [mə́ːrtʃəndàiz]
n. (집합적) 상품
v. 매매하다, 거래하다

things bought and sold
[n] merchandiser 상인   [a] merchandising 거래[판매]의
[syn] wares, commodity, goods

All of this merchandise is to be shipped immediately to our customer in China.
The Internet is the quickest way to merchandise products.

---

03 creed [kriːd]
n. 신조, 신념

a statement of belief or principles, especially religious
[syn] dogma, faith, doctrine

All human beings are bound to the common creed of humanity, brotherhood and tolerance.

---

04 juvenile [dʒúːvənl]
n. 청소년, 어린이

a child or young person
[syn] adolescence, teenager, youth   [ant] adult

The police arrested two juveniles for the crime of frequent shoplifting.

---

05 conjunction [kəndʒʌ́ŋkʃən]
n. 결합, 연결, 접속사

the state of combining different things
[a] conjunctive 결합하는, 연결한
[syn] combination, connection, union   [ant] detachment, division, separation

Police are working in conjunction with the FBI to track a serial killer.
A conjunction typically connects two clauses of a sentence that express complete ideas.

---

06 ratio [réiʃou]
n. 비, 비율

a fixed relationship between two similar things
[syn] proportion, quotient, rate

The ratio of students to teachers is very low in this school.

---

01 Clive의 가장 큰 약점은 다른 사람들의 괴롭힘을 견디지 못한다는 것이다. 02 이 모든 상품은 중국에 있는 고객에게 즉시 선적될 것입니다. 인터넷은 상품을 거래하는 가장 빠른 방법이다. 03 모든 인간은 인간애, 동포애, 관용과 같은 공통의 신념을 지킬 의무가 있다. 04 경찰은 상점의 물건을 상습적으로 훔친 죄로 두 명의 청소년을 체포했다. 05 경찰은 연쇄살인범을 추적하기 위해 FBI와 합동수사를 하고 있다. 접속사는 일반적으로 완전한 개념을 표현하는 하는 하나의 문장에서 두 개의 절을 연결한다. 06 이 학교의 교사 대비 학생의 비율은 낮다.

07 vocal [vóukəl]
a. 목소리의, 음성의

of or produced by the voice

[n] vocalization 발성 [v] vocalize 목소리로 내다 [ad] vocally 목소리로, 구두로

[syn] voiced, vocalized [ant] written

Vocal cords, lips, tongue and teeth are involved in producing the sounds of speech.

08 concise [kənsáis]
a. 간결한, 간명한

short and clear, without using too many words

[n] concision 간결, 간명 [ad] concisely 간결하게

[syn] brief, succinct, condensed [ant] lengthy, long, prolix

Keep in mind that a report should be concise and clear.

09 vigorous [vígərəs]
a. 원기 왕성한, 힘찬, 강력한

strong or energetic in mind and body

[n] vigor 활기, 박력 [ad] vigorously 발랄하게, 힘차게

[syn] active, powerful, robust [ant] impotent, inactive, frail

It is not advisable to engage in vigorous exercise late at night.

10 gross [grous]
a. 전체의, 총계의

total amount before taxes and expenses are deducted

[syn] entire, whole, aggregate [ant] partial, net

The store owner deducted his expenses from the gross receipts to figure out his actual profit.

11 reckless [réklis]
a. 무모한, 부주의한

acting or done without thinking of the consequence

[n] recklessness 무모함 [ad] recklessly 무모하게

[syn] thoughtless, rash, careless, heedless [ant] cautious, prudent, careful

The reckless statement caused much harm to the relationship between the two countries.

12 tacit [tǽsit]
a. 무언의, 조용한

unspoken but understood

[n] tacitness 무언임, 조용함 [ad] tacitly 무언으로, 조용하게

[syn] implicit, unexpressed, silent [ant] explicit, express

Her parents gave their tacit permission for her to go out with him.

13 authentic [ɔːθéntik]
a. 진짜의, 믿을 만한

not fake or copied

[n] authenticity 신빙성 [ad] authentically 확실하게

[syn] genuine, trustworthy, real [ant] counterfeit, fake, phony

This restaurant can be proud of its authentic French menu and tasteful decor.

---

07 성대, 입술, 혀, 이는 말소리를 만드는 데 관여한다. 08 보고서는 명확하고 간결해야 한다는 것을 명심하십시오. 09 밤늦게 심한 운동을 하는 것은 피하시는 것이 좋습니다. 10 그 가게 주인은 실제 수입을 계산하기 위해 총 수령액에서 비용을 뺐다. 11 그 무모한 발언은 두 나라의 관계에 엄청난 악영향을 미쳤다. 12 그녀의 부모님은 그와 데이트를 해도 좋다는 무언의 허락을 해주셨다. 13 이 식당은 정통 프랑스 메뉴와 세련된 인테리어를 자랑한다.

14 foremost [fɔ́ːrmòust]
a. 맨 앞의, 주요한
ad. 맨 먼저

first in place, time, etc.
[syn] first, leading, primary [ant] last, minor

Mohammed Ali is considered one of the foremost boxers in the history of the sport.

Foremost, we should recognize that we have an advantage at this time.

15 crude [kruːd]
a. 가공하지 않은, 조잡한

in a raw or natural condition
[n] crudeness 노골적임, 조야함 [ad] crudely 교양 없이, 노골적으로
[syn] rough, unpolished, harsh [ant] finished, polished, refined

Prices for crude oils are usually based on three main regional crude oil benchmarks - WTI, Dubai and Brent.

These prehistoric cave murals look crude and primitive but are very valuable objects of study.

16 absurd [æbsə́ːrd]
a. 불합리한, 어리석은

so unreasonable as to be ridiculous
[n] absurdity 어리석음, 불합리 [ad] absurdly 불합리하게, 모순되게
[syn] illogical, stupid [ant] logical, rational, reasonable

The committee felt that my expensive proposal was absurd since they had very little money.

17 eerie [íəri]
a. 무시무시한, 섬뜩한

strange and frightening
[n] eeriness 무시무시함, 섬뜩함 [ad] eerily 무시무시하게, 섬뜩하게
[syn] uncanny, weird, frightful, spooky

The boys saw an eerie sight late at night while they were driving home.

18 mutate [mjúːteit]
v. 변화하다, 돌연변이하다

to change or alter
[n] mutation 변화, 돌연변이 [a] mutant 변화된, 돌연변이의
[syn] modify, vary, sport [ant] remain, stay

The bacteria's genes mutated to create a super germ.

19 attain [ətéin]
v. 달성하다, 이르다

to gain or achieve something
[n] attainment 달성, 도달 [a] attainable 달성할 수 있는
[syn] accomplish, succeed [ant] abandon, fail, lose

My father has finally attained his political goal of becoming a senator.

---

14 Mohammed Ali는 스포츠 역사상 최고의 복싱선수로 여겨진다. 맨 먼저, 우리는 현재 유리한 상황에 있다는 것을 알아야 합니다. 15 원유가는 각 지역을 대표하는 기준 원유-서부텍사스 중질유, 두바이유, 브렌트유를 바탕으로 책정된다. 이 선사시대의 동굴 벽화는 조야하고 투박해 보이지만 상당한 연구 가치가 있다. 16 재정이 충분치 않았기 때문에 위원회는 비용이 많이 드는 내 제안을 터무니없다고 생각했다. 17 어젯밤 소년들이 차를 타고 집으로 돌아오면서 섬뜩한 광경을 목격했다. 18 박테리아의 유전자는 슈퍼세균으로 돌연변이를 일으켰다. 19 아버지는 마침내 상원위원이 되겠다는 정치적 목적을 달성했다.

20 override [òuvəráid]
v. 우위에 서다, 결정권을 갖다, 무효화하다

to be more important than something else

ⓐ overriding 최우선의, 결정적인

ⓢⓨⓝ dominate, overrule

People realize that health overrides everything else only after getting sick.

The congress may override the president's veto through a vote.

---

21 advocate [ǽdvəkèit / -kət]
v. 옹호하다, 지지하다
n. 옹호자, 변호사

to speak or write in support of another or a cause

ⓝ advocacy 변호, 옹호, 지지   ⓐ advocatory 옹호자의

ⓢⓨⓝ encourage, promote, support   ⓐⓝⓣ criticize, oppose, protest

The political candidate advocates taking tough stance against North Korea.

Brandon is a fervent advocate of the vegetable diet.

---

22 uphold [ʌphóuld]
v. 지지하다, 떠받치다

to support or maintain something, especially against opposition

ⓝ upholder 지지자, 옹호자

ⓢⓨⓝ back, defend, sustain   ⓐⓝⓣ criticize, protest, oppose

The U.S. president swears to uphold the Constitution when he assumes the office of the president.

---

23 swell [swel]
v. 부풀다, 증가하다
n. 팽창, 증가

to become bigger than usual, especially used for part of body

ⓐ swelling 커지는, 부푼

ⓢⓨⓝ expand, distend, bulge   ⓐⓝⓣ compress, shrink, decrease

The organizers were happy to see the hall swell with spectators in time for the grand show.

There is a swell of opposition to China's violent suppression of Tibetan marchers.

---

24 scribble [skríbl]
v. 휘갈겨 쓰다

to write carelessly and hastily, sometimes illegibly

ⓢⓨⓝ scrawl, scrabble

My substitute teacher scribbled the formula on the blackboard, and no one in my class could read it.

---

25 testify [téstəfài]
v. 증명하다, 증언하다

to give evidence, especially under oath in court

ⓝ testification 증명, 증언

ⓢⓨⓝ prove, affirm, attest

The woman testified that she saw the man rob the store.

---

20 사람들은 아프고 나서야 비로소 건강이 제일 중요하다는 것을 깨닫게 된다. 국회는 투표를 통해 대통령의 거부권을 무효로 만들 수 있다. 21 그 국회의원 출마자는 대북 강경책을 지지한다. Brandon은 채식의 열렬한 옹호자이다. 22 미국 대통령은 취임식 때 헌법을 충실히 따르겠다는 맹세를 한다. 23 주최자는 대공연 시간에 맞춰 관객들로 홀이 가득 차는 것을 보고 즐거워했다. 티베트인 시위자들에 대한 중국의 무력 진압에 반대하는 물결이 증대되고 있다. 24 대리 선생님이 칠판에 공식을 휘갈겨 써서 우리 반 누구도 그것을 읽을 수가 없었다. 25 여인은 그 남자가 가게를 터는 것을 보았다고 증언했다.

Exercise

Score /20

Word Check 각 단어의 뜻으로 알맞은 것을 찾아 연결하시오.

01 tacit   ⓐ unusual, unexpected and scary

02 scribble   ⓑ to make a formal statement of fact in a court

03 merchandise   ⓒ to write down something quickly and untidily

04 testify   ⓓ goods that are being bought, sold and traded

05 eerie   ⓔ understood something without being actually said

Syn & Ant Check 주어진 단어의 동의어, 반의어를 골라 쓰시오.

accomplish	oppose	primary	robust	refined
advantage	combination	brief	reasonable	prudent

06 concise =   11 shortcoming ↔

07 foremost =   12 absurd ↔

08 attain =   13 crude ↔

09 vigorous =   14 reckless ↔

10 conjunction =   15 advocate ↔

Sentence Practice 문장을 읽고 빈칸에 알맞은 단어를 고르시오.

16 The judge passed a light sentence on the _____ as it was his first offense.

 ⓐ creed   ⓑ conjunction   ⓒ merchandise   ⓓ juvenile

17 Sociologists are concerned at the imbalance in the _____ between males and females in several developing countries.

 ⓐ advocate   ⓑ creed   ⓒ shortcoming   ⓓ ratio

18 _____ handcrafted items were among the main attractions at the annual fair.

 ⓐ Foremost   ⓑ Gross   ⓒ Authentic   ⓓ Vigorous

19 A junior officer can _____ the order of a senior one if the order is illegal or immoral.

 ⓐ override   ⓑ swell   ⓒ uphold   ⓓ testify

20 Scientists are working to understand the process by which normal cells _____ into cancerous ones.

 ⓐ attain   ⓑ advocate   ⓒ mutate   ⓓ scribble

❖ not, without

a, an

a + **theist** (유신론자) = **atheist** 무신론자

She is a confirmed atheist that has denied the existence of supreme beings.
그녀는 신의 존재를 믿지 않는 확고한 무신론자이다.

ab, abs

ab + **normal** (정상적인) = **abnormal** 비정상적인

Parents are heartbroken when they learn their child is abnormal.
아이들이 비정상적인 것을 알면 부모들은 가슴이 미어진다.

de

de + **grade** (등급을 매기다) = **degrade** 강등시키다

You should not degrade yourself by making you do careless remarks.
경솔한 언사를 함으로써 자신의 품위를 낮춰서는 안 된다.

dis

dis + **inherit** (상속받다) = **disinherit** 상속권을 빼앗다

Her mother said she would disinherit her if she married a normal salary man.
그녀의 엄마는 그녀가 보통 월급쟁이와 결혼을 하면 상속을 박탈하겠다고 했다.

in, il, im, ir

in + **finite** (유한한) = **infinite** 무한한

The Internet has enabled us to access to an infinite amount of information.
인터넷은 무한한 양의 정보로의 접근을 가능하게 한다.

un

un + **conditional** (조건부의) = **unconditional** 무조건의

The China government insisted on Tibetan's unconditional surrenders.
중국정부는 티베트 국민들의 무조건적인 항복을 주장했다.

non

non + **fiction** (허구) = **nonfiction** 사실

The books of autobiography are found on the non-fiction shelves in the library.
자서전은 도서관 비소설분야 서가에서 찾을 수 있다.

ig

ig + **noble** (고귀한) = **ignoble** 비열한

She seems ignoble because she has done everything to achieve her success.
그녀는 성공을 하기 위해 무엇이든 하기 때문에 비열해 보인다.

Review test Day 1 ~ Day 5

Score /25

A 영어 풀이에 알맞은 단어를 보기에서 찾아 쓰시오.

paradox	withstand	casualty	eloquent	advocate

01 injured or killed in an accident or battle   _____

02 forceful and fluent, especially in speech and writing   _____

03 to support something or someone, especially in public   _____

04 a statement or situation containing two opposing ideas   _____

05 to be strong enough not to be harmed or changed by something   _____

B 문장을 읽고 문맥에 적절한 단어를 고르시오.

06 The witness came forward to (testify/inquire) against the accused in the sensational case.

07 Rarely do the children's summer recesses (coincide/confront) with their parents' work vacation schedules.

08 Bill never had to (encounter/exert) some of the more difficult instructors who were infamous for giving a lot of homework.

09 We are having a hard time (replicating/restraining) the results of the first experiments.

C ▨▨▨▨ 표시된 부분과 뜻이 가장 가까운 것을 고르시오.

10 A juvenile faces the unique problem of being neither a child nor an adult.

    ⓐ propaganda   ⓑ corpse   ⓒ spectator   ⓓ adolescence

11 Ivan the Terrible was a tyrant who ruled without compassion, kindness or pity.

    ⓐ rebel   ⓑ recruit   ⓒ despot   ⓓ realm

12 People most often choose a parent, spouse, sibling or friend to confide in about their problems.

    ⓐ disclose   ⓑ dismay   ⓒ accord   ⓓ avail

13 The government will lay down strict rules to ban sexual advertisements that degrade women.

    ⓐ demote   ⓑ deprive   ⓒ classify   ⓓ compass

D 표시된 부분의 반대말로 가장 알맞은 것을 고르시오.

14 The teachings of Confucius are known to be both simple and profound.
    ⓐ secondary   ⓑ superficial   ⓒ bleak   ⓓ partial

15 Many British criminals were banished to Australia during the 18th Century.
    ⓐ roamed   ⓑ flung   ⓒ deplored   ⓓ welcomed

16 The company symbol on the pack reassures us that this is an authentic product.
    ⓐ counterfeit   ⓑ mischievous   ⓒ filthy   ⓓ intimate

17 The distraught father could only plead with the doctors to save his child.
    ⓐ affirm   ⓑ surpass   ⓒ command   ⓓ grin

E 주어진 단어를 알맞은 형태로 바꿔 빈칸에 쓰시오.

18 My parents attempted to never show _____ to either me or my sister. (partial)

19 The proposal was an absolute _____ because of our situation. (absurd)

20 He took his _____ route to work each day except for this morning. (norm)

21 The student questioned the _____ of the class to train him well for the job. (adequate)

F 빈칸에 알맞은 단어를 보기에서 찾아 쓰시오. (필요한 경우 형태를 바꾸시오.)

excavate	cowardice	immerse	recruit	crude
accumulate	prehistoric	vigorous	shortcoming	agenda

22 파키스탄 지역에서 발굴된 선사시대 유물은 여태까지 밝혀지지 않은 공룡이 존재했다는 것을 암시한다.
    → _____ remains _____ at a site in Pakistan point to the existence of a hitherto unknown dinosaur.

23 오늘의 주요 협의 사항은 회사의 판매 전략을 검토하는 것입니다.
    → The main item on today's _____ is the review of the company's sales strategies.

24 몸매를 유지하기 위해서 늘 심한 운동을 할 필요는 없다.
    → It is not always necessary to engage in _____ exercise in order to stay fit.

25 새로 오신 신입 직원들은 인사부에서 유니폼과 ID배지를 수령하실 수 있습니다.
    → New _____ can collect their uniforms and ID badges from the Human Resources Department.

➤ 영어를 우리말로 옮기시오.

01	confront		31	vacuum
02	extraterrestrial		32	hurl
03	deduct		33	mutate
04	advocate		34	fluctuate
05	classify		35	concise
06	accord		36	avail
07	norm		37	swell
08	dismay		38	grin
09	dilemma		39	recruit
10	surpass		40	teem
11	eloquent		41	fling
12	intimate		42	amend
13	degrade		43	realm
14	attain		44	deplore
15	exert		45	obese
16	crude		46	laborious
17	cowardice		47	adequate
18	filthy		48	override
19	assess		49	modify
20	timber		50	inquire
21	restrain		51	vigorous
22	secondary		52	accumulate
23	elevate		53	rebel
24	encounter		54	reckless
25	banish		55	immerse
26	magnificent		56	abnormal
27	testify		57	shortcoming
28	boost		58	depict
29	merchandise		59	halt
30	abound		60	flee

➤ 우리말을 영어로 옮기시오.

61 역설 _____
62 의제, 일정 _____
63 헛된 _____
64 동기, 이유 _____
65 결합, 연결 _____
66 청소년 _____
67 사상자 _____
68 넘어지다 _____
69 황량한 _____
70 범위, 영역 _____
71 불합리한 _____
72 발굴하다 _____
73 갈다, 빻다 _____
74 진짜의 _____
75 부분적인 _____
76 (사람의) 시체 _____
77 표류하다 _____
78 비, 비율 _____
79 가속하다 _____
80 나침반 _____
81 절박한 _____
82 질질 끌며 걷다 _____
83 선전 _____
84 논제, 논문 _____
85 의류 _____
86 휘갈겨 쓰다 _____
87 일치하다 _____
88 손상시키다 _____
89 이해, 불안 _____
90 복제하다 _____

91 신조, 신념 _____
92 장난이 심한 _____
93 박탈하다 _____
94 조예가 깊은 _____
95 헤매다 _____
96 고동치다 _____
97 견디다 _____
98 무시무시한 _____
99 신성한 장소 _____
100 비웃다 _____
101 혼돈, 무질서 _____
102 폭군 _____
103 관통하다 _____
104 도살하다 _____
105 폭발, 분출 _____
106 암시적인 _____
107 맨 앞의 _____
108 무언의 _____
109 신용하다 _____
110 선사의 _____
111 단언하다 _____
112 가볍게 두드림 _____
113 지지하다 _____
114 떨림, 전율 _____
115 얽히게 하다 _____
116 감독하다 _____
117 총계의 _____
118 영양분을 주다 _____
119 유약, 광택 _____
120 배회하다 _____

Part 2

Day 6

🎧 **01 tissue** [tíʃuː]
n. 조직, (얇은) 직물

a group of cells having similar function or structure
ⓐ tissuey 조직 같은

Oils like rosehip oil and emu oil help to heal scars and sun-damaged skin tissue.
She only uses purely cotton tissue products because of her sensitive skin.

02 aviation [èiviéiʃən]
n. 비행(술), 항공(술)

the science or practice of flying or making aircraft
ⓝ aviator 비행사, 조종사
syn flying, flight, aeronautics

Modern aviation is considered to have begun with the efforts of the Wright Brothers.

03 altitude [ǽltətjùːd]
n. 고도, 높이

the height of a thing, especially above sea level
ⓐ altitudinal 고도의, 표고의
syn elevation, height ant abyss, depth

They flew at a very low altitude in order to avoid being caught by enemy fighters.

04 utensil [juːténsəl]
n. 기구, 도구

a tool or object with a particular use
syn implement, equipment, instrument, apparatus

I bought some new gardening utensils to plant some flowers.

05 sermon [sə́ːrmən]
n. 설교, 교훈

a talk about a religious subject, usually in a church and based on the Bible
ⓐ sermonic 설교의, 설교적인 ⓥ sermonize 설교하다
syn preaching, discourse, lesson

My pastor gave a wonderful sermon about the resurrection of Jesus Christ last Sunday.

06 draft [dræft]
n. 초안, 밑그림
a. 초안의

an early version of writing or plan that is unfinished
syn outline, sketch

The architect drew a draft of the plans of the new building.
The draft treaty will be revised and finished by the congress this week.

---

01 들장미 열매 오일과 에뮤 오일과 같은 오일은 상처와 태양으로부터 손상된 피부 조직을 치료하는 데 도움을 준다. 그녀는 피부가 너무 민감하기 때문에 순면 직물 제품만 사용한다. 02 현대 항공술은 Wright 형제의 노고에서 시작되었다고 여겨진다. 03 적군에게 들키지 않기 위해서 그들은 낮은 고도로 비행했다. 04 나는 꽃을 심으려고 정원 손질 도구를 몇 개 샀다. 05 목사님은 지난 일요일에 예수의 부활에 관한 훌륭한 설교를 해주셨다. 06 건축가는 새 건물 설계 초안을 그렸다. 이번 주에 의회는 협정의 초안을 수정해 완성할 것이다.

07 slump [slʌmp]

n. 슬럼프, 폭락
v. 떨어지다, 폭락하다

a sudden decline in something

[syn] falloff, drop, descent [ant] rise, soar

Everyone takes the recent economic slump as proof of an impending recession.

Most experts expect that the shares will continue to slump for a few weeks.

08 transparent [trænspέərənt]

a. 투명한, 명백한

clear and easy to be seen through

[n] transparency 투명 [v] transparentize 투명하게 하다

[syn] pellucid, limpid, crystalline [ant] translucent, opaque, unclear

Our boat's transparent base allowed us a great view of the marine life around the island.

The reporter easily identified the transparent motive for his committing the murder.

09 sufficient [səfíʃənt]

a. 충분한, 적당한

as many or as much as is necessary

[n] sufficiency 충분(한 상태) [ad] sufficiently 충분히

[syn] adequate, enough, ample [ant] inadequate, insufficient, deficient

There are sufficient resources in the world to cater to man's legitimate needs.

10 ruthless [rú:θlis]

a. 무정한, 무자비한

without pity or compassion

[n] ruthlessness 무자비함, 잔인함 [ad] ruthlessly 무자비하게, 잔인하게

[syn] cruel, merciless, inhuman, relentless [ant] compassionate, merciful

Hitler was a ruthless dictator who attempted to conquer the entire world.

11 sturdy [stə́:rdi]

a. 견고한, 튼튼한

firm and strong, especially of construction

[ad] sturdily 튼튼히, 기운차게

[syn] hardy, stalwart, solid, well-made [ant] weak, feeble

The sturdy structure kept the men safe during the violent storm.

12 tranquil [trǽŋkwil]

a. 조용한, 평온한

pleasantly calm, quiet and peaceful

[n] tranquility 평정, 평온 [ad] tranquilly 조용하게, 평온하게

[syn] gentle, serene, placid, still [ant] loud, noisy

Try to have a tranquil moment even in the middle of your busy and hectic day.

---

07 모든 사람들이 최근의 경기 침체를 갑작스러운 경기 후퇴의 증거로 여긴다. 대부분의 전문가들은 주식이 몇 주 동안은 계속해서 떨어질 것이라고 전망하고 있다. 08 배의 바닥이 투명했기 때문에 우리는 섬 주위의 해양 생물을 자세히 볼 수 있었다. 기자는 어려움 없이 그가 살해를 저지른 명백한 동기를 규명했다. 09 세계에는 인간의 정당한 욕구를 충족시켜줄 수 있는 만큼의 충분한 자원이 있다. 10 Hitler는 전 세계를 정복하고자 했던 무자비한 독재자였다. 11 견고한 구조물 때문에 격렬한 폭풍이 치는 동안에도 사람들은 안전할 수 있었다. 12 정신이 바쁜 날이라 해도 평온한 순간을 가지려고 애쓰세요.

13 customary [kʌ́stəmèri]
a. 관습의, 습관적인

according to a traditional activity or practice

n custom 관습, 습관 ad customarily 습관적으로, 관습으로

syn conventional, habitual, accustomed ant abnormal, unusual, unfamiliar

It is customary to leave a tip for a waiter or waitress in the US.

14 animate [ǽnəmèit]
v. 생기 있게 하다
a. 생명이 있는

to make someone or something alive

n animation 생기, 활발 a animated 생기가 있는, 활발한

syn enliven, breathing, live ant inanimate, dead, lifeless

The work of several artists helps to animate our favorite cartoon characters.

The professor studies only animate creatures in the desert.

15 deform [difɔ́ːrm]
v. 변형시키다, 불구로 만들다

to change the usual form and make less useful or ugly

n deformity 기형, 불구 a deformable 변형할 수 있는 a deformed 흉하게 변형된

syn disfigure, cripple ant adorn, beautify, embellish

Wearing high heels makes you look better but it can deform your feet.

16 precede [prisíːd]
v. 앞서다, 우선하다

to happen or exist before something else

n precedence 앞섬, 상위 n precedent 전례, 선례 a preceding 이전의, 선행하는

syn predate, antecede ant succeed, follow

Violent disagreements over the issue of slavery preceded the outbreak of the American Civil War.

17 exclaim [ikskléim]
v. 외치다, 감탄하다

to cry out suddenly and forcefully

n exclamation 외침, 절규 a exclamatory 감탄하는

syn cry, yell, shout ant whisper

People went into the streets and exclaimed hurrah for Korean independence on March 1st, 1919.

18 beam [biːm]
v. 밝게 미소 짓다, 빛을 발하다
n. 광선, 빛

to smile at someone in a happy way

a beaming 밝게 빛나는, 명랑한

syn shine, radiate, smile ant frown, scowl

He was beaming with pride after receiving the gold medal for the men's 100-meter swimming.

The light year is a distance that a beam of light can travel in a year and one light-year is about 9.44 trillion km.

---

13 미국에서는 웨이터나 웨이트리스에게 팁을 남기는 것이 관례다. 14 몇몇 예술가의 노력이 우리가 좋아하는 만화 캐릭터에 생명을 불어 넣었다. 그 교수는 오직 사막의 살아있는 생명체만을 연구한다. 15 하이힐은 신으면 좀 더 예뻐보이긴 하겠지만 그건 네 발을 변형시킬 수도 있어. 16 미국 남북 전쟁 발발에 앞서 노예 문제에 대한 격렬한 반발이 있었다. 17 1919년 3월 1일에 사람들은 거리로 나와 대한독립만세를 외쳤다. 18 그는 남자부 100미터 수영경기에서 금메달을 받은 후에 자부심을 가지고 밝게 미소 지었다. 광년은 한 줄기 빛이 1년 동안 이동하는 거리로 1광년은 약 9조 4천 4백 킬로미터이다.

19 graze [greiz]
v. 풀을 뜯어 먹다

to feed on growing grass

n grazing 방목, 목장

syn pasture, browse

The shepherd took his flock of sheep to graze in a meadow where he could easily watch over them.

20 discern [disə́:rn]
v. 식별하다, 인식하다

to recognize something by thinking about it

n discernment 인식(력), 식별(력)   a discerning 통찰력이 있는, 분별 있는

syn distinguish, perceive, notice   ant disregard, neglect, overlook

How do you discern an authentic hand bag from fake ones?

21 assail [əséil]
v. 습격하다, 비난하다

to attack in some way

n assailant 공격자, 가해자   a assailable 공격할 수 있는

syn assault, criticize   ant defend, withdraw, support

The newspaper article assailed the senator's remarks on the peace treaty.

22 minimize [mínəmàiz]
v. 최저[최소]로 하다, 경시하다

to reduce to or estimate at a minimum

n minimization 최소한도로 함, 깔봄

syn minify, decrease, despise   ant maximize, exaggerate

Efforts are currently on to minimize the losses caused by the workers' strike.

23 glide [glaid]
v. 미끄러지다, 활주하다

to move smoothly and effortlessly

gliding n 미끄러지기, 활주 a 미끄러지는, 활주하는

syn slide, waft, coast, float

A fox squirrel moves around the forest by gliding between trees.

24 paralyze [pǽrəlàiz]
v. 마비시키다, 무능[무력]하게 만들다

to make unable to do or feel

n paralysis 마비, 무(기)력   a paralyzed 마비된

syn cripple, incapacitate   ant invigorate, strengthen

The traffic accident killed my uncle and paralyzed my older brother's leg.

25 shiver [ʃívər]
v. 떨다, 흔들거리다
n. 떨림, 전율

to shake lightly because someone is cold or frightened

syn quiver, shudder, tremor

Children in the theater were screaming and shivering with the fear.
The cold breeze made a shiver run down my spine.

---

19 양치기는 양떼들이 풀을 뜯어먹을 수 있게 양들을 잘 지켜볼 수 있는 초원으로 양떼들을 몰고 갔다. 20 어떻게 명품 핸드백과 모조품을 구별하나요? 21 그 신문 기사는 평화 조약에 대한 그 상원의원의 발언을 비난했다. 22 현재는 노동자들의 파업으로 인한 손실을 최소화하는 데 노력을 쏟고 있다. 23 여우 다람쥐는 숲에서 나무 사이를 활공하면서 이동한다. 24 그 교통사고로 삼촌이 돌아가셨고 오빠의 다리가 마비됐다. 25 영화관에 있던 아이들은 공포로 소리를 지르고 떨었다. 차가운 바람이 등골을 오싹하게 만들었다.

Exercise

Score / 20

Word Check 각 단어의 뜻으로 알맞은 것을 찾아 연결하시오.

01 transparent   ⓐ to criticize someone strongly

02 shiver   ⓑ able to be seen through something

03 deform   ⓒ to change the shape or form of something

04 aviation   ⓓ a shaking or trembling movement of the body

05 assail   ⓔ the act of producing, designing and operating aircraft

Syn & Ant Check 주어진 단어의 동의어, 반의어를 골라 쓰시오.

| rise | placid | adequate | enliven | frown |
| equipment | succeed | distinguish | maximize | feeble |

06 tranquil =   11 sturdy ↔

07 utensil =   12 slump ↔

08 animate =   13 precede ↔

09 sufficient =   14 beam ↔

10 discern =   15 minimize ↔

Sentence Practice 문장을 읽고 빈칸에 알맞은 단어를 고르시오.

16 Places at high _____ are cooler than lower ones because they receive less heat through radiation.

    ⓐ utensils   ⓑ altitudes   ⓒ aviation   ⓓ sermons

17 The _____ gangster killed and robbed a large number of innocent people for years.

    ⓐ transparent   ⓑ sturdy   ⓒ ruthless   ⓓ tranquil

18 In India it is _____ to fold one's hands in greeting or as a mark of respect.

    ⓐ animate   ⓑ draft   ⓒ sufficient   ⓓ customary

19 I could not help but _____ at the sheer grandeur of the palace and its surroundings.

    ⓐ exclaim   ⓑ graze   ⓒ glide   ⓓ minimize

20 The neurotoxins in some kinds of snake venom help to _____ the victim and thus prevent escape.

    ⓐ shiver   ⓑ discern   ⓒ deform   ⓓ paralyze

Day 7

01 alley [ǽli]
n. 골목, 오솔길

a narrow street behind or between buildings
syn lane, pathway, path

Walking through the long winding alley in Venice was an unforgettable experience.

---

02 shed [ʃed]
n. 오두막, 헛간

a small structure for shelter or storage
syn hut, barn

What tools do I need to build a shed in the backyard?

---

03 epilogue [épəlɔ̀ːg]
n. 에필로그, 후기

a short speech or writing added to end of a movie, book or play
syn afterword, postlude, postscript   ant preface, prelude, prologue

The author wrote an informative epilogue about the characters.

---

04 aristocracy [ærəstάkrəsi]
n. 귀족, 명문

a class of persons holding exceptional rank and privileges
n aristocrat 귀족   a aristocratic 귀족의, 상류의
syn gentry, nobility, patrician   ant commoner, plebeian

With his great success, the man finally became a member of the aristocracy.

---

05 toxic [tάksik]
a. 독성의, 유독한

containing a poisonous substance
n toxin 독소   n toxicity 독성, 유독성
syn noxious, venomous   ant non-lethal, nonpoisonous, nontoxic

The workman is charged with discarding toxic chemicals into a river.

---

06 proficient [prəfíʃənt]
a. 능숙한, 숙달한

well-advanced or competent in something
n proficiency 숙달, 숙련   ad proficiently 숙련되게, 능숙하게
syn adept, skillful, expert   ant incompetent, inept, unskilled

The most proficient student in the class stands to win a full scholarship.

---

07 dormant [dɔ́ːrmənt]
a. 휴면 중인, 잠자는

a state of rest or inactivity
n dormancy 수면[휴면] 상태
syn inactive, asleep   ant active, awake

The dormant volcano has not erupted for over 400 years.

---

01 길고 꾸불꾸불한 Venice의 골목을 걸었던 것은 잊지 못할 경험이었다. 02 뒤뜰에 헛간을 지으려고 하는데 어떤 도구가 필요한가요? 03 작가는 등장인물에 대한 정보를 주는 에필로그를 썼다. 04 크게 성공해 그 남자는 드디어 귀족이 되었다. 05 그 노동자는 강에 독성 화학물질을 방류한 혐의로 기소되었다. 06 반에서 가장 뛰어난 학생이 전액 장학금을 받게 될 것이다. 07 그 휴화산은 400년이 넘는 동안 폭발하지 않았다.

08 **upright** [ʌ́pràit]
a. 직립한, 정직한

standing or sitting straight

[n] uprightness 정직함, 직립 [ad] uprightly 정직하게, 똑바로

[syn] erect, straight, truthful [ant] bent, dishonest, deceptive

Sit upright in your chair when the teacher enters the room!
Even the most upright man is tempted to tell a lie from time to time.

09 **unanimous** [ju:nǽnəməs]
a. 만장일치의, 합의의

in complete agreement

[n] unanimity 합의, 만장일치 [ad] unanimously 만장일치로

[syn] consentaneous, consentient, agreed

The decision was unanimous to establish a nonprofit organization for parents of autistic children.

10 **optimal** [ɑ́ptəməl]
a. 최선의, 최적의

most favorable or best

[n] optimum 최적 조건 [ad] optimally 최선으로, 최적으로

[syn] greatest [ant] least, worst

Passing the test places me in an optimal position to graduate early.

11 **righteous** [ráitʃəs]
a. 옳은, 정직한

morally right or justifiable

[n] righteousness 정의, 정직 [ad] righteously 옳게, 정당하게

[syn] just, honest, equitable, impartial [ant] corrupt, dishonest, unrighteous

King Solomon was known to be incredibly wise and unfailingly righteous in his judgments.

12 **pathetic** [pəθétik]
a. 측은한, 불쌍한

arousing pity or sympathy

[n] pathos 비애감, 애수 [ad] pathetically 불쌍하게, 정서적으로

[syn] pitiful, sad, piteous, miserable [ant] comical

What makes him even more pathetic is there isn't one single person who he has Christmas with.

13 **prone** [proun]
a. 경향이 있는, 엎드린

having a tendency to do something

[syn] inclined, apt, tending

Pregnant women are more prone to suffer from depression due to the change in hormone secretion.
Studies show that the risk of the sudden infant death syndrome is higher when infants sleep in the prone position.

08 선생님이 교실로 들어오실 때에는 똑바로 앉아 있어라! 가장 정직한 사람일지라도 때때로 거짓말의 유혹에 빠진다. 09 자폐아를 둔 부모님들을 위한 비영리 단체를 세우자는 결정은 만장일치로 통과되었다. 10 시험에 통과하면 조기 졸업을 할 수 있는 가장 유리한 입장에 있게 된다. 11 Solomon 왕은 놀라울 정도로 지혜롭고 한쪽에 치우치지 않는 정직한 판단을 한 것으로 유명했다. 12 그를 더욱 애처롭게 만드는 것은 크리스마스를 같이 보낼 사람이 한 명도 없다는 것이다. 13 호르몬의 변화 때문에 임신한 여성들은 우울증에 걸리기 쉽다. 여러 연구는 아이를 엎드려 재울 때 영유아 돌연사 위험이 더 크다는 것을 보여주었다.

14 conceal [kənsíːl]

v. 숨기다

to hide or keep secret

ⓝ concealment 은닉, 잠복　ⓐ concealable 숨길 수 있는

syn veil, cover, disguise　ant disclose, divulge, uncover, reveal

All plans to conceal the truth were defeated by the startling new evidence.

---

15 revere [rivíər]

v. 숭배하다, 경외하다

to regard with deep respect, love, etc.

ⓝ reverence 숭상, 존경

syn venerate, adore, admire, esteem　ant despise, scorn

Gandhi is still revered as one of the greatest moral and political leaders in the world.

---

16 seize [siːz]

v. 꽉 잡다, 이해하다

to take or grab something especially by force

seizing　ⓝ 잡기, 붙잡기　ⓐ 주목할 만한

syn clutch, grip, apprehend　ant relinquish, release

A great panic seized the Japanese as nuclear weapons were dropped on Hiroshima and Nagasaki.

I couldn't seize what the director tried to express in the movie.

---

17 formulate [fɔ́ːrmjulèit]

v. 공식화하다, 체계화하다

to express something in certain forms or terms

ⓝ formulation 공식화, 체계화

syn formularize, codify

A Russian mathematician and meteorologist Alexander Friedmann formulated the Big Bang Theory in 1992.

---

18 infuse [infjúːz]

v. 불어넣다, 고취하다

to put into or fill with something

ⓝ infusion 고취, 불어넣기　ⓐ infusible 주입할 수 있는

syn implant, inculcate, inspire

The teacher infused the class with curiosity about insects.

---

19 compile [kəmpáil]

v. 편집하다, 수집하다

to collect and assemble from various sources

ⓝ compilation 편집, 편찬

syn edit, collect, accumulate　ant disperse, scatter, separate

My mom compiled stories in a book about my brother's football career for ten years.

---

14 진실을 감추려던 모든 계획은 놀라운 새 증거로 인해 수포로 돌아갔다. 15 간디는 여전히 세계에서 가장 위대한 윤리적, 정치적 지도자 중 한 명으로 존경 받고 있다. 16 히로시마와 나가사키에 핵폭탄이 투하되었을 때 일본인들은 엄청난 공포에 사로잡혔다. 나는 감독이 그 영화에서 표현하고자 했던 것이 무엇인지 이해할 수 없었다. 17 러시아의 수학자이자 기상학자인 Alexander Friedmann은 1992년에 빅뱅 이론을 체계화했다. 18 그 교사는 학생들에게 곤충에 관한 호기심을 불어 넣었다. 19 엄마는 10년 동안의 오빠의 미식 축구 인생에 대한 이야기를 모아서 책을 만들었다.

20 **contend** [kənténd]

v. 싸우다, 다투다

to fight, argue or compete

n contender 경쟁자 n contention 말다툼, 논쟁 a contentious 다투기를 좋아하는

syn contest, battle, dispute ant agree, harmonize

The two teams will contend for the championship on Sunday.

21 **empower** [impáuər]

v. 권한[권능]을 부여하다

to make someone or something able to do something

n empowerment 권한 부여

syn enable, commission, authorize ant disallow, hinder, prevent

The committee should be empowered to make decisions for the residential project.

22 **secrete** [sikrí:t]

v. 분비하다

to form and release a substance

n secretion 분비

syn exude, release, emit ant absorb

The venom secreted by the snake's poison glands is used to make its antidote.

23 **combat** [kəmbǽt / kámbæt]

v. 싸우다, 투쟁하다

n. 전투, 투쟁

to fight or contend against someone or something

combatant n 전투원 a 싸우는, 전투적인

syn battle, oppose, struggle ant agree, compromise, cooperate

Emergency measures were taken to combat the spread of SARS in East Asia.

24 **fuss** [fʌs]

v. 야단법석하다, 불평하다

n. 야단법석, 소동

to become upset or complain over trifles

a fussy 법석을 떠는 ad fussily 떠들썩하게, 신경질적으로

syn niggle, disturbance, agitation ant calm

She was an ill-tempered person who always found things to fuss about.

The customer made a fuss over the broken lamp shade.

25 **recess** [rí:ses]

v. 휴정[휴교, 휴회]하다

n. 휴식, 휴지

to halt temporarily

syn adjourn, interval

The judge recessed the important trial for the day.

The chairman asked for a recess so he could go over the agenda.

---

20 두 팀은 일요일에 챔피언 자리를 놓고 싸우게 될 것이다. 21 위원회가 지역 사업에 대한 결정을 내리려면 권한을 부여 받아야 한다. 22 뱀의 독 샘에서 분비된 독은 해독제를 만드는 데 사용된다. 23 사스의 확산을 막기 위해 동아시아에 긴급 조치가 내려졌다. 24 그녀는 언제나 트집 잡을 거리를 찾는 심술궂은 사람이었다. 그 손님은 전등의 갓이 부서졌다고 소동을 일으켰다. 25 판사는 중요한 재판을 하루 동안 휴정했다. 의장이 휴정을 요청해 안건에 대해 살펴볼 수 있었다.

Exercise

Word Check 각 단어의 뜻으로 알맞은 것을 찾아 연결하시오.

01 optimal   ⓐ able to do something very well

02 recess   ⓑ a small building for storing things

03 shed   ⓒ to develop something as a plan, theory, etc.

04 formulate   ⓓ having the most favorable and desirable quality

05 proficient   ⓔ a temporary break from work, especially in parliament, law courts, etc.

Syn & Ant Check 주어진 단어의 동의어, 반의어를 골라 쓰시오.

nonpoisonous	corrupt	piteous	disclose	release
inspire	authorize	battle	calm	truthful

06 upright =   11 fuss ↔

07 combat =   12 seize ↔

08 empower =   13 toxic ↔

09 infuse =   14 righteous ↔

10 pathetic =   15 conceal ↔

Sentence Practice 문장을 읽고 빈칸에 알맞은 단어를 고르시오.

16 The _____ of Shakespeare's play *The Tempest* is both a tribute and a farewell to the stage.

   ⓐ epilogue   ⓑ aristocracy   ⓒ shed   ⓓ alley

17 Plant seeds contain _____ life that is awakened upon receiving favorable conditions.

   ⓐ dormant   ⓑ toxic   ⓒ proficient   ⓓ pathetic

18 The urban population was _____ in their choice of leader for the city improvement program.

   ⓐ upright   ⓑ unanimous   ⓒ prone   ⓓ optimal

19 All ancient civilizations were known to _____ and worship the forces of nature.

   ⓐ seize   ⓑ empower   ⓒ revere   ⓓ combat

20 Our pancreases _____ the insulin which helps to process sugar in the body.

   ⓐ fuss   ⓑ secrete   ⓒ recess   ⓓ compile

🎧 01 **venue** [vénjuː]

n. 모임 장소, 행위[사건]의 현장, 재판지

a place where people go for an arranged activity

syn locale, scene, locus

The lawyer asked the judge for a change of venue for the trial.

02 **margin** [máːrdʒin]

n. 여백, 가장자리, (득표 등의) 차, 이문

the empty space of a written or printed page

ⓐ marginal 가장자리의, 주변의

syn blank, border, edge, profit   ant center, inside

Make sure you do not write in the left or right margin of the page.

The politician won the election by a wide margin.

03 **feedback** [fíːdbæk]

n. 반응, 피드백

a statement made to respond to a inquiry or request, etc.

syn answer, reply, response

We need your feedback in order to improve the quality of our service and products.

04 **rear** [riər]

n. 뒤, 후방

a. 뒤쪽의, 후방의

the back part

syn posterior, backside, rearward   ant forepart, front

The only space available for rent here is at the rear of the building.

The thief broke into the house through a rear window and stole several items.

05 **textile** [tékstail]

n. 직물

any material made by weaving

syn fabric, cloth

Textiles made in Bangladesh are not only inexpensive but also comfortable to wear.

06 **exploit** [éksplɔit/iksplɔ́it]

n. 영웅적 행위, 위업

v. 개발하다, 이용하다

a brave, exciting and interesting action

syn achievement, adventure, feat, utilize, apply

The director described the exploits of John F. Kennedy and disclosed his death in the movie.

Children are still exploited for cheap labor in many Asian and African countries.

---

01 변호사는 판사에게 그 공판의 재판지를 바꿔줄 것을 요청했다. 02 페이지의 왼쪽과 오른쪽 여백에 글을 쓰지 않도록 주의해 주십시오. 그 정치가는 큰 차이로 선거에서 승리했다. 03 저희는 서비스와 상품의 질을 향상시키기 위해 여러분들의 피드백이 필요합니다. 04 지금 여기서 임대가 가능한 곳은 건물의 뒤쪽 뿐입니다. 도둑이 뒤쪽 창문으로 침입해 몇 가지 물품을 훔쳐갔다. 05 방글라데시에서 만들어지는 직물은 저렴할 뿐만 아니라 입기에도 편하다. 06 감독은 영화에서 John F. Kennedy의 업적을 묘사하고 그의 죽음을 파헤쳤다. 많은 아시아와 아프리카 국가에서 여전히 아이들이 값싼 노동력으로 착취당하고 있다.

07 **avalanche** [ǽvəlæ̀ntʃ]
n. (눈, 산)사태, 쇄도

a large mass of loosened snow, earth, etc., sliding down a mountain

syn landslide, deluge, rush   ant lack, insufficiency

The sudden avalanche missed the skiers near the mountain.

---

08 **puberty** [pjúːbərti]
n. 사춘기, 청춘기

the period or age at which a person changes from a child to an adult

syn pubescence, adolescence

Many of the students in my class are just reaching puberty.

---

09 **petition** [pətíʃən]
n. 청원, 탄원(서)
v. 청원하다, 탄원하다

a request sent to an authority, especially one signed by many people

n petitioner 청원자   a petitionary 청원[탄원]의

syn application, request, entreat

The committee drew up a petition for a new recycling plant.

We petitioned the judge for a new hearing on the matter.

---

10 **filter** [fíltər]
n. 여과기
v. 거르다, 여과하다

something that gas or liquid is put through to remove unwanted substances

a filterable 여과할 수 있는   a filterability 여과성   v filtrate 여과하다

syn sieve, percolate, permeate   ant muddle, combine, mix

Regularly changing the oil filter will make your car last longer.

Traffic policemen wear masks to filter out the noxious fumes emitted by vehicles.

---

11 **accustomed** [əkʌ́stəmd]
a. 익숙해진

familiar with something by constant use, habit or practice

v accustom ~에 익숙하게 하다   ad accustomedly 평소대로

syn usual, customary, habitual   ant unaccustomed, unusual

People are getting accustomed to ordering products on the Internet.

---

12 **intelligible** [intélədʒəbl]
a. 이해할 수 있는, 명료한

able to be clearly understood

n intelligibility 이해할 수 있음, 명료

syn apprehensible, understandable, plain   ant unintelligible, unclear

Alison was too scared and exhausted to tell her story in an intelligible manner.

---

13 **plausible** [plɔ́ːzəbl]
a. 그럴듯한, 정말 같은

seemingly true, trustworthy and honest

n plausibility 그럴싸함   ad plausibly 그럴싸하게, 정말같이

syn probable, believable, likely   ant improbable, implausible, unlikely

The man told the guard a plausible story, so he released him.

---

07 갑자기 일어난 눈사태로 산 근처에서 스키를 타던 사람들이 실종되었다. 08 우리 반의 많은 학생들이 이제 갓 청소년이 되었다. 09 위원회는 새 재활용 공장을 요청하는 탄원서를 작성했다. 우리는 판사에게 그 사건의 재심을 청원했다. 10 정기적인 오일 필터 교환은 자동차의 수명을 연장해 줍니다. 교통경찰은 차량에서 배출되는 유독 가스를 걸러주는 마스크를 쓴다. 11 사람들은 인터넷으로 물건을 주문하는 것에 점점 익숙해지고 있다. 12 Alison은 너무 무섭고 피곤했기 때문에 그녀의 이야기를 명료하게 할 수가 없었다. 13 그 남자는 교도관에게 그럴듯한 이야기를 했고 교도관은 그 남자를 풀어주었다.

14 foretell [fɔːrtél]
v. 예고[예언]하다

to tell what will happen beforehand

ⓝ foreteller 예언자

syn foresee, predict, prophesy, foreknow

Even the Weather Department could not foretell the damage that would be done by the fierce hurricane.

15 stir [stəːr]
v. 섞다, 움직이다
n. 움직임, 동요

to move something around to mix using one's hand or a tool

ⓐ stirless 움직이지 않는

syn agitate, mix

Add egg mixture to the flour mixture and stir until they are well combined.
The latest report caused a stir among scientists.

16 astound [əstáund]
v. 깜짝 놀라게 하다

to surprise or shock someone

ⓝ astoundment 대경실색   ⓐ astounding 놀라운   ad astoundingly 간담이 서늘하여

syn amaze, startle, stun   ant bore, dull

She was astounded to hear that she was nominated as the best actress.

17 suck [sʌk]
v. 빨다, 흡수하다

to draw something into the mouth, especially liquid

ⓝ suction 빨기, 흡인(력)   ⓐ sucking 빠는, 흡수하는

syn absorb, extract, imbibe   ant discharge, emit

One of the best treats during the hottest days of summer is to suck on a snow cone.

18 mislead [mislíːd]
v. 오도하다, 속이다

to lead someone in a wrong direction

ⓐ misleading 오도하는, 그릇된

syn misguide, misdirect, delude, deceive

Advertisements should not mislead customers about the quality of the products advertised.

19 obsess [əbsés]
v. 사로잡다, 괴롭히다

to think about someone or something all the time

ⓝ obsession 사로잡힘   ⓐ obsessive 강박관념의, 망상의

syn haunt, engross, possess, preoccupy

Mike became obsessed with the idea that the whole school gossiped about him.

---

14 기상청 조차도 맹렬한 허리케인이 가져올 피해를 예측할 수 없었다. 15 계란 반죽을 밀가루 반죽에 넣고 잘 섞일 때까지 저어주세요. 최근 연구보고서가 과학자들 사이에 동요를 일으켰다. 16 그녀는 자신이 여우주연상 후보에 올랐다는 사실을 듣고는 깜짝 놀랐다. 17 무더운 여름 날 우리에게 가장 즐거움을 주는 것 중의 하나는 빙과를 빨아먹는 것이다. 18 광고는 소비자들에게 제품의 품질을 속여서는 안 된다. 19 Mike는 온 학교가 그에 대해 험담을 한다는 생각에 사로잡혀 있었다.

20 mount [maunt]

v. 오르다

to go up something

[syn] rise, climb, ascend [ant] descend

The speaker mounted the high stage very slowly before his speech.

---

21 terminate [tə́ːrmənèit]

v. 끝내다, 종결시키다

to end or finish something

[n] termination 종료, 결말 [a] terminative 종결시키는, 결정적인

[syn] complete, close, conclude [ant] begin, initiate, commence

The company terminated the project of developing alternative fuel vehicles due to lack of funds.

---

22 enrage [inréidʒ]

v. 격분하게 하다

to make someone very angry

[n] enragement 분노 [n] rage 격노, 분노

[syn] anger, provoke, infuriate [ant] calm, appease, pacify, soothe

Many people were enraged by the government's decision to raise the income tax.

---

23 decrease [dikríːs/díkriːs]

v. 감소하다, 줄다

n. 감소, 감퇴

to make or become less in some way

[a] decreasing 감소하는 [ad] decreasingly 감소하게

[syn] lessen, diminish, reduce [ant] increase, multiply

As the company announced plans to decrease the employee welfare budget, the employees went on strike.

There has been a decrease in the birth rate and an increase in the number of elderly people.

---

24 glare [glɛər]

v. 노려보다, 눈부시게 빛나다

n. 노려봄, 섬광

to stare fiercely

[a] glaring 눈부신, 반짝거리는

[syn] glower, glow, shine, dazzle [ant] smile

The woman glared at the clerk for not giving her the correct change.

He gave her a steady glare until she saw him.

---

25 paste [peist]

v. 붙이다

n. 풀, 밀가루 반죽

to stick or glue two things together

[syn] attach, adhere [ant] loosen, unfasten, separate

The children pasted the heart-shaped colored paper onto the cards for Valentine's Day.

The recipe says to make a thick paste of flour and milk.

---

20 연사는 연설하기 전에 높은 무대로 천천히 올라갔다. 21 그 회사는 자금의 부족으로 대체 연료 차량 개발을 끝냈다. 22 많은 사람들이 소득세를 올리겠다는 정부의 결정에 격분했다. 23 회사가 직원 복지 예산을 줄이겠다는 계획을 발표하자 직원들은 파업에 돌입했다. 출생률이 감소하고 고령 인구가 증가하고 있다. 24 그 여인은 정확한 거스름돈을 거슬러 주지 않았기 때문에 점원을 노려보았다. 그는 그녀가 볼 때까지 그녀를 뚫어지게 쳐다보았다. 25 아이들은 하트 모양의 색종이를 발렌타인데이 카드에 붙였다. 요리법에는 걸쭉한 밀가루 우유 반죽을 만들라고 쓰여 있어.

Exercise

Word Check 각 단어의 뜻으로 알맞은 것을 찾아 연결하시오.

01 astound
02 puberty
03 accustomed
04 avalanche
05 suck

ⓐ used to doing something
ⓑ to draw liquid into the mouth
ⓒ to make someone feel surprised and shocked
ⓓ the stage in humans when they become physically mature
ⓔ a sudden movement of a large mass of snow, ice, etc. down a mountain

Syn & Ant Check 주어진 단어의 동의어, 반의어를 골라 쓰시오.

blank	predict	descend	commence	pacify
response	apprehensible	front	increase	adhere

06 feedback = _____
07 margin = _____
08 paste = _____
09 intelligible = _____
10 foretell = _____

11 decrease ↔ _____
12 enrage ↔ _____
13 terminate ↔ _____
14 rear ↔ _____
15 mount ↔ _____

Sentence Practice 문장을 읽고 빈칸에 알맞은 단어를 고르시오.

16 The _____ was changed at the last minute owing to the unseasonable rain.
   ⓐ avalanche   ⓑ venue   ⓒ textile   ⓓ puberty

17 Many concerned citizens are lining up to sign the _____ to prevent future forest fires.
   ⓐ exploit   ⓑ rear   ⓒ feedback   ⓓ petition

18 A stalker will _____ over his victim and may even follow or hurt him or her.
   ⓐ obsess   ⓑ paste   ⓒ mislead   ⓓ foretell

19 I thought his reasons for being delayed were not entirely _____.
   ⓐ intelligible   ⓑ plausible   ⓒ accustomed   ⓓ rear

20 The class was cowed into silence by the teacher's angry _____.
   ⓐ glare   ⓑ paste   ⓒ margin   ⓓ filter

01 tablet [tǽblit]
n. 정제, 알약

a small piece of medicine

syn pill, capsule

I'm sorry but this particular cold and flu tablet is currently out of stock.

02 fatigue [fətíːg]
n. 피로, 피곤
v. 지치게 하다

extreme mental or physical tiredness after work, activity, effort, etc.

a fatigued 지친

syn exhaustion, weariness   ant energy, strength, vigor

If you work twenty four seven, you could die of fatigue.

I am fatigued with my mother's frequent visits and endless nagging.

03 fraud [frɔːd]
n. 사기, 기만, 사기꾼

the act of deceiving someone to gain money, things, etc.

syn trickery, deception, cheat   ant fairness, honesty, integrity

There has been an increase in the number of frauds against older people living alone.

I knew the man was a dangerous fraud when he told me his plan.

04 heredity [hərédəti]
n. 유전, 상속

the passing of characteristics from parent to offspring through genes

a hereditary 유전(성)의, 세습의

syn inheritance

The researchers are investigating the role of heredity in heart disease.

05 rally [rǽli]
n. 대회, 집회
v. 다시 모으다, 규합하다

a gathering for some purpose

a rallier 집회참가자

syn assembly, demonstration, assemblage, muster

Many peace rallies were organized in response to an attack on Iraq.

Environmentalists rallied to protest commercial whaling in Washington D.C.

06 blunder [blʌ́ndər]
n. 큰 실수

a foolish mistake

syn lapse, oversight   ant achievement, success

I have just realized that I made a big blunder in my report.

---

01 죄송하지만 이 감기 독감 약은 현재 재고가 없습니다. 02 계속 일만 하다간 과로사 할 수도 있어. 나는 엄마의 잦은 방문과 끝없는 잔소리에 지쳤어. 03 독거노인을 상대로 한 사기가 증가하고 있다. 그가 그의 계획을 얘기했을 때 나는 그 남자가 위험한 사기꾼이라는 것을 알아챘다. 04 연구원들은 유전이 심장병에 어떠한 영향을 미치는지를 조사하고 있다. 05 많은 평화 집회가 이라크 공격에 대응하여 결성되었다. 환경 운동가들이 상업적인 포경에 반대하기 위해 Washington D.C.에 다시 모였다. 06 나는 방금 막 내가 보고서에 큰 실수를 했다는 것을 깨달았어.

07 precaution [prikɔ́:ʃən]
n. 조심, 예방 조치

an action taken to prevent or avoid a risk or danger

ⓐ precautious 조심하는, 주의 깊은   ⓐ precautionary 예방의, 경계의

syn caution, forethought, carefulness

People thought of a list of wise precautions for the next hurricane.

---

08 fraction [frǽkʃən]
n. 일부, 조금

a small part or amount

ⓐ fractional 부분적인   ⓥ fractionalize 분할하다, 나누다

syn portion, part, fragment   ant entirety, total, whole

We offer package tours to Brazil for a fraction of the normal cost.

---

09 abundant [əbʌ́ndənt]
a. 풍부한, 많은

more than enough in quantity

ⓝ abundance 풍부, 충만   ad abundantly 풍부하게

syn teeming, ample, plentiful   ant lacking, meager, scarce

They brought us an abundant number of textbooks for the new course.

---

10 rampant [rǽmpənt]
a. 유행하는, 만연하는

growing and spreading in an uncontrolled way

ⓝ rampancy 유행, 만연   ad rampantly 분방하게

syn epidemic, pandemic, widespread

The country has experienced rampant inflation during the past three years.

---

11 feasible [fí:zəbl]
a. 실현 가능한

able to be done or accomplished

ⓝ feasibility 실현 가능성   ad feasibly 실행할 수 있게

syn probable, possible   ant impossible, unfeasible

To travel around the world in 80 days is feasible if we have enough money.

---

12 tame [teim]
a. 길든

changed from wildness to a gentle state

syn domesticated   ant untamed, undomesticated, savage

The ferocious-looking bulldog turned out to be very tame and even-tempered.

---

13 conscientious [kὰnʃién̩ʃəs]
a. 세심한, 양심적인

showing a lot of care and attention

ⓝ conscience 양심   ad conscientiously 양심적으로

syn careful, scrupulous, thorough   ant careless, unconscientious, dishonest

Our hospital doctors are very conscientious toward the terminally-ill patients.

---

07 사람들은 다음 허리케인을 대비하여 신중하게 예방조치 리스트에 대해 생각했다. 08 저희는 정상 가격에 비교해 아주 저렴한 브라질 여행 상품을 제공합니다. 09 그들은 우리에게 새 교과과정에 쓰일 많은 교과서를 가져왔다. 10 그 나라는 지난 3년 동안 고질적인 인플레이션을 겪고 있다. 11 우리에게 충분한 돈만 있으면 80일 만에 세계 일주를 할 수 있어. 12 사나워 보이는 그 불독은 잘 길들여져 순했다. 13 저희 병원의 의사들은 말기 환자들에게 매우 정성을 쏟고 있습니다.

14 explicit [iksplísit]

a. 명백한, 명확한, 노골적인

clearly stated or shown

[n] explicitness 명백함, 솔직함 [ad] explicitly 명백하게, 명확하게

[syn] plain, definite, unambiguous [ant] implicit, ambiguous, obscure

There must be an explicit reason why he was not promoted.

The sexually explicit movie was banned from viewing in the U.S.

15 trifling [tráifliŋ]

a. 사소한, 하찮은

of little importance

[n] trifle 시시한 것 [ad] triflingly 하찮게, 근소하게

[syn] trivial, frivolous, insignificant, unimportant [ant] important, significant

The most trifling problems could become big enough to cause serious trouble if not dealt with in a timely fashion.

16 trim [trim]

a. 말쑥한, 잘 정돈된

v. 정돈하다, 치다

fit and healthy in appearance

[syn] neat, tidy, orderly [ant] disordered

She has a trim look through diet and exercise after her ex-boyfriend dumped her.

I asked a hairdresser to trim my fringe a bit but he made me look like Frankenstein.

17 lessen [lésn]

v. 줄이다, 감소시키다

to make or become less in size, quantity or degree

[syn] decrease, diminish, dwindle [ant] grow, increase

The doctor was able to lessen the effects of the illness on the girl's development.

18 thrive [θraiv]

v. 번영[번성]하다

to grow heathly and vigorous

[n] thrift 번영, 번성 [a] thriving 번영[번성]하는

[syn] flourish, prosper [ant] weaken, languish

The economy will thrive when businesses invest more and consumers buy more.

19 dispatch [dispǽtʃ]

v. 급파하다, 발송하다

n. 급파, 발송

to send someone or something for a certain reason

[n] dispatcher 발송인

[syn] transmit, forward [ant] hold, keep, retain, delay

The Korean government agreed to dispatch additional troops to Iraq.

After you confirm your order, we will inform you by email the order details and the date of dispatch.

---

14 그가 승진하지 못한 명백한 이유가 있을 거야. 성적으로 노골적인 그 영화는 미국에서 상영이 금지되었다. 15 가장 사소한 문제도 제때에 해결하지 않으면 심각한 문제를 초래하는 큰 문제가 될 수 있다. 16 그녀는 전 남자친구에게 차이고 난 후 운동과 다이어트를 통해 말쑥해졌다. 나는 미용사에게 앞머리를 조금만 쳐 달라고 했는데 프랑켄슈타인처럼 보이게 해 놓았다. 17 의사는 그 병이 소녀의 성장에 미치는 영향을 줄 일 수 있었다. 18 사업체들이 더 많은 금액을 투자하고 소비자들이 더 많은 물건을 살 때 경제가 번영한다. 19 한국 정부는 이라크에 더 많은 군사를 파견하는 데 동의했다. 주문을 확인하시면 저희가 이메일을 통해 주문 상세내역과 발송일을 알려드리겠습니다.

20 ponder [pándər]
v. 숙고하다

to think deeply about something or someone

a ponderable 일고의 가치가 있는

syn deliberate, consider, contemplate

He is pondering over how to refuse her offer without offending her.

21 relay [rí:lei]
v. 중계하다

to get and pass on something, especially news, a message, etc.

syn communicate, transmit

All football matches will be relayed live to every continent.

22 scatter [skǽtər]
v. 흩뿌리다

to separate or throw in many directions

a scattered 흩뿌려진, 산재해 있는

syn disperse, dispel, dissipate   ant assemble, congregate, unite

The gunshot made the animals scatter from the hunter and scurry for cover.

23 interpret [intə́:rprit]
v. 해석하다, 설명하다

to restate what is said into another language

n interpretation 해석, 해설   n interpreter 해석자, 통역자

syn translate, explain

The woman was able to interpret the speech into seven different languages.

The teacher interpreted the humanity revealed in Shakespeare's tragedies.

24 prescribe [priskráib]
v. 규정하다, 처방하다

to order or direct, especially medicine

n prescription 처방전

syn specify, stipulate

I will prescribe several pills that you can pick up at the pharmacy across the street.

25 amid [əmíd]
prep. ~의 사이에, ~의 한복판에

in the middle of or among

syn amidst, among, between, mid   ant beyond, outside

Jason was sitting amid a group of people waiting for his name to be called.

---

20 그는 그녀의 기분을 상하게 하지 않고 어떻게 그녀의 제안을 거절할 것인가를 고민하고 있다. 21 모든 축구 경기는 생방송으로 모든 대륙에 중계될 것이다. 22 총성으로 동물들이 사냥꾼으로부터 흩어져서 숨을 곳을 찾아 황급히 달렸다. 23 그 여성은 그 연설을 7개국어로 통역할 수 있었다. 선생님은 Shakespeare의 비극에서 드러나는 인간성을 설명해 주셨다. 24 길 건너 약국에서 약을 받을 수 있도록 몇 가지 약을 처방 해드릴게요. 25 Jason은 자신의 이름이 불리기를 기다리면서 한 무리의 사람들 속에 앉아 있었다.

Exercise

Word Check 각 단어의 뜻으로 알맞은 것을 찾아 연결하시오.

01	thrive	ⓐ very careful to do something
02	precaution	ⓑ to do well or successful financially
03	conscientious	ⓒ capable of being done or achieved
04	ponder	ⓓ to consider something deeply and carefully
05	feasible	ⓔ something done in order to avoid danger, failure, injury, etc.

Syn & Ant Check 주어진 단어의 동의어, 반의어를 골라 쓰시오.

weariness	demonstration	meager	ambiguous	domesticated
neat	entirety	increase	congregate	among

06	trim	=	11	fraction	↔
07	rally	=	12	scatter	↔
08	tame	=	13	lessen	↔
09	amid	=	14	explicit	↔
10	fatigue	=	15	abundant	↔

Sentence Practice 문장을 읽고 빈칸에 알맞은 단어를 고르시오.

16 The "miracle medicine" never really helped anybody and turned out to be a _____.

  ⓐ fraud   ⓑ rally   ⓒ blunder   ⓓ fraction

17 People tend to ascribe their flaws or shortcomings to the vagaries of _____ instead of taking personal responsibility.

  ⓐ tablet   ⓑ precaution   ⓒ fatigue   ⓓ heredity

18 The United Nations is working very hard to solve the problem of hunger _____ throughout Africa.

  ⓐ trim   ⓑ feasible   ⓒ conscientious   ⓓ rampant

19 It was shocking to see the good friends fall out over a(n) _____ matter they could have overlooked.

  ⓐ trifling   ⓑ explicit   ⓒ tame   ⓓ abundant

20 We have been asked to _____ this order to the Bahamas by express delivery.

  ⓐ prescribe   ⓑ thrive   ⓒ ponder   ⓓ dispatch

🎧 01 **kinship** [kínʃip]
n. 혈족 관계

family relationship or close connection

[syn] affinity, consanguinity

Primitive tribe societies were bound by strong kinship ties, which provided security and intimacy.

02 **affectation** [æfektéiʃən]
n. 체하기, 뽐냄

insincere or unnatural behavior intended to impress someone

[v] affect 가장하다, ~체하다

[syn] pretending, pretentiousness   [ant] genuineness

We value teammates who speak honestly and without any affectation.

03 **turmoil** [tɔ́ːrmɔil]
n. 소란, 소동

a state of confusion, excitement and trouble

[syn] agitation, riot, disturbance   [ant] order, quiet

The business suffered from economic turmoil for a few years.

04 **apparatus** [æpərǽtəs]
n. (한 벌의) 기구, 장치

a set of instruments, tools, machines, etc., used for a specific purpose

[syn] appliance, machinery, equipment, device

The circus star wore a safety apparatus during the dangerous performance.

05 **excerpt** [éksəːrpt]
n. 발췌록, 인용구

a passage selected or quoted from a book, film, etc.

[a] excerptible 인용[발췌]할 수 있는

[syn] extract, citation, quotation

My teacher read a fascinating excerpt from Jim Elliot's biography.

06 **metropolis** [mitrápəlis]
n. 중심 도시

a large and important city of a country or area

[a] metropolitan 주요 도시의, 대도시의

[syn] capital, municipality

Brian's family lives in a quiet area away from the bustling metropolis of Chicago.

---

01 원시 부족 사회는 강한 혈족 관계로 결속되어 있었고 이것이 안정과 친밀감을 주었다. 02 우리는 가식없이 정직하게 말하는 팀 동료를 소중하게 여긴다. 03 그 사업체는 몇 년 동안 경제적인 혼란을 겪었다. 04 그 서커스 배우는 위험한 공연을 하는 동안 안전장치를 착용했다. 05 선생님은 Jim Elliot의 전기에서 감동적인 발췌문을 읽어주셨다. 06 Brian의 가족은 혼잡한 중심도시인 Chicago에서 떨어진 한가로운 지역에 살고 있다.

07 slope [sloup]
n. 기울기, 비탈
v. 경사지다

a piece of ground or surface that has a incline
[syn] gradient, side, lean, tilt   [ant] flat, plain, level

Students learned how to measure the slope of the tangent without using a grid and a ruler.

The plateaus of the South Asian subcontinent slope gently towards the sea.

08 supreme [səprí:m]
a. 최고의, 최대의

highest in position, power or importance
[n] supremacy 최고, 우위   [ad] supremely 최고로, 대단하게
[syn] greatest, paramount, ultimate   [ant] lowest, minor

The president acts as supreme commander of the military in times of peace or war.

09 compelling [kəmpéliŋ]
a. 강제적인, 위압적인, 마음을 끄는

having great power so one cannot resist
[v] compel 강제[강요]하다   [ad] compellingly 강제적으로
[syn] constraining, powerful, forcing, overpowering   [ant] unconvincing

Fossil discoveries have continued to provide new and compelling evidence to support the theory of evolution.

Martin Luther King Jr. gave compelling speeches against racial segregation in America.

10 fuzzy [fʌ́zi]
a. 불분명한, 모호한

not easy to understand or not having clear details
[ad] fuzzily 흐릿하게
[syn] indistinct, imprecise, obscure, vague   [ant] clear, distinct

My son always gives me fuzzy answers about what he wants for his birthday present.

11 frigid [frídʒid]
a. 몹시 추운, 냉랭한

extremely cold in temperature
[n] frigidity 한랭, 냉담   [ad] frigidly 차갑게, 냉담하게
[syn] freezing, refrigerated, chilly   [ant] burning, hot, warm

The weatherman warned people about the frigid weather.

12 vulnerable [vʌ́lnərəbl]
a. 상처[공격] 받기 쉬운, 취약한

easily hurt or affected
[n] vulnerability 상처 받기 쉬움, 취약함
[syn] susceptible, weak, unprotected   [ant] guarded, invulnerable

Korean industry is highly vulnerable to changes in the exchange rate due to the lack of raw materials.

---

07 학생들은 격자와 자를 사용하지 않고 접선의 기울기를 측정하는 법을 배웠다. 남아시아 대륙의 고원 지대는 바다를 향해 완만하게 경사져 있다. 08 대통령은 전시나 평화시를 막론하고 군 최고 사령관 역할을 한다. 09 화석의 발견은 진화론을 뒷받침해 주는 새롭고 강력한 증거를 계속해서 제시해 주고 있다. Martin Luther King Jr.는 미국의 인종 차별에 반대하는 강력한 연설을 했다. 10 내 아들은 항상 생일 선물로 무엇을 받고 싶으냐는 말에 모호한 대답을 한다. 11 예보관은 사람들에게 날씨가 매울 추울 것이라고 알렸다. 12 한국의 산업은 원자재의 부족 때문에 환율 변화에 매우 취약하다.

13 render [réndər]
v. ~이 되게 하다, 주다

to cause someone or something to be in a certain condition
[syn] present, leave, give

The news of my mother's death rendered me speechless.
The man rendered aid to accident victims until the ambulance arrived.

14 seal [siːl]
v. 날인하다, 봉하다
n. 인장

to close something tightly
[syn] enclose, fasten   [ant] unseal

Please seal this register in an envelope and sign over the flap.
The knight broke the king's seal with a knife as soon as he received the letter from king.

15 clarify [klǽrəfài]
v. 명백히 하다

to make or become clear
[n] clarification 정확, 설명
[syn] define, elucidate, explain   [ant] confuse, muddle, obfuscate

We would like you to clarify the current situation regarding the contract agreement.

16 perplex [pərpléks]
v. 당황케 하다, 혼란케 하다

to make someone feel confused
[n] perplexity 당황, 혼란   [a] perplexed 당황한
[syn] puzzle, confound, bewilder, confuse

The disappointing result of the final match perplexed everyone on our team.

17 recede [risíːd]
v. 물러 나다, 철회하다

to move away until something disappears
[syn] withdraw, back, retreat   [ant] advance, approach

What could be more fun than watching tides as they surge forward and recede?

18 thrust [θrʌst]
v. 밀어내다

to push something with force
[syn] drive, force, shove   [ant] pull

He was thrust into a bad situation from the first day he arrived at the company.

19 retain [ritéin]
v. 보유하다, 간직하다

to keep or continue to have something
[n] retention 보유, 보존   [a] retentive 보존하는
[syn] hold, maintain, preserve   [ant] lose

Please make sure you retain this ticket stub until after the performance.

13 어머니가 돌아가셨다는 소식이 할 말을 잃게 만들었다. 남자는 구급차가 도착하기 전에 사고 부상자를 치료해 주었다. 14 이 신청서를 봉투에 넣어 봉하고 접는 부분에 서명 해주십시오. 왕으로부터 편지를 받자마자 기사는 왕의 인장을 칼로 뜯었다. 15 계약 체결에 관한 현재 상황을 분명히 밝혀주십시오. 16 결승 전 결과가 실망스러워서 우리 팀의 모든 사람들이 당황했다. 17 조류가 밀려들어왔다 나가는 것을 지켜보는 것만큼 즐거운 일이 또 있을까? 18 그 회사에 입사 한 첫날에 그는 좋지 않은 상황에 말려들었다. 19 공연이 끝난 후까지 표의 나머지 부분을 가지고 계십시오.

20 dissent [disént]
v. 의견을 달리하다
n. 불찬성, 이의

to have a different opinion from someone else

[a] dissentient 반대하는   [ad] dissentingly 의견을 달리하여

[syn] disagree, oppose, object   [ant] assent, approve, concur

It is infinitely easier to agree with the majority than to dissent.

There was a lot of political dissent in the country because of the upcoming election.

21 polish [páliʃ]
v. 닦다, 윤을 내다
n. 광택제

to make something smooth and shine by rubbing

[syn] burnish, gloss

Try to use a banana peel to polish your leather goods.

My brother bought some shoe polish for dad's shoes.

22 concur [kənkə́:r]
v. 동의하다, 일치하다

to agree with someone or something

[n] concurrence 일치, 동의, 동시 발생   [a] concurrent 일치하는, 의견이 같은

[syn] accede, consent, assent   [ant] disagree, object, oppose

Neil seemed to concur with his parents' decision regarding the new job.

23 deteriorate [ditíəriərèit]
v. 악화시키다, 저하시키다

to make or become worse

[n] deterioration 악화   [a] deteriorative 악화[저하] 하는

[syn] depreciate, worsen, decay   [ant] improve, strengthen, ameliorate

His health condition has dramatically deteriorated due to complications of the diabetes.

24 steer [stiər]
v. 키를 잡다, 이끌다

to control the direction of something

[n] steering 조종, 지도   [a] steerable 조종 가능한

[syn] direct, drive, guide

His advisor steered him into a different major and he became a well-known astronomer.

25 crawl [krɔːl]
v. 기어가다
n. 서행

to move on hands and knees or with the body on the ground

[syn] creep, clamber   [ant] hurry, rush

A baby starts to crawl as early as 6 months and as late as 11 months.

The traffic slowed to a crawl in the snow storm.

---

20 다수의 사람에게 반대하는 것보다 동의하는 것이 훨씬 쉽다. 곧 있을 선거 때문에 그 나라는 정치적 이견이 분분했다. 21 가죽 제품을 닦을 때 바나나 껍질을 사용해 봐. 오빠가 아빠 신발을 닦으려고 구두약을 샀다. 22 Neil은 새 직업에 대해서 부모님의 결정에 동의한 것처럼 보였다. 23 그의 건강 상태는 당뇨 합병증으로 급속히 악화되었다. 24 그의 지도 교수는 그를 다른 전공으로 이끌었고 그는 유명한 천문학자가 되었다. 25 아기는 빠르면 6개월, 늦으면 11개월 무렵에 기기 시작한다. 눈보라 속에서 차들이 서행했다.

Exercise

Word Check 각 단어의 뜻으로 알맞은 것을 찾아 연결하시오.

01 perplex   ⓐ to make someone confused

02 kinship   ⓑ to have a different idea with someone

03 polish   ⓒ connection made by blood, adoption or marriage

04 dissent   ⓓ the large and important city of the country or region

05 metropolis   ⓔ substance that makes something smooth and glossy by rubbing it

Syn & Ant Check 주어진 단어의 동의어, 반의어를 골라 쓰시오.

pretentiousness	inferior	unconvincing	burning	susceptible
muddle	worsen	maintain	quotation	rush

06 vulnerable = _____

07 deteriorate = _____

08 affectation = _____

09 retain = _____

10 excerpt = _____

11 compelling ↔ _____

12 clarify ↔ _____

13 crawl ↔ _____

14 supreme ↔ _____

15 frigid ↔ _____

Sentence Practice 문장을 읽고 빈칸에 알맞은 단어를 고르시오.

16 The _____ in the laboratory was modern enough to satisfy the most exacting researcher.

    ⓐ kinship   ⓑ apparatus   ⓒ seal   ⓓ affectation

17 I'm sorry to say that the details of this project are still a little _____ to most of the staff.

    ⓐ frigid   ⓑ supreme   ⓒ compelling   ⓓ fuzzy

18 The French Revolution was followed by an era of great _____ and upheaval.

    ⓐ turmoil   ⓑ excerpt   ⓒ dissent   ⓓ metropolis

19 Mr. Faulkner was granted the privilege of _____ the keynote address at the seminar.

    ⓐ thrusting   ⓑ polishing   ⓒ rendering   ⓓ crawling

20 Residents in the beachfront area are asked to wait until the flood waters _____.

    ⓐ perplex   ⓑ recede   ⓒ deteriorate   ⓓ dissent

❖ before

ante : **ante**cipate 예상하다, **ante**date ~보다 앞서다

Our ancestors used to **ante**cipate a good harvest when they had a lot of snow in winter.
우리 조상들은 겨울에 눈이 많이 오면 풍년을 기대하곤 했다.

pre : **pre**scient 선견지명이 있는, **pre**cede 앞장서다, **pre**cise 정확한

The prophet gave **pre**scient warnings before the troops' attacking.
그 예언자는 군대의 공격이 있기 전에 선견지명이 있는 경고를 했다.

fore : **fore**see 예견하다, **fore**bear 조상, **fore**head 이마

It's impossible to **fore**see exactly how our future will be.
우리의 미래가 어떻지 정확히 예측하기란 불가능하다.

❖ after

post : **post**erity 후대, **post**dated ~후에 오다, **post**humous 사후에 생긴

The photojournalist who was killed during the war recorded the war scene on video for **post**erity.
전쟁 중에 죽은 그 사진기자는 후대를 위해 전쟁 장면들을 비디오로 녹화해 놓았다.

epi, meta : **epi**logue 끝맺는 말, **epi**taph 비명, **meta**physics 형이상학

The novelist said that the hardest work is to write the **epi**logue.
그 소설가는 후기를 쓰는 것이 가장 어렵다고 했다.

❖ back

retro : **retro**gression 역행, 후퇴, **retro**spect 회상, **retro**active 반동적인

There was a **retro**gression of human rights during the medieval ages.
중세시대에 인권의 후퇴 시기가 있었다.

❖ new

neo : **neo**logism 신조어, **neo**lithic 신석기의, **neo**classical 신고전주의의

Oxford University Press has updated its dictionaries every year to include the latest **neo**logisms.
OUP는 매년 사전에 최신 조어들을 수록하기 위해 업데이트 한다.

❖ again

re : **re**activate 부활시키다, **re**collect 회상하다, **re**arrange 다시 정리하다

You may cancel or **re**arrange your schedule before the end of this month.
당신은 이번 달 말일 전에 스케줄을 취소하거나 재조정할 수 있습니다.

A 영어 풀이에 알맞은 단어를 보기에서 찾아 쓰시오.

| paralyze | unanimous | petition | blunder | deteriorate |

01 sharing the same opinion or view _____

02 a stupid or embarrassing mistake _____

03 to make someone unable to move or feel _____

04 to become worse in quality, character or value _____

05 to make a written formal request to a government or organization _____

B 문장을 읽고 문맥에 적절한 단어를 고르시오.

06 Cindy could not help but (exclaim/clarify) in wonder at the beauty of the mountainside.

07 Professor Mason's exceptionally difficult papers and assignments always (preceded/ perplexed) his students.

08 Jake (receded/obsessed) with the math problem for two hours before finally grasping the principles to solve it.

09 My room gets (abundant/transparent) light because of its tall windows facing the morning sunshine of the east.

C 표시된 부분과 뜻이 가장 가까운 것을 고르시오.

10 It's great to see the children thrive in this kindergarten's atmosphere of affection and care.

    ⓐ animate   ⓑ fuss   ⓒ dissent   ⓓ flourish

11 We'll recess for an hour before continuing on with our monthly departmental review at 12:40.

    ⓐ formulate   ⓑ adjourn   ⓒ compile   ⓓ dissent

12 The view of the mainland was fuzzy this morning because of the mist coming in off the ocean.

    ⓐ frigid   ⓑ optimal   ⓒ indistinct   ⓓ tranquil

13 Lorna always felt uncomfortable during puberty because she was no longer a girl but not yet a woman.

    ⓐ adolescence   ⓑ venue   ⓒ fatigue   ⓓ affectation

D 표시된 부분의 반대말로 가장 알맞은 것을 고르시오.

14 The two friends will contend for the same prize in today's exciting contest.
ⓐ harmonize　　　ⓑ seize　　　ⓒ assail　　　ⓓ combat

15 The champion asserted that he was supreme because he had defeated all his rivals.
ⓐ ruthless　　　ⓑ lowest　　　ⓒ righteous　　　ⓓ optimal

16 My bank has no plausible explanation for the discrepancy in my recent account statements.
ⓐ accustomed　　　ⓑ intelligible　　　ⓒ conscientious　　　ⓓ improbable

17 The pile of dry leaves scattered in the strong autumn wind and covered the yard.
ⓐ seize　　　ⓑ decrease　　　ⓒ assemble　　　ⓓ paste

E 주어진 단어를 알맞은 형태로 바꿔 빈칸에 쓰시오.

18 The child was born with a slight physical ＿＿＿＿＿. (deform)

19 Some personal ＿＿＿＿＿ is necessary for healthy living. (vulnerable)

20 The worker's ＿＿＿＿＿ progress on the project amazed his boss. (astound)

21 The objective of this study is to evaluate the ＿＿＿＿＿ of producing biodiesel from a variety of oils such as soy, corn. (feasible)

F 빈칸에 알맞은 단어를 보기에서 찾아 쓰시오. (필요한 경우 형태를 바꾸시오.)

accustomed	terminate	feedback	retain	seize
aristocracy	concur	seal	fatigue	seize

22 London의 쌀쌀한 날씨에 적응하는 데 며칠이 걸렸다.
　→ It took us a few days to get ＿＿＿＿＿ to the cold weather in London.

23 이 설문지를 작성해주십시오. 저희 가게에 대한 고객님의 의견을 듣고자 합니다.
　→ We request you to give us your ＿＿＿＿＿ on our store by filling in this questionnaire.

24 포장이 훼손되었거나 봉인이 뜯겨져 있으면 이 상품을 사용하지 마십시오.
　→ Do not use this product if the packaging is damaged or the ＿＿＿＿＿ is broken.

25 군이 권력을 장악한 이후로 귀족의 권세는 서서히 사라졌다.
　→ The dominance of the ＿＿＿＿＿ faded for ever after the army ＿＿＿＿＿ power.

> 영어를 우리말로 옮기시오.

01 proficient		31 textile	
02 apparatus		32 abundant	
03 perplex		33 amid	
04 intelligible		34 suck	
05 fraction		35 dormant	
06 clarify		36 dissent	
07 mount		37 plausible	
08 fatigue		38 supreme	
09 sturdy		39 venue	
10 scatter		40 unanimous	
11 rally		41 exploit	
12 vulnerable		42 customary	
13 astound		43 blunder	
14 deteriorate		44 revere	
15 glide		45 paralyze	
16 prone		46 recess	
17 deform		47 implore	
18 concur		48 shiver	
19 precaution		49 dispatch	
20 transparent		50 obsess	
21 seize		51 minimize	
22 mislead		52 metropolis	
23 assail		53 infuse	
24 contend		54 terminate	
25 glare		55 explicit	
26 frigid		56 rampant	
27 fuss		57 compile	
28 recede		58 paste	
29 conscientious		59 empower	
30 slump		60 aviation	

우리말을 영어로 옮기시오.

61	조직		91	유독한	
62	익숙해진		92	실현 가능한	
63	번성하다		93	예고[예언]하다	
64	사소한, 하찮은		94	정직한, 직립한	
65	길든	,	95	고도, 높이	
66	옳은, 정직한		96	최선의, 최적의	
67	유전, 상속		97	귀족, 명문	
68	에필로그, 후기		98	이끌다	
69	격분하게 하다		99	빛을 밝히다	
70	설교, 교훈		100	기구, 도구	
71	재단사		101	섞다	
72	(눈, 산)사태		102	감소하다	
73	소란, 소동		103	여백	
74	충분한, 적당한		104	잘 정돈된	
75	오두막, 헛간		105	체하기, 뽐냄	
76	숙고하다		106	보유하다	
77	사춘기, 청춘기		107	무자비한	
78	강제적인		108	식별하다	
79	불분명한		109	탄원(서)	
80	사기, 기만		110	골목, 오솔길	
81	~이 되게 하다		111	통역하다	
82	분비하다		112	정제, 알약	
83	조용한, 평온한		113	중계하다	
84	초안의		114	날인하다	
85	뒤, 후방의		115	공식화하다	
86	줄이다		116	밀어내다	
87	숨기다		117	앞서다	
88	처방하다		118	광택제	
89	혈족 관계		119	측은한	
90	풀을 뜯어 먹다		120	외치다	

Part 3

Day 11

01 criterion [kraitíəriən]
n. 기준, 표준

something by which a thing can be judged
[syn] standard, norm, touchstone

The main criterion in choosing home furniture should be its durability.

02 peep [pi:p]
n. 엿보기, 훔쳐 보기
v. 엿보다, 훔쳐 보다

a quick look at someone or something
[syn] peek, glimpse, glance

I sneaked into the room for a peep at my friend's wedding dress.
The children were peeping through the curtains before the play.

03 proportion [prəpɔ́ːrʃən]
n. 비율, 균형, 넓이

a comparative part or number of a whole
[a] proportional 비례하는, 균형 잡힌 [v] proportionate 균형 잡히게 하다
[syn] ratio, balance, dimension [ant] imbalance

The proportion of boys to girls in this class is higher than before.

04 drawback [drɔ́ːbæ̀k]
n. 장애, 약점

something that can cause a difficulty
[syn] disadvantage, deficiency, obstacle [ant] advantage

Her biggest drawback is a hesitation to take on new challenges at work.

05 antibiotic [æ̀ntibaiátik]
n. 항생 물질
a. 항생(작용)의

a medical drug that is used to kill bacteria and cures infections
[syn] antitoxin, antibacterial

The doctor wrote me a prescription for an antibiotic.
Antibiotic medication must be taken only under the advice of a physician.

06 foe [fou]
n. 적, 원수

someone who is opposed to someone else
[syn] antagonist, adversary, enemy, rival [ant] friend

The two men were sworn foes although they pretended to be friends in public.

---

01 가정용 가구를 고르는 주된 기준은 내구성이어야 한다. 02 나는 친구의 웨딩 드레스를 슬쩍 들여다보려고 방으로 몰래 들어갔다. 아이들은 연극이 시작되기 전에 장막 안을 훔쳐보고 있었다. 03 이 학급의 여학생 대 남학생의 비율이 전보다 높아졌다. 04 그녀의 가장 큰 약점은 회사에서 새로운 일을 하는 것을 주저하는 것이다. 05 의사는 나에게 항생제를 처방해 주었다. 항생 작용을 하는 약은 의사와 상의하여 복용해야만 한다. 06 사람들 앞에서는 친구인 척하지만 그 두 사람은 불구대천의 원수지간이다.

07 trait [treit]

n. 특성, 특징

a distinguishing quality or characteristic

[syn] attribute, feature

I described his good traits to my grandparents before they met him.

08 preoccupied [priːɑ́kjupàid]

a. 몰두한, 선취된

completely absorbed in one's own thoughts

[n] preoccupation 선점, 선취 [v] preoccupy 점유하다, 선취하다

[syn] engrossed, engaged

Bridget is preoccupied with the preparation of Mark's birthday party.
We decided not to disturb a preoccupied caterer who was busy making arrangements for the party.

09 utter [ʌ́tər]

a. 완전한, 철저한

complete or absolute

[syn] thorough, perfect [ant] incomplete

News of the proposed demolition has come as an utter shock to the building's residents.

10 magnetic [mægnétik]

a. 자석의, 매력이 있는

having the power of a magnet to attract

[n] magnet 자석, 매혹하는 물건[사람] [ad] magnetically 자석으로, 자기로

[syn] magnetized, charming, attractive [ant] antimagnetic, unattractive

The card has a magnetic strip on the back which holds some important information.
She has a magnetic personality that drew admirers like bees to honey.

11 ambiguous [æmbígjuəs]

a. 애매한, 확실치 않은

having an unclear meaning

[n] ambiguity 모호함, 불명료 [ad] ambiguously 애매하게, 모호하게

[syn] vague, obscure, uncertain [ant] explicit, definite, unambiguous

Lawyers sometimes use ambiguous and complicated legal jargon to badger witnesses.

12 attribute [ətríbjuːt/ǽtribjùːt]

v. ~의 탓으로 하다
n. 속성, 특성

to regard that an event or situation is caused by something

[n] attribution 돌리기, 특성 [a] attributable ~ 탓에 의한

[syn] ascribe, impute, character, quality

It is common to attribute failures to others' lapses while taking credit for our successes.
Among the attributes of a good leader is the ability to recognize and respect others' strengths.

---

07 나는 조부모님이 그를 만나기 전에 그에 대한 좋은 점을 말씀 드렸다. 08 Bridget은 Mark의 생일파티 준비에 열중하고 있다. 우리는 파티를 준비하느라 바쁜 연회업자를 방해하지 않기로 했다. 09 철거 계획 통지로 빌딩 거주자들이 완전히 충격에 휩싸였다. 10 카드의 뒤쪽에는 중요한 정보가 담겨있는 자기 띠가 있다. 벌이 꿀을 좋아하듯 그녀는 사람을 끄는 매력적인 성격의 소유자이다. 11 증인들을 괴롭히기 위해 변호사들은 가끔 애매하고 복잡한 법률 용어를 사용한다. 12 성공은 자신의 공으로 삼고 실패는 다른 사람의 과오라고 탓하는 경우가 종종 있다. 훌륭한 지도자의 특성 중에는 다른 사람들의 장점을 발견하고 그것을 존중하는 것이 있다.

13 intimidate [intímədèit]
v. 겁주다, 협박하다

to make someone afraid with threats

[n] intimidation 위협   [a] intimidatory 협박적인

[syn] frighten, terrify, threaten   [ant] calm, encourage

The men intimidated the women with their harsh words and angry gestures.

14 undertake [ʌ̀ndərtéik]
v. 떠맡다, 책임을 지다, 착수하다

to accept to do something, especially a duty or task

[n] undertaking 떠맡기, 인수

[syn] assume, assure, commence   [ant] abstain, refuse

Our architects will undertake the project and complete it well within the deadline.

15 ascertain [æ̀sərtéin]
v. 확인하다, 알아내다

to discover or find out something

[n] ascertainment 확인, 규명   [a] ascertainable 확인할 수 있는

[syn] confirm, determine, identify

The judge ascertained the important facts during the trial so he sentenced her to one year in prison.

16 incite [insáit]
v. 자극하다, 격려하다

to urge someone to do something

[n] incitement 격려, 자극물   [a] incitant 자극하는

[syn] stimulate, provoke, motivate, prompt   [ant] discourage, dissuade

Police fear the activist's speech will incite trouble in the city because it was so inflammatory.

17 equip [ikwíp]
v. 설치하다, 갖추다

to provide what is needed

[n] equipment 설비, 장비

[syn] furnish, outfit, supply   [ant] disassemble, unready

The car is equipped with many special features such as a navigation system, object detection and airbags.

18 soar [sɔːr]
v. 솟다, 날아오르다

to rise or fly high into the air

[a] soaring 높이 나는, 치솟은

[syn] increase, ascend, mount   [ant] descend, plunge

The space shuttle Discovery soared into the sky on July 26, 2 years after the 2003's Columbia disaster.

---

13 그 남자들은 거친 말과 화난 동작을 하면서 여자들을 협박했다. 14 저희 건축가가 그 일을 착수해 마감일까지 마무리할 것입니다. 15 판사는 재판을 하는 동안 중요한 사실을 알게 되었고 그녀에게 징역 1년형을 선고했다. 16 경찰은 활동가의 연설이 너무 선동적이었기 때문에 도시에서 문제를 일으킬까 봐 염려하고 있다. 17 그 자동차에는 네비게이션 시스템, 물체 탐지 기능, 에어백과 같은 많은 특별한 장치들이 설치되어 있다. 18 우주 왕복선 Discovery호는 2003년 Columbia호 대참사 2년 후인 7월 26일 하늘을 날아올랐다.

19 toss [tɔːs]
v. (가볍게) 던지다

to throw lightly
[syn] fling, cast   [ant] catch
I love watching my mother toss pancakes up and flip them over deftly.

---

20 intrude [intrúːd]
v. 침입하다, 참견하다, 방해하다

to force in without invitation or permission
[syn] interfere, meddle, trespass, encroach
Harry had to be reminded not to intrude in the personal matters of his colleagues.

---

21 convey [kənvéi]
v. 나르다, 운송하다

to transport or carry someone or something to a certain place
[n] conveyance 운반, 수송   [a] conveyable 운송[전달]할 수 있는
[syn] communicate, send, transmit   [ant] maintain, retain, withhold
Arterial blood conveys oxygen and nourishment to the cell tissues in our body.

---

22 outlive [àutlív]
v. 보다 더 오래 살다

to live longer than something or someone else
[syn] outlast, survive
My desktop has outlived its usefulness and I am going to buy a new one.

---

23 segregate [ségrigèit]
v. 분리하다, 차별하다

to separate one group of people from the others
[n] segregation 분리, 인종 차별   [a] segregated 분리된, 인종 차별을 하는
[syn] isolate, separate, discriminate   [ant] amalgamate, desegregate, integrate
The teachers segregated the classes according to learning skills.

---

24 mediate [míːdièit]
v. 조정[중재]하다, 화해시키다

to settle differences between persons, nations, etc., through intervention
[n] mediation 중재, 조정
[syn] reconcile, arbitrate, intercede, interpose
The CEO and union leader are mediating a settlement for better facilities for workers.

---

25 escort [éskɔːrt]
v. 호위하다, 동행하다
n. 호위, 호위병

to accompany or attend someone or something
[syn] chaperon, guard   [ant] abandon, desert, leave
The men always escort the president everywhere he goes.
Some hotel visitors have an armed escort with them.

---

19 나는 엄마가 능숙하게 팬케이크를 던져 뒤집는 것을 보는 걸 좋아한다. 20 Harry는 사적인 문제로 그의 동료들을 방해하면 안 된다는 것을 상기해야 했다. 21 체내에서 동맥혈은 산소와 영양분을 세포 조직에 전달한다. 22 내 컴퓨터가 수명이 다 되어 새것을 구입할 예정이다. 23 그 교사는 학습 능력에 따라 학생들을 편애했다. 24 CEO와 조합 대표는 노동자들의 더 나은 편의를 제공하기 위해 협상을 조정하고 있다. 25 그 남자들은 대통령이 어디를 가든지 대통령을 호위한다. 무장한 호위병이 몇몇 호텔 방문객들을 따라다닌다.

Exercise

Word Check 각 단어의 뜻으로 알맞은 것을 찾아 연결하시오.

01	trait	ⓐ able to attract something or someone
02	outlive	ⓑ to make someone frightened with threats
03	intimidate	ⓒ to be alive longer than someone or something else
04	mediate	ⓓ to resolve an argument, dispute, etc. between two parties
05	magnetic	ⓔ a particular quality or characteristic of something or someone

Syn & Ant Check 주어진 단어의 동의어, 반의어를 골라 쓰시오.

advantage	standard	incomplete	abandon	interfere
furnish	enemy	assure	dissuade	integrate

06	foe	=	11	incite	↔
07	intrude	=	12	segregate	↔
08	equip	=	13	utter	↔
09	criterion	=	14	drawback	↔
10	undertake	=	15	escort	↔

Sentence Practice 문장을 읽고 빈칸에 알맞은 단어를 고르시오.

16 He _____ his success to his hard work and the support of his team.

ⓐ attributes　　ⓑ escorts　　ⓒ intimidates　　ⓓ soars

17 The leader tried to evade the media's probing questions with _____ answers.

ⓐ ambiguous　　ⓑ magnetic　　ⓒ antibiotic　　ⓓ preoccupied

18 Tom stole into the attic for a _____ at the "treasures" inside the wooden chest.

ⓐ proportion　　ⓑ drawback　　ⓒ foe　　ⓓ peep

19 Clara _____ her bridal bouquet out of the car window as she left with her new husband.

ⓐ intruded　　ⓑ undertook　　ⓒ segregated　　ⓓ tossed

20 Brian was too _____ to take active part in our discussion today.

ⓐ utter　　ⓑ ambiguous　　ⓒ preoccupied　　ⓓ magnetic

01 core [kɔːr]

n. 핵심, 중요 부분, 속

the central part of something

[syn] nucleus, center, focus [ant] exterior, outside, perimeter

The core of our problem is that we don't have enough evidence to convince the jury.

Although the apple looked fresh and juicy from the outside, its core was rotten.

02 morale [mərǽl]

n. 의욕, 사기, 도덕

a mental condition related to courage, confidence, enthusiasm, etc.

[syn] spirit, confidence

The good news increased morale among the team members.

03 installment [instɔ́ːlmənt]

n. 분할분, 월부

a series of regular payments until full price is paid

You can pay back your car loan through monthly or quarterly installments.

04 conspiracy [kənspírəsi]

n. 음모, 공모

an unlawful plot

[a] conspiratorial 공포의, 음모의 [v] conspire 음모를 꾸미다

[syn] intrigue, collusion [ant] faithfulness, loyalty

The men were part of a conspiracy to smuggle cocaine into the U.K.

05 delinquency [dilíŋkwənsi]

n. 직무 태만, 불법 행위

behavior that is illegal or socially unacceptable

[a] delinquent 태만한, 직무를 게을리하는

[syn] misconduct, default, dereliction [ant] dutifulness

Police say the hardened criminal had started off as a petty troublemaker charged with delinquency.

06 temperament [témpərəmənt]

n. 성질, 기질

a person's basic nature

[a] temperamental 기질의, 신경질적인

[syn] character, disposition, temper

This breed of the dog has a very friendly temperament.

---

01 우리 문제의 핵심은 우리에게는 배심원단을 설득할만한 충분한 증거가 없다는 것이다. 겉으로 봐선 사과가 신선하고 먹음직스러웠지만 속은 썩어 있었다. 02 좋은 소식은 우리 팀 멤버들의 사기를 북돋아주었다. 03 자동차 융자는 매달 또는 분기마다 분할해서 상환하실 수 있습니다. 04 그 남자들은 코카인을 영국으로 밀수입하려는 모의의 가담자들이었다. 05 그 비정한 범죄자는 처음에는 범법행위로 기소된 문제아였을 뿐이었다고 경찰은 말하고 있다. 06 이런 품종의 개는 성질이 순하다.

07 intermediate [ìntərmíːdiət]
a. 중간의, 중급의

in the middle or laying between two points, extremes, etc.

n intermediary 중개자, 매개물

syn medium, halfway, in-between

The stock markets are in an intermediate phase after the alternating gains and losses of last month.

08 immune [imjúːn]
a. 면역(성)의

not affected by a particular disease

n immunity 면역, 면역성 v immunize 면역성을 주다

syn resistant ant susceptible

The immune system is an important part of the human body.

09 untimely [ʌntáimli]
a. 때 아닌, 시기 상조의

happening at an inappropriate time

syn ill-timed, inopportune, premature ant timely, punctual, opportune

Your gaiety in the context of this serious discussion is quite untimely.

10 shield [ʃiːld]
v. 방패로 막다, 보호하다
n. 방패, 보호물

to protect someone from a danger or risk

syn cover, guard, safeguard ant endanger, expose

Snails have hard shells that shield their soft bodies from injury.
The Spartans used a unique shield in battle against the Persians.

11 transmit [trænsmít]
v. (물건 등을) 보내다, 전하다

to send out or pass on

n transmission 전달, 전송 a transmissve 전달하는, 보내는

syn dispatch, forward, convey, transfer ant receive

The ship transmitted distress signals as soon as the crew discovered it to be in danger.

12 mumble [mʌ́mbl]
v. 중얼거리다
n. 중얼거림

to speak something indistinctly or unclearly

syn mutter, murmur ant articulate, enunciate

She mumbled her words so that I could not understand her.
The young man spoke in a low mumble to the policeman.

13 stagnate [stǽgneit]
v. 침체[정체]하다, 흐르지 않다, 썩다

to stop developing or improving

n stagnation 굄, 침체 a stagnant 고여 있는, 발전이 없는

syn rot, decay ant rise

The greatest minds can stagnate if they do not accept new ideas or challenges.

---

07 주식 시장은 지난달 이익과 손실이 교차한 이후로 중간 수준을 유지하고 있다. 08 면역체계는 인간의 신체에서 중요한 기능을 한다. 09 당신이 심각한 토론을 하는 자리에서 즐거워하는 것은 정말 상황에 맞지 않는 행동이군요. 10 달팽이는 단단한 껍질을 가지고 있어서 부상으로부터 자신의 부드러운 몸을 보호한다. 스파르타 사람들은 페르시아 사람들과 전쟁을 할 때 독특한 방패를 사용했다. 11 선원이 배가 위험에 처해 있다는 것을 발견하자마자 그 배는 조난 신호를 보냈다. 12 중얼거리며 얘기를 해서 그녀의 말을 이해할 수 없었다. 그 젊은 남자는 낮게 중얼거리면서 경찰에게 말했다. 13 위대한 인물은 새로운 사상이나 도전을 받아들이지 않으면 성장하지 않기도 한다.

14 suffocate [sʌ́fəkèit]

v. 숨을 막다, 질식시키다

to lack or prevent access to air

n suffocation 질식　ad suffocatingly 질식하도록, 숨막힐 듯이

syn stifle, smother, strangle, choke

The man was suffocated by the dense smoke during the fire.

---

15 avenge [əvéndʒ]

v. 복수를 하다

to take revenge on someone

a avenging 복수의, 보복의　ad avengingly 보복으로

syn retaliate, requite, chastise　ant excuse, forgive, pardon

They must avenge their brother's death after identifying the real culprit.

---

16 withdraw [wiðdrɔ́:]

v. 그만두다, 철회하다, 철수하다.

to remove or take something away

n withdrawal 물러나기

syn remove, rescind, retreat　ant remain, stay

Korean troops will withdraw from Afghanistan on condition that they release the hostages.

Sponsors have said they may withdraw funds for the program unless it is implemented immediately.

---

17 strive [straiv]

v. 애쓰다, 노력하다, 싸우다

to try to do something with a great effort

syn endeavor, struggle

The artist is continually striving for perfection in his paintings.

He strived against injustice and inequality throughout his entire life.

---

18 snatch [snætʃ]

v. 낚아채다, 움켜 잡다

n. 잡아 채기, 조각, 단편

to take something or someone suddenly, especially by force

syn grasp, seize

The girl quickly snatched old woman's money and started running.

The boy only heard a snatch of conversation between the two thieves.

---

19 urge [ə:rdʒ]

v. 재촉하다, 격려하다, 강요하다

n. 몰아댐, 충동

to strongly advise someone to do something

n urgency 긴급, 긴급한 일　a urgent 긴박한

syn induce, prompt, compel, spur　ant discourage

We urge you to reconsider the decision to step down as president of this organization.

We had a sudden urge to eat ice cream after supper.

---

14 그 남자는 화재 속에서 짙은 연기 때문에 질식사했다. 15 진범을 밝힌 후 그들은 동생의 죽음을 복수를 해야 한다. 16 그들이 인질을 풀어주는 조건으로 한국군은 아프가니스탄에서 철군할 것이다. 후원자들은 그 프로그램이 즉시 실행되지 않으면 자금을 회수할 수도 있다고 말했다. 17 그 예술가는 자신의 그림에 완벽을 기하기 위해 끊임없이 노력한다. 그는 평생동안 불의와 불평등에 맞서 투쟁했다. 18 소녀는 노부인의 돈을 낚아채 뛰기 시작했다. 그 소년은 도둑들이 하는 대화의 일부를 들었을 뿐이다. 19 저희는 의장님께서 사직하시기로 한 결정을 다시 생각해 주셨으면 합니다. 우리는 저녁을 먹은 후에 갑자기 아이스크림이 먹고 싶은 충동을 느꼈다.

20 groan [groun]

v. 신음하다, 투덜대다
n. 신음소리

to make a deep sound expressing pain, distress, etc.

syn moan, complain

His nightmare made him jump up from sleep and groan in sheer terror.

The woman made a loud groan of pain after she fell on the stairs.

21 litter [lítər]

v. 쓰레기를 버리다
n. 쓰레기, 잡동사니

to make untidy or messy by throwing away rubbish

syn dirty, clutter, garbage

You are especially reminded not to litter the trail while on this trip up the mountainside.

The ground was filled with litter after the celebrations of the previous night.

22 stray [strei]

v. 길을 잃다, 방황하다
a. 길 잃은, 헤매는

to move away from a safe or familiar area

n strayer 길 잃은 사람 a astray 길을 잃고

syn rove, roam, meander, wander

If there is a lack of love and guidance from parents, teenagers tend to stray from the right path and make a wrong choice.

My sister found a stray cat behind the old shed in the garden.

23 enrich [inrítʃ]

v. 풍부하게 하다, (가치 등을) 높이다

to make better in quality or value

n enrichment 부유, 강화 a enriched 풍부한

syn augment, enhance ant degenerate, deprive, impoverish

Art and culture enrich our lives by showing us the extent of human creativity.

24 merge [məːrdʒ]

v. 합병하다

to absorb or combine

n mergence 합병

syn join, unite, consolidate ant separate, split

The two baseball teams merged to form a new team.

25 namely [néimli]

ad. 즉, 다시 말하면

specifically

syn expressly, that is to say

We now come to the final part of the program-namely the vote of thanks.

---

20 그는 악몽 때문에 잠에서 벌떡 일어나 공포에 빠져 신음했다. 그 여인은 계단에서 구르고 아파서 신음했다. 21 여러분은 산을 오르면서 오솔길에 쓰레기 버리면 안 된다는 것을 명심하셔야 합니다. 어젯밤의 축하 행사로 바닥은 쓰레기로 가득 차 있었다. 22 부모님의 사랑이나 지도가 없으면 십대들은 올바른 길에서 벗어나 잘못된 선택을 하기 쉽다. 내 동생은 정원의 낡은 창고에서 주인 잃은 고양이를 발견했다. 23 예술과 문화는 인간이 창조해 낼 수 있는 범위를 보여줌으로써 우리의 삶을 풍요롭게 해준다. 24 두 야구팀은 새로운 단일팀을 구성하기 위해 합병되었다. 25 지금 우리는 프로그램의 마지막 순서, 즉 감사결의만을 남겨놓고 있습니다.

Exercise

Word Check 각 단어의 뜻으로 알맞은 것을 찾아 연결하시오.

01 litter   ⓐ to carry or transport something

02 urge   ⓑ to incite someone to do something

03 transmit   ⓒ rubbish scattered in a public place

04 temperament   ⓓ one's natural character or feature

05 conspiracy   ⓔ a secret plot to do something harmful and illegal

Syn & Ant Check 주어진 단어의 동의어, 반의어를 골라 쓰시오.

exterior	dutifulness	medium	articulate	stifle
forgive	struggle	rove	enhance	receive

06 suffocate = _____

07 intermediate = _____

08 stray = _____

09 enrich = _____

10 strive = _____

11 core ↔ _____

12 transmit ↔ _____

13 mumble ↔ _____

14 avenge ↔ _____

15 delinquency ↔ _____

Sentence Practice 문장을 읽고 빈칸에 알맞은 단어를 고르시오.

16 Your first monthly _____ is due within 30 days of the issue of this letter.

ⓐ core   ⓑ morale   ⓒ installment   ⓓ temperament

17 The spectators were disappointed when the injured player was forced to _____ from the game.

ⓐ withdraw   ⓑ strive   ⓒ litter   ⓓ mumble

18 Regular and timely vaccinations help young children become _____ to illnesses.

ⓐ untimely   ⓑ immune   ⓒ intermediate   ⓓ stray

19 The audience _____ sadly when their favorite contestant missed the final question.

ⓐ groaned   ⓑ merged   ⓒ stagnated   ⓓ snatched

20 It is _____ to celebrate when people here are mourning the loss of a loved one.

ⓐ stray   ⓑ immune   ⓒ intermediate   ⓓ untimely

🎧 **01 excursion** [ikskə́:rʒən]

n. 짧은 여행, 소풍

a short trip for a special purpose

ⓝ excursionist 유람 여행자

syn journey, tour, outing

This year we plan to go on an excursion to the underground caves near Blackstone Creek.

---

02 compliment [kámpləmənt]

n. 찬사, 칭찬

v. 찬사를 말하다, 칭찬하다

an expression of approval or admiration for one's achievements or qualities

ⓐ complimentary 찬사의, 칭찬의

syn commend, praise   ant disapprove, denounce, criticize

Nora received several compliments on her scintillating talk at the seminar.

The teacher complimented her students on their good test scores.

---

03 duplicate [djú:plikət/-kèit]

n. 복제, 사본

v. 복사하다

an exact copy of something

syn replica, counterpart, reproduction   ant original, master

Please keep a duplicate of the lease and give the original to the landlord.

The secretary duplicated the magazine article for me.

---

04 blaze [bleiz]

n. 불길, 화재, 강한 빛

a bright burst of flame or lights

syn fire, conflagration, flare

The firemen fought the enormous blaze in the warehouse.

---

05 doom [du:m]

n. 멸망, 비운

v. 운명 짓다, ～할 운명이다

a tragic event that someone is unable to prevent or escape

syn destruction, tragedy, destine, fate

The men on the ship faced certain doom in the horrible storm.

Lack of support had doomed the museum project to failure.

---

06 stunt [stʌnt]

n. 묘기, 곡예

a dangerous action to gain attention from or entertain people

syn trick, exploit, performance

I'm always amazed at the gymnastic stunts performed by circus trapeze artists high above the crowds.

---

01 우리는 올해 Blackstone Creek 근처에 있는 지하 동굴로 소풍을 갈 계획이다. 02 Nora는 세미나에서 재치 넘치는 연설로 많은 찬사를 받았다. 선생님이 학생들의 높은 시험 성적을 칭찬했다. 03 임대차 계약서의 사본은 보관하시고 원본은 집주인에게 주십시오. 비서는 나에게 잡지 기사를 복사해 주었다. 04 그 소방관은 창고에서 커다란 화염과 싸우고 있다. 05 배에 있던 사람들은 무서운 폭풍을 맞아 피할 수 없는 비운에 직면했다. 지원 부족으로 박물관 사업은 실패로 끝났다. 06 관중들 위로 높이 그네를 타는 곡예사의 묘기는 나를 항상 놀라게 한다.

07 zeal [ziːl]

n. 열의, 열정

great interest and eagerness

ⓐ zealous 열심인, 열중한   ⓐ zealless 열의가 없는

syn enthusiasm, passion, ardor   ant apathy, indifference, lethargy

It is heartening to see the students take on this challenge with zeal and commitment.

08 outskirts [àutskə́ːrts]

n. 변두리, 교외

the parts that are away from the center of a city or a town

syn suburbs, environs

Ted's farmhouse is very spacious and quiet but is in the outskirts of the town of Claremont.

09 perseverance [pə̀ːrsəvíərens]

n. 인내(력), 참을성

the ability of persisting or persevering something

ⓐ perseverant 불요불굴의, 참을성 있는   ⓥ persevere 인내하다, 견디어내다

syn persistence, patience   ant impatience

Her perseverance in working on this project finally paid off by being promoted.

10 salvation [sælvéiʃən]

n. 구제자, 구조, 구원

a person or thing that prevents loss, damage or failure

ⓐ salvational 구조의

syn deliverance, rescue   ant damnation, downfall, destruction

Your generous donations have been the salvation of the disaster victims.

Nearly all religions offer salvation in the afterlife for believers who follow a certain code of conduct.

11 tactic [tǽktik]

n. 전략, 전술

a skillful method to achieve something

ⓐ tactical 전술상의, 전술적인

syn strategy, stratagem

Most games are won through the timely use of appropriate moves and tactics.

12 shrewd [ʃruːd]

a. 약삭빠른, 빈틈없는, 영리한

good at judging people or situations in a successful way

ⓝ shrewdness 빈틈없음   ⓐⓓ shrewdly 빈틈없이, 약삭빠르게

syn astute, ingenious, sharp, intelligent   ant stupid

The shrewd official saved many lives by preparing for the disaster.

07 열정과 책임을 가지고 도전을 받아들이는 학생들을 보니 마음이 든든하다. 08 Ted의 농가는 넓고 고요하지만 Claremont 시의 변두리에 있다. 09 이 프로젝트를 하면서 보여준 그녀의 인내심은 승진으로 보상 받았다. 10 여러분들의 관대한 기부가 재난 피해자들에게 구원자의 역할을 하고 있습니다. 거의 모든 종교는 그 종교의 강령을 따른 신자들에게 내세에서의 구원을 약속한다. 11 대부분 게임은 적시에 알맞은 수를 옮기고 적절한 전략을 사용하면 이길 수 있다. 12 기민한 공무원이 재난을 대비해 많은 생명을 구할 수 있었다.

13 stingy [stíndʒi]
a. 인색한

not willing to spend money or share something

n stinginess 인색함, 구두쇠 짓　ad stingily 인색하게, 구두쇠처럼

syn miserly, penny-pinching, ungenerous　ant generous

The man as stingy as Scrooge cannot be expected to contribute money.

14 divine [diváin]
a. 신의, 신성한

having the qualities of or coming from God

n divinity 신성, 신의 힘　ad divinely 신성하게

syn sacred, holy　ant profane, unholy

Prayer brings us close to the divine power that guides the world.

15 predominant [pridámənənt]
a. 우세한, 두드러진

more common or superior

n predominance 우세, 우월　v predominate 우세하다, 눈에 띄다

syn prevailing, prominent, dominant　ant minor, subsidiary

The predominant theme of the book is respect for human life.

16 atomic [ətámik]
a. 원자의, 원자력의, 원자 폭탄의

involving atoms

n atom 원자　ad atomically 원자력을 사용하여

syn atom-powered, nuclear

Fission generates energy by altering elements like uranium at the atomic level.

The new atomic power plant will help meet the growing energy requirements of the state.

17 spank [spæŋk]
v. 찰싹 때리다

to hit on the buttocks with the open hand

n spanking 손바닥으로 때리기

syn slap, smack

As children we were spanked if we were either disobedient or untruthful.

18 sip [sip]
v. 조금씩 마시다, 홀짝거리다
n. 한 모금, 홀짝거림

to drink a little at a time

syn taste

Kelli likes to sip water from her glass while Greg drinks it straight from the bottle.

The sick child swallowed a sip of cool water before bed.

---

13 Scrooge처럼 인색한 그 남자는 돈을 기부하지 않을 거야. 14 기도는 세상을 인도하는 신력에 우리를 더 가까이 다가가게 해준다. 15 그 책의 주요 주제는 인간 생명에 대한 존경이다. 16 핵분열은 우라늄과 같은 분자를 원자 상태로 바꿔 에너지를 발생시킨다. 새 원자력 발전소는 그 주의 증가하는 에너지 수요를 충족시키는 데 도움을 줄 것이다. 17 어렸을 때 우리는 말을 듣지 않거나 거짓말을 한 경우에 엉덩이를 찰싹 맞았다. 18 Greg이 물을 병째 마시는 반면 Kelli는 컵에 따라 조금씩 마시는 것을 좋아한다. 병에 걸린 아이는 잠자리에 들기 전에 시원한 물을 한모금 삼켰다.

19 vanish [vǽniʃ]
v. 사라지다

to disappear suddenly

syn evanesce, fade　ant appear

The magician made the card **vanish** and recovered it from an old lady in the audience.

---

20 invert [invə́ːrt]
v. 뒤집다, 반대로 하다

to make something move backwards

syn reverse, turn

You will spill all its contents if you **invert** this container without closing its lid.

---

21 dispel [dispél]
v. 쫓아버리다, 흩어지게 하다

to scatter or drive away

syn displace, disperse　ant collect, gather

My mother **dispelled** a terrible rumor about my aunt.

---

22 choke [tʃouk]
v. 질식시키다

to prevent someone from breathing

n choking 질식, 숨막힘　a choked 숨막히는

syn strangle, stifle, suffocate　ant breathe

Many workers were **choked** by the heavy poisonous gas.

---

23 exile [égzail]
v. 추방하다
n. 국외 추방, 망명(자)

to force to leave one's country

syn banish, fugitive, deportee　ant repatriate

The king **exiled** the minister when he was found guilty of treason.
The unhappy woman lived in **exile** for the rest of her life.

---

24 kidnap [kídnæp]
v. 유괴하다, 납치하다

to take someone illegally and demand money for his return

n kidnapper 유괴자, 유괴범

syn abduct　ant ransom, release

The man **kidnapped** her son and demanded a ransom of $500,000 for safe return.

---

25 capture [kǽptʃər]
v. 붙잡다, 획득하다, 점령하다
n. 포획(물), 포로

to take by force

syn seize, apprehend, arrest　ant free, liberate, release

The first speaker **captured** my attention with his introduction.
The author wrote about the **capture** of the enemy army.

---

19 마술사는 카드를 사라지게 했다가 관중들 중 한 노부인에게서 찾아냈다. 20 뚜껑을 닫지 않고 용기를 뒤집으면 내용물이 쏟아질 거야. 21 엄마가 이모에 대한 끔찍한 소문을 불식시켰다. 22 많은 노동자가 짙은 유독 가스에 질식했다. 23 왕은 장관이 반역죄를 저지른 것을 알고 장관을 추방했다. 그 불쌍한 여인은 여생을 망명자 신분으로 지냈다. 24 남자는 그녀의 아들을 납치해 안전하게 되돌려주는 대가로 5십만 달러를 몸값으로 요구했다. 25 첫번째 연사의 연설 도입 부분이 나의 관심을 사로잡았다. 그 저자는 적군의 포로에 대해 글을 썼다.

Exercise

Word Check 각 단어의 뜻으로 알맞은 것을 찾아 연결하시오.

01 excursion   ⓐ unwilling to spend money

02 invert   ⓑ to catch something with one's hand

03 stingy   ⓒ to turn something the other way or upside down

04 capture   ⓓ the act of saving someone or something in danger

05 salvation   ⓔ a short journey, usually for pleasure and enjoyment

Syn & Ant Check 주어진 단어의 동의어, 반의어를 골라 쓰시오.

denounce	minor	counterpart	appear	ransom
impatience	sacred	passion	disperse	banish

06 duplicate   = _____   11 predominant ↔ _____

07 zeal   = _____   12 vanish   ↔ _____

08 divine   = _____   13 kidnap   ↔ _____

09 dispel   = _____   14 compliment   ↔ _____

10 exile   = _____   15 perseverance ↔ _____

Sentence Practice 문장을 읽고 빈칸에 알맞은 단어를 고르시오.

16 Bad planning by the city councilmen _____ the ambitious road project from the outset.

　　ⓐ vanished　　　　ⓑ captured　　　　ⓒ kidnapped　　　　ⓓ doomed

17 Anita has turned out to be a(n) _____ manager despite her lack of formal training.

　　ⓐ shrewd　　　　ⓑ divine　　　　ⓒ atomic　　　　ⓓ stingy

18 In peak traffic it takes more than an hour to reach the city from the _____.

　　ⓐ stunt　　　　ⓑ blaze　　　　ⓒ salvation　　　　ⓓ outskirts

19 Putting the troublemaker in charge of the group was a brilliant _____.

　　ⓐ tactic　　　　ⓑ zeal　　　　ⓒ perseverance　　　　ⓓ compliment

20 I noticed that little Brenda was _____ on a large piece of candy.

　　ⓐ dispelling　　　　ⓑ spanking　　　　ⓒ choking　　　　ⓓ inverting

Day 14

Loading 375 Words 375 of 625

01 **advent** [ǽdvent]
n. (중요한 시대 · 사건 등의) 도래, 출현

a coming of an important person or thing
syn onset, beginning, appearance ant end, exit

The **advent** of the Internet and email seems to have made letter-writing redundant.

02 **peasant** [péznt]
n. 소작인

a small farmer or laborer
syn farmhand

Even in poverty the **peasant** refused to sell the land of his forefathers.

03 **mob** [mɑb]
n. 군중, 폭도, 무리
v. 떼지어 모이다

a disorderly and lawless crowd
syn gang, throng, mass

The police finally controlled the violent **mob** from the city.
The shoppers **mobbed** the sale racks at the department store in the mall.

04 **monarch** [mɑ́nərk]
n. 군주

a person who rules a state with hereditary right
a monarchical 군주(국)의, 군주정치의
syn sovereign, ruler

Countries such as Britain, Holland and Spain continue to have **monarchs** as titular heads of government.

05 **utmost** [ʌ́tmòust]
n. 최대한, 극한
a. 최대의, 극대의

the greatest or highest amount, degree or extent
a uttermost, maximum, extreme ant moderate, halfway

The coach asked his players to do their **utmost** for the team.
This matter is of the **utmost** urgency and must be dealt with immediately.

06 **intuition** [ìntjuíʃən]
n. 직관

the ability to know something without the facts
a intuitional 직관의 ad intuitionally 직관적으로
syn instinct, insight ant intellect

I trusted my **intuition** to guide me in this decision.

01 인터넷과 전자메일 도입은 손으로 쓰는 편지를 필요없는 것으로 만든 것 같다. 02 소작인은 가난 속에서도 조상이 물려준 땅을 팔라는 제의를 거절했다. 03 경찰은 마침내 도시의 난폭한 폭도를 제압할 수 있었다. 쇼핑객들은 쇼핑몰에 있는 백화점 세일 진열대에 떼지어 모였다. 04 영국, 네덜란드, 스페인과 같은 국가에서 명목상의 국가수반으로 군주가 계속해서 존재한다. 05 코치는 선수들에게 팀을 위해 최선을 다해달라고 부탁했다. 이런 문제는 극도로 긴급하기 때문에 즉시 처리해야 한다. 06 나는 이런 결정하게 한 내 직관을 믿어.

07 coverage [kʌ́vəridʒ]
n. (신문 · 방송의) 보도, (보험의) 보상

the amount covered by something

syn extent, reimbursement

The news coverage has been very good about the recent election.

To apply for insurance coverage is always difficult, involving complicated paperwork.

---

08 assault [əsɔ́:lt]
n. 습격, 맹공격
v. 습격하다

a violent attack

syn onslaught, assail   ant defense

The man committed an assault with a deadly weapon.

The men assaulted each other after a bitter argument over some soccer tickets.

---

09 eligible [élidʒəbl]
a. 적격의, 적당한

having the appropriate ability or competence to do something

n eligibility 적임, 적격성

syn qualified, fit, suitable   ant unfit, ineligible, disqualified

Graduates awaiting results of their final year exams are also eligible for this position.

---

10 numb [nʌ́m]
a. 감각을 잃은, 마비된
v. 마비시키다

unable to feel anything

ad numbly (일시) 감각을 잃어, 마비되어

syn paralyzed, anesthetized   ant sensitive

My sister was numb with grief after her friend died suddenly.

The doctor numbed my hand before she performed the operation.

---

11 rigorous [rígərəs]
a. 엄격한, 혹독한

strict and harsh

n rigor 엄함, 엄격   ad rigorously 엄격히, 엄밀히

syn severe, austere, stringent

To qualify for the armed forces one must be prepared to go through rigorous training.

---

12 weary [wíəri]
a. 지친, 피곤한, 지루한

physically and mentally tired

n weariness 권태, 피로   ad wearily 지쳐서

syn exhausted, fatigued   ant energetic, lively

All of us were hungry and weary at the end of our day-long camping expedition.

---

07 이 기사는 최근 선거에 대해 자세하게 다루고 있다. 보험사에 보상을 청구하는 것은 항상 복잡한 서류 절차가 수반되어 어렵다. 08 그 남자는 살상무기를 가지고 공격을 감행했다. 남자들은 축구 경기 표를 가지고 심한 언쟁을 벌인 후 서로 치고 받았다. 09 마지막 학기 시험을 치르고 성적을 기다리는 졸업생 또한 이 직업에 지원할 수 있습니다. 10 내 동생은 친구의 갑작스러운 죽음으로 인해 슬픔에 빠져 멍해 있다. 의사는 수술하기 전에 내 손을 마취했다. 11 군대에 지원하고자 하는 사람은 엄격한 훈련을 받을 준비가 되어 있어야 한다. 12 우리는 모두 하루 종일 계속된 야영으로 매우 허기지고 지쳐 있었다.

13 cunning [kʌ́niŋ]
a. 교활한, 간사한

able to achieve something in a deceitful way
[ad] cunningly 교활[간사]하게
[syn] crafty, tricky, sly [ant] gullible, naive, honest
The cunning spy reached safety across the border, at last.

---

14 engender [indʒéndər]
v. 일으키다, 낳다, 야기시키다

to cause or produce something
[n] engenderment 야기, 초래
[syn] arouse, generate, provoke
The development of tourism has engendered the growth of several small businesses in the area.

---

15 circulate [sə́:rkjulèit]
v. 순환하다, 돌다, 유포시키다

to move or go round, usually in a fixed route
[n] circulation 순환 [a] circulatory 순환의
[syn] circle, spread [ant] block, conceal
The heart makes blood circulate through the blood vessels in the body.

---

16 torture [tɔ́:rtʃər]
v. 고문하다
n. 고문

to inflict mental or physical pain on someone
[a] torturous 고문의, 고통스러운
[syn] rack, excruciate, torment [ant] alleviate, relieve
The guard tortured the man for the whereabouts of the money.
Hundreds of unfortunate people suffered torture and were burned for heresy during the Catholic Inquisitions.

---

17 cling [kliŋ]
v. 달라붙다, 매달리다

to hold tightly
[a] clingy 접착력이 강한 [a] clinging 밀착성의, 달라붙는
[syn] adhere, stick, clutch [ant] detach, release
The rescuers clung to the side of the mountain during the snowstorm.

---

18 divert [divə́:rt]
v. 전환하다, (주의 등을) 돌리다

to change the direction or purpose of something
[n] diversion 전환 [a] diverting 기분 전환이 되는
[syn] avert, disturb, distract [ant] maintain, focus
The dam diverted the flow of water to the north.

---

19 arouse [əráuz]
v. 깨우다, 자극하다

to cause to feel or act
[syn] provoke, awaken, stimulate [ant] calm, lull, pacify
Many years later I realized that my professor's remarks had aroused me from diffidence into confident action.

---

13 그 교활한 스파이는 마침내 국경을 건너 안전한 곳에 도착했다. 14 관광 산업의 발달로 그 지역의 소기업이 성장하고 있다. 15 심장은 우리 체내의 혈관을 통해 피를 순환하게 한다. 16 간수는 돈의 소재를 파악하기 위해 그 남자를 고문했다. 가톨릭 종교재판이 진행되는 동안 수백만 명의 불운한 사람들이 이단으로 몰려 고문을 당하고 화형당했다. 17 구조원들은 눈보라가 치는 동안 산모퉁이에 달라붙어 있었다. 18 그 댐은 물길을 북쪽으로 유입하게 한다. 19 많은 시간이 지난 후에야 교수님의 말씀이 내가 수줍음을 극복하고 자신감 있게 행동할 수 있도록 일깨워 줬다는 것을 깨달았다.

20 initiate [iníʃièit]
v. 시작하다

to start or introduce
initiative ⓝ 시작 ⓐ 처음의, 발단의
syn commence, launch, originate   ant conclude, complete

The government will initiate a new population policy to increase the birth rate.

---

21 seduce [sidʒúːs]
v. 부추기다, 유혹하다

to attract someone to do something
ⓝ seduction 유혹   ⓐ seductive 유혹적인, 매력 있는
syn allure, entice, tempt

We were seduced into renting the house by the persuasive charm of the property agent.

---

22 assent [əsént]
v. 동의하다
n. 동의, 찬성

to agree with something
syn consent, approval   ant dissent, disagree, disapprove

There was no choice but to assent to the conditions mentioned by the landlord.

We were told that our loan could not be sanctioned without the assent of the top authorities.

---

23 spur [spəːr]
v. 박차를 가하다, 자극하다

to make something happen faster
syn encourage, promote, boost

The band director spurred her on to practice the trumpet.

---

24 prolong [prəlɔ́ːŋ]
v. 연장하다, 늘이다

to make something continue
ⓝ prolongment 연장, 연기   ⓐ prolonged 오래 끄는, 장기의
syn lengthen, protract, extend   ant abbreviate, shorten

The director prolonged the concert because of the audience's loud applause.

---

25 imprint [ímprint]
v. 인상지우다, (마음에) 새기다
n. 자국, 인상

to mark or have a lasting effect
ⓝ imprinting 각인
syn engrave, mark, impress, stamp

The picture will be imprinted in my memory for the rest of my life.

Among my most priceless treasures is an ink imprint of my little daughter's hand.

---

18 정부는 출산율을 높이기 위해 새로운 인구 정책을 시작할 것이다. 19 부동산 업체는 그럴듯한 말로 그 집을 임대하라며 우리를 부추겼다. 22 집주인이 말한 조건에 동의하는 수밖에 다른 선택의 여지가 없었다. 우리는 은행장의 승인 없이는 대출을 받을 수 없다고 얘기 들었다. 23 그 밴드 지휘자는 그녀가 트럼펫 연습을 하도록 격려했다. 24 지휘자는 관객의 성원에 콘서트를 연장했다. 25 그 그림은 남은 생애 동안 내 기억에 남아 있을 것이다. 돈으로 살 수 없는 소중한 것들 중의 하나는 잉크를 발라 찍은 내 작은 딸의 손자국이다.

Exercise

Word Check 각 단어의 뜻으로 알맞은 것을 찾아 연결하시오.

01 intuition   ⓐ to stimulate someone to do something

02 spur   ⓑ to give a strong impression of something

03 torture   ⓒ the act of inflicting metal or physical suffering

04 imprint   ⓓ having the necessary ability or skill to do something

05 eligible   ⓔ the ability to realize something without proof or evidence

Syn & Ant Check 주어진 단어의 동의어, 반의어를 골라 쓰시오.

sovereign	detach	maximum	paralyzed	energetic
defense	avert	provoke	disapprove	conclude

06 utmost = _____   11 assent ↔ _____

07 monarch = _____   12 weary ↔ _____

08 numb = _____   13 cling ↔ _____

09 divert = _____   14 initiate ↔ _____

10 arouse = _____   15 assault ↔ _____

Sentence Practice 문장을 읽고 빈칸에 알맞은 단어를 고르시오.

16 The minister's personal attention to the project has _____ hopes of its timely completion.

     ⓐ tortured   ⓑ engendered   ⓒ diverted   ⓓ initiated

17 The _____ of the sewing machine helped to make the garment industry more productive.

     ⓐ advent   ⓑ intuition   ⓒ peasant   ⓓ monarch

18 This is live and exclusive _____ of the film awards from Berlin.

     ⓐ coverage   ⓑ utmost   ⓒ assault   ⓓ mob

19 Latest rumors _____ in the company suggest that Paul Iverson will be the new CEO.

     ⓐ prolonging   ⓑ clinging   ⓒ imprinting   ⓓ circulating

20 The _____ congressman ensured his supremacy by dividing his opponents and making them weak.

     ⓐ weary   ⓑ cunning   ⓒ eligible   ⓓ utmost

01 ailment [éilmənt]
n. (가볍거나 만성적인) 병

a mild illness
[a] ailing 앓고 있는, 병든 [v] ail 아픔을 느끼다
[syn] infirmities, disease, illness, malady [ant] health

You need to watch out for throat ailments and skin allergies this season.

02 hypocrisy [hipákrəsi]
n. 위선, 위선적 행위

the act of pretending to believe something which one does not
[syn] affectation [ant] honesty, sincerity

Having the chain-smoking superstar endorse the latest anti-smoking campaign seemed an exercise in hypocrisy.

03 particle [pá:rtikl]
n. 극소량, 작은 조각

a tiny part
[syn] scrap, fragment, shred, bit

Yellow dust particles cause eye and respiratory disease because they contain heavy metals and other dangerous materials.

04 acclaim [əkléim]
n. 갈채, 환호
v. 갈채를 보내다, 환호하다

applause for someone or something
[a] acclaimed 갈채를 받고 있는
[syn] cheering, clapping [ant] jeer, heckle, hiss

Mathew Jardine's latest book has received acclaim from critics in London, New York and Paris.
A special meeting was held that acclaimed the award-winning team of designers.

05 concord [kánkɔ:rd]
n. 일치, 조화, 평화

agreement and harmony
[syn] consensus, accord [ant] discord, disagreement

There was complete concord regarding the new environmental policy among the member countries.
There was lasting concord between the two nations, at last.

06 predator [prédətər]
n. 약탈자, 육식 동물

an animal that kills and eats other animals
[a] predatory 약탈하는, 육식(성)의
[syn] carnivore, marauder [ant] prey

The killer whale is the most fearsome of all marine predators.

01 이 시기에는 목 질환과 피부 알레르기를 조심해야 합니다. 02 줄담배를 피우는 슈퍼스타가 흡연에 반대하는 캠페인을 하는 것이 위선적인 행동으로 보였다. 03 황사 입자들은 중금속과 다른 위험 물질을 포함하고 있기 때문에 눈과 기관지 질환을 일으킨다. 04 Mathew Jardine의 최근 저서는 London, New York 그리고 Paris의 비평가들에게서 호평을 받았다. 디자이너 상을 받은 팀을 환호하기 위한 특별 모임이 있었다. 05 회원국들 간에 환경 정책에 대한 의견이 완전히 일치했다. 마침내, 두 나라에 영원한 평화가 공존하게 되었다. 06 범고래는 모든 해양 생물들 중에서 가장 무시무시한 포식 동물이다.

07 grant [grænt]
n. 하사금, 보조금
v. 주다, 허가하다

an amount of money given for a certain purpose
[syn] reward, subsidy, award [ant] discount, deprivation, deduction

According to the latest reports the grant for research in genetics has been doubled.

The president granted special pardons to ten people convicted of bribery and misconduct.

---

08 haunt [hɔ:nt]
n. 자주 드나드는 곳
v. 출몰하다

a place often visited
[n] haunting 자주 다님, 출몰

This coffeehouse has been the haunt of aspiring actors, artists and writers for several decades.

Local residents believe that the spirit of the slain maiden haunts the house every moonlit night.

---

09 decimal [désəməl]
a. 10진법의, 소수의
n. 소수

based on the number ten
[syn] denary

The Dewey decimal system is widely used to arrange books in the library.

Third grade students were taught how to change fractions to decimals and they had a hard time understanding it.

---

10 sacred [séikrid]
a. 신성한, 성스러운

relating to a god or religion
[syn] holy, divine, godly [ant] profane, secular

Giving alms and feeding the hungry are considered as sacred as saying prayers.

---

11 exempt [igzémpt]
a. (의무 등이) 면제된
v. 면제하다

free from a duty or rule
[n] exemption 면제, 해제
[syn] absolved, released, relieve [ant] responsible, liable, enforce

Many people are exempt from military service for various reasons.

My school exempted me from gym classes as I had sprained my ankle.

---

12 flunk [flʌŋk]
v. (시험 등에) 낙제하다, 실패하다

to fail, especially in school

Carl flunked 3 of his exams because he didn't study but managed to pass 2 others.

---

07 최근 보고에 따르면 유전학 분야의 연구 보조금이 두 배로 증가했다. 대통령은 뇌물 수수와 비리로 유죄가 선고된 10명에 대해 특별사면을 단행했다. 08 이 커피숍은 야심 있는 배우, 예술가, 작가들이 수십 년 동안 자주 드나드는 곳이다. 지역 거주민들은 살해된 처녀 유령이 달빛 비치는 밤에 출몰한다고 생각한다. 09 듀이식 십진 시스템은 오늘날 도서관에서 책을 정리하는 데 널리 이용된다. 3학년 학생들이 분수를 소수로 바꾸는 방법을 배웠지만 그것을 이해하는 데 어려움을 겪었다. 10 자선품을 나누어 주고 배고픈 사람들에게 먹을 것을 주는 것은 기도를 드리는 것만큼이나 성스럽게 여겨진다. 11 많은 젊은이들이 여러 가지 이유로 병역을 면제 받는다. 발목이 삐었기 때문에 학교 측은 나를 체육수업에서 빼주었다. 12 Carl은 공부를 하지 않았기 때문에 시험에서 세 과목은 낙제를 했고 두 과목은 간신히 통과할 수 있었다.

13 pledge [pledʒ]

v. 서약하다
n. 서약, 맹세

to promise something

[syn] swear, vow, promise

Doctors pledge to respect and protect human life when they receive their medical degrees.

The president didn't fulfill his pledge to create five million new jobs.

14 relish [réliʃ]

v. 즐기다, 좋아하다
n. 맛, 흥미, 즐거움

to get enjoyment from something

[a] relishable 맛있는, 재미있는

[syn] enjoy, fancy   [ant] dislike

The woman didn't relish the thought of going back to work.

I have little relish for having long conversations on the phone.

15 inhabit [inhǽbit]

v. 살다, 거주하다

to live in

[n] inhabitant 거주자   [a] inhabited 사람이 살고 있는

[syn] populate, abide, dwell, reside

The island of Madagascar is one of the few areas in the world inhabited by lemurs.

16 omit [oumít]

v. 생략하다, 빠뜨리다

to not include either by accident or purpose

[n] omission 생략, 탈락   [a] omissible 생략할 수 있는

[syn] exclude, eliminate   [ant] add, include

The student omitted an answer to the last question on the test.

17 entrust [intrʌ́st]

v. (책임·임무 등을) 맡기다, 위임하다

to give someone a responsibility

[syn] assign, consign, commit

I entrust you with the task of recruiting researchers for the new assignment.

18 justify [dʒʌ́stəfài]

v. 정당화하다, 옳다고 하다

to give an acceptable explanation for something

[n] justification 정당화

[syn] vindicate, legitimize

The city official justified the committee's decision to the mayor.

19 deem [diːm]

v. 간주하다, 생각하다

to consider something in a particular way

[syn] regard, view, reckon

The teacher deemed the assignment worthy of repeating.

---

13 의사들은 의사 면허를 받을 때 인간의 생명을 존중하고 보호하겠다고 서약한다. 대통령은 5백 만개의 일자리를 창출하겠다는 공약을 지키지 못했다. 14 여인은 다시 일을 해야 한다는 사실이 탐탁스럽지 않았다. 나는 전화로 통화를 길게 하는 것을 별로 좋아하지 않는다. 15 Madagascar 섬은 여우 원숭이가 서식하는 세계 몇 안 되는 곳 중 하나이다. 16 학생은 시험의 맨 마지막 문제 푸는 것을 빼먹었다. 17 새로운 연구를 할 연구원들을 뽑는 임무를 당신에게 맡기겠습니다. 18 그 시 공무원은 시장에게 위원회의 결정이 옳다고 했다. 19 교사는 그 과제를 되풀이해서 내도 되겠다고 생각했다.

20 salute [səlúːt]

v. 인사하다, 경의를 표하다
n. 경례, 예포

to greet and show respect

n salutation 인사   a salutatory 인사의, 환영의

syn honor, tribute

The sergeant jumped up to salute the general as he entered the command tent.

The ships fired a 21-gun salute in honor of the admiral's arrival.

21 bluff [blʌf]

v. 속이다, (허세를 부려서) ~시키다
a. 퉁명스러운

to deceive or mislead someone

syn dupe, delude, blunt

Steve was bluffing during the card game because he could not win.

Jason is seemingly rather bluff but he has a very warm heart.

22 grasp [græsp]

v. 붙잡다, 이해하다
n. 붙잡음, 이해

to take and hold firmly

a grasping 쥐는, 붙잡는

syn clutch, seize, apprehend, grab   ant release

The climber carefully grasped the rope and moved his feet up.

The main point of her argument was beyond his grasp.

23 trigger [trígər]

v. (사건 등을) 일으키다, 유발하다
n. 방아쇠, (기계의) 제동기

to make something happen

syn cause, generate, provoke   ant check, halt, stop

The sleeping driver triggered the large accident last night.

The criminal pulled the trigger on the gun, but fortunately, it didn't fire.

24 magnify [mǽgnəfài]

v. 확대하다, 과장하다

to make something appear larger or more important

n magnification 확대, 과장

syn amplify, expand, overstate   ant minimize, understate

My older brother always magnifies the trifle matters and fusses over them.

25 discriminate [diskrímənèit]

v. 구별하다, 차별 대우하다

to treat differently and unfairly

n discrimination 구별, 차별 대우   n discriminative 구별되는, 특이한

syn differentiate, distinguish, segregate   ant indiscriminate

No one should discriminate against people of other races or countries.

---

20 하사관은 장군이 사령부 막사로 들어오자 경례하려고 벌떡 일어났다. 함선은 해군 장성이 도착하자 경의를 표하기 위해 21발의 예포를 발사했다. 21 Steve는 카드 게임에서 이길 수 없었기 때문에 패가 센 것처럼 허풍을 떨었다. Jason은 겉으로는 좀 무뚝뚝해 보이지만 따뜻한 마음을 가진 사람이다. 22 등산가는 등산을 하는 동안 조심스럽게 로프를 붙잡고 발을 움직였다. 그는 그녀가 주장하는 요점을 이해하기가 어려웠다. 23 졸음 운전자는 어젯밤 대형 사고를 일으켰다. 그 범죄자가 총의 방아쇠를 당겼지만 다행히도 총알이 발사되지 않았다. 24 오빠는 항상 사소한 일을 과장해 난리법석을 떤다. 25 그 누구도 다른 인종이나 다른 나라의 사람들을 차별해서는 안 된다.

Exercise

Score / 20

Word Check 각 단어의 뜻으로 알맞은 것을 찾아 연결하시오.

01 grant   ⓐ a feeling of enjoyment
02 trigger   ⓑ to give something formally
03 relish   ⓒ to cause something to happen
04 haunt   ⓓ relating to the system based number ten
05 decimal   ⓔ to appear in a place regularly, especially as a ghost or sprit

Syn & Ant Check 주어진 단어의 동의어, 반의어를 골라 쓰시오.

jeer	carnivore	disagreement	profane	vow
dwell	include	release	expand	segregate

06 inhabit   = _____   11 concord   ↔ _____
07 predator   = _____   12 grasp   ↔ _____
08 magnify   = _____   13 sacred   ↔ _____
09 discriminate = _____   14 acclaim   ↔ _____
10 pledge   = _____   15 omit   ↔ _____

Sentence Practice 문장을 읽고 빈칸에 알맞은 단어를 고르시오.

16 We think it is unfair not to give Francis a chance to _____ his actions.

ⓐ deem   ⓑ trigger   ⓒ magnify   ⓓ justify

17 The change in weather has brought its customary share of minor _____ like colds and coughs.

ⓐ ailments   ⓑ predators   ⓒ grants   ⓓ acclaim

18 Damon had to _____ about his whereabouts to protect his younger brother Leslie.

ⓐ grasp   ⓑ bluff   ⓒ entrust   ⓓ exempt

19 His discomfort was due to the _____ of food stuck in his throat.

ⓐ particle   ⓑ hypocrisy   ⓒ concord   ⓓ haunt

20 Donations to this fund are _____ from income tax under the country's laws.

ⓐ sacred   ⓑ decimal   ⓒ exempt   ⓓ bluff

✤ between, within

inter : **inter**ject 끼워 넣다, **inter**act 상호작용하다, **inter**fere 방해하다
People mirror each other's postures and interject feedback such as nods.
사람들은 서로의 태도를 보며 끄덕임 같은 반응을 보인다.

intro : **intro**vert 내성적인 사람, **intro**spect 내성하다, **intro**versive 내성적인
He used to be very sociable but he became an introvert now.
그는 매우 사교적이었지만 지금은 내성적인 사람이 되었다.

circum : **circum**stance 주변 사정, **circum**flight 궤도 비행, **circum**ference 원주
Force of circumstance caused him to leave his family.
주위 상황 때문에 어쩔 수 없이 그는 가족을 떠났다.

✤ near, side

cis : **cis**atlantic 대서양 이쪽편의, **cis**tern 저수탱크, **cis**alpine 알프스 남쪽의
The cistern was built to hold rainwater to be used for watering the plants and washing the car.
물탱크는 꽃에 물을 주거나 세차할 때 사용할 수 있는 빗물을 저장할 목적으로 만들어졌다.

peri : **peri**cardial 심장주위의, **peri**scope 잠망경, **peri**anth 꽃덮이
This research shows the natural history of pericardial effusion after cardiac surgery.
이 연구는 심장 수술 후 심장주위의 혈액 흐름의 자연력을 보여준다.

para : **para**phrase 의역, **para**biosis 병체결합, **para**ble 비유 담
Jesus told many parables to his followers such as the Good Samaritan.
예수는 제자들에게 착한 사마리아 사람과 같은 많은 우화를 들려줬다.

✤ under

sub : **sub**marine 잠수함, **sub**acid 약간 신, **sub**agent 부대변인
It is unfair that the agent could appoint a subagent without notice.
대리인이 알리지 않고 부대변인을 선임할 수 있다는 것이 부당합니다.

infra : **infra**structure 하부조직, **infra**costal 늑골 아래의, **infra**human 인간 이하의
The question is to improve the country's financial infrastructure.
문제는 국가의 재정적 하부구조를 개선하는 것입니다.

A 영어 풀이에 알맞은 단어를 보기에서 찾아 쓰시오.

criterion	strive	divine	numb	magnify

01 unable to feel or move _____

02 relating to God or a god _____

03 to try very hard to achieve something _____

04 to make something appear larger or louder _____

05 a standard or principle used to judge something or someone _____

B 문장을 읽고 문맥에 적절한 단어를 고르시오.

06 We heard on the news that hired thugs are being used to (intimidate/initiate) loan defaulters.

07 Bright plumage and courtship displays help male birds attract, woo and (salute/seduce) females.

08 I (entrust/justify) you with the responsibility to supervise this project in my absence.

09 Wisdom (dispels/captures) ignorance in the same way that light does darkness.

C ▨▨▨▨ 표시된 부분과 뜻이 가장 가까운 것을 고르시오.

10 Special Detective Mike Connor is being sent to mediate for the release of the hostages.

ⓐ intrude   ⓑ incite   ⓒ kidnap   ⓓ intercede

11 One of the predominant features of this region is that it has black soil suitable for growing cotton.

ⓐ antibiotic   ⓑ magnetic   ⓒ prominent   ⓓ divine

12 Although this chapter will be omitted from this year's syllabus it would be good for you to go through it.

ⓐ excluded   ⓑ flunk   ⓒ trigger   ⓓ segregate

13 Birds are seen to engage in hectic nesting activities at the advent of spring.

ⓐ trait   ⓑ core   ⓒ beginning   ⓓ excursion

D 표시된 부분의 반대말로 가장 알맞은 것을 고르시오.

14 The patient's family received ambiguous replies in response to their frantic questions about their son's condition.
  ⓐ utmost   ⓑ cunning   ⓒ explicit   ⓓ stingy

15 All societies are guilty of hypocrisy when they profess regard for women and then exploit them.
  ⓐ peep   ⓑ honesty   ⓒ conspiracy   ⓓ monarch

16 The organizers announced the results in reverse order so they could prolong the audience's suspense.
  ⓐ outlive   ⓑ segregate   ⓒ imprint   ⓓ abbreviate

17 An untimely shower forced the postponement of the much-awaited final match.
  ⓐ shrewd   ⓑ eligible   ⓒ rigorous   ⓓ opportune

E 주어진 단어를 알맞은 형태로 바꿔 빈칸에 쓰시오.

18 The _____ activity of the animal is the same as for other members of its species. (predator)

19 She will _____ in her endeavors despite any failure or disappointment. (perseverance)

20 His strong _____ sense warned him against accepting the terms of the offer. (intuition)

21 It was difficult to believe that the queen herself had _____ to overthrow the king. (conspiracy)

F 빈칸에 알맞은 단어를 보기에서 찾아 쓰시오. (필요한 경우 형태를 바꾸시오.)

merge	torture	escort	salvation	morale
arouse	relish	assent	pledge	avenge

22 우리는 최근 앨범에서 좀 더 많은 청중에게 다가가기 위해 클래식 음악과 현대 리듬을 혼합했습니다.
 → Our latest album has _____ classical music with contemporary rhythms to reach out to a wider audience.

23 Simon은 변덕스러운 팀의 사기를 유지하는 골치 아픈 일을 하고 있다.
 → Simon has the unenviable job of keeping up the _____ of his volatile team.

24 우리는 항상 엄마가 요리해주시는 간소하고 건강한 식사를 즐긴다.
 → We always _____ the simple, wholesome meals cooked by our mother.

25 우리 그룹은 우리 지도자의 죽음에 앙갚음 하고 그의 오명을 벗기자는 엄숙한 맹세를 했다.
 → Our group took a solemn _____ to _____ our leader's death and clear his name.

▶ 영어를 우리말로 옮기시오.

01 intimidate		31 urge	
02 kidnap		32 doom	
03 withdraw		33 outlive	
04 prolong		34 mob	
05 justify		35 hypocrisy	
06 duplicate		36 dissent	
07 advent		37 invert	
08 magnetic		38 assent	
09 combat		39 ambiguous	
10 stagnate		40 acclaim	
11 decimal		41 ascertain	
12 entrust		42 feedback	
13 salvation		43 avenge	
14 equip		44 shrewd	
15 stingy		45 incite	
16 shield		46 toss	
17 sacred		47 monarch	
18 trait		48 groan	
19 bluff		49 intrude	
20 ailment		50 exempt	
21 assault		51 delinquency	
22 discriminate		52 trigger	
23 installment		53 compliment	
24 mediate		54 segregate	
25 plead		55 cling	
26 numb		56 divine	
27 stray		57 untimely	
28 atomic		58 choke	
29 seduce		59 merge	
30 utter		60 enrich	

우리말을 영어로 옮기시오.

61 ~의 탓으로 하다

62 전략, 전술

63 약탈자

64 음모, 공모

65 목소리의

66 일으키다, 낳다

67 적, 원수

68 일치, 조화

69 중얼거리다

70 열의, 열정

71 직관

72 장애, 약점

73 서약하다

74 날아오르다

75 낚아 채다

76 우세한

77 호위하다

78 짧은 여행

79 확대하다

80 적격의, 적당한

81 즐기다

82 엄격한, 혹독한

83 간주하다

84 사라지다

85 깨우다, 자극하다

86 면역(성)의

87 엿보기

88 박차를 가하다

89 붙잡다, 이해하다

90 살다, 거주하다

91 숨을 막다

92 변두리, 교외

93 지친, 지루한

94 적용 범위

95 몰두한, 선취된

96 운송하다

97 불길, 화염

98 의욕, 사기

99 항생 물질

100 애쓰다

101 인내력

102 성질

103 쓰레기

104 추방하다

105 책임을 지다

106 비율, 균형

107 고문하다

108 최대한, 극한

109 생략하다

110 전환하다

111 경의를 표하다

112 중간의, 중급의

113 인상지우다

114 찰싹 때리다

115 극소량

116 다시 말하면

117 보내다, 전하다

118 하사금, 보조금

119 쫓아버리다

120 기준, 표준

Part 4

Day 16

🎧 01 **malfunction** [mælfʌ́ŋkʃən]
n. (기계 등의) 고장, 오작동
v. (기계 등이) 제대로 작동하지 않다

failure to function correctly
ⓐ malfunctioning 제대로 기능하지 못하는
syn breakdown, impairment   ant function

The malfunction in the DVD player was very difficult to repair correctly.
The TV malfunctioned last night, so I am having it fixed, today.

02 **multitude** [mʌ́ltətjùːd]
n. 다수, 군중

a large number
ⓐ multitudinous 다수의, 아주 많은
syn mass, throng, mob, crowd

The official spoke to the unhappy multitude about the recent changes to the employment policy.

03 **counterpart** [káuntərpàːrt]
n. 대응하는 사람[것], 사본

a person or thing that has the same function or character as another
syn copy, equal, equivalent

The office manager phoned his counterpart in the Los Angeles office.

04 **doctrine** [dáktrin]
n. (종교의) 교의, (정치의) 주의, 정책

belief or set of beliefs, especially religious or political
ⓐ doctrinal 교리의
syn principle, tenet, policy, dogma

The students asked questions about the church's doctrine of the Holy Trinity.

05 **contract** [kántrækt]
n. 계약
v. 계약하다, 수축하다

a legal agreement between two companies or people
syn compact, pledge, covenant, constrict   ant disagreement, expand

The two companies will make a contract to work together for the next five years.
Our lungs expand when we inhale and contract when we exhale.

06 **prophet** [práfit]
n. 예언자, 선지자

a religious leader who teaches people and foretells future events
ⓐ prophetic 예언(자)의   ⓥ prophesy 예언하다
syn seer, prophesier, vaticinator, diviner

Famine and drought swept through the land when its people refused to heed the prophet's words.

---

01 DVD 고장은 정확하게 수리하기가 매우 어렵다. 텔레비전이 어젯밤에 제대로 작동하지 않아서 오늘 수리를 할거야. 02 그 임원은 불만에 찬 군중에게 고용 정책에 대한 최근 변화에 대해 말했다. 03 사무소장은 Los Angeles 지점의 사무소장에게 전화했다. 04 학생들은 교회의 삼위일체론 교리에 대해 질문했다. 05 그 두 회사는 앞으로 5년 동안 동업을 하기로 계약할 것이다. 우리의 폐는 공기를 들여 마실 때 팽창하고 내쉴 때 수축한다. 06 사람들은 예언자의 말에 주의를 기울이지 않았고 기근과 가뭄이 그 지역을 휩쓸었다.

07 ornament [ɔ́ːrnəmənt]

n. 장신구, 장식
v. 장식하다

something used to decorate a person or thing

n ornamentation 장식, 치레   a ornamental 장식용의, 장식적인

syn decoration, adornment, embellish

This is a traditional ornament worn on the forearm like an amulet.

The ceremonial attire of royal personages was often ornamented with real gems.

08 monitor [mɑ́nitər]

n. (컴퓨터, TV 등의) 모니터, 감시자
v. 감시[조정]하다

a device or person that regulates performance

n monitoring 감시, 관찰

syn overseer, supervisor, supervise

The test monitor told me to sit in the third row.

The chemistry teacher monitored the experiment during science class.

09 acquaintance [əkwéintəns]

n. 아는 사이[사람], 알고 있음

someone who one knows slightly, but not well

a acquainted 알고 있는, 아는 사이인   v acquaint 소개하다

syn familiarity, awareness   ant unfamiliarity, stranger

Toby is a new acquaintance of mine who works in the same building as I do.

10 confidential [kɑ̀nfədénʃəl]

a. 기밀의, 비밀의, 신뢰할 수 있는

intended to be kept secret

n confidentiality 기밀성, 비밀성

syn secret, classified, trusted   ant known, open, public

Everyone is concerned at the mysterious disappearance of the file containing confidential information.

11 ubiquitous [juːbíkwətəs]

a. 어디에나 존재하는

seeming to be everywhere at the same time

n ubiquity 도처에 있음, 편재   ad ubiquitously 편재하여, 도처에 존재하는 식으로

syn omnipresent, ever-present, universal   ant rare, scarce

My work would have been infinitely harder without the help of my ubiquitous personal assistant.

12 vague [veig]

a. 막연한, 애매한, 흐릿한

unclear in some way

n vagueness 막연함   ad vaguely 막연하게, 애매하게

syn indefinite, obscure, hazy   ant certain, positive, definite

She had a vague idea about what to do after her graduation.

---

07 이것은 부적처럼 팔뚝에 차고 다니는 전통 장신구이다. 왕가 명사의 예복은 종종 진짜 보석으로 장식되었다. 08 시험 감독관이 나에게 세 번째 줄에 앉으라고 했다. 화학 선생님은 과학 시간에 실험을 지켜보았다. 09 Toby는 나와 같은 건물에서 일하는 새로 알게 된 사람이다. 10 모든 사람들은 기밀 정보가 담긴 파일이 신비하게 흔적도 없이 사라진 것을 걱정하고 있다. 11 어디를 가든 나를 따라다니는 개인 비서의 도움이 없다면 일을 하기가 매우 힘들었을 것이다. 12 그녀는 졸업 후 무엇을 할 것인지에 대해 막연한 생각을 가지고 있다.

13 tremble [trémbl]

v. 떨리다, 떨다

to shake from cold, fear, etc.

trembling [n] 떨림, 전율 [a] 떨리는, 떠는

[syn] quiver, shudder, shiver [ant] calm, steady

The little child trembled with fear when he woke up from a nightmare.

14 revise [riváiz]

v. 개정하다, 수정하다

to change or improve something

[n] revision 개정, 교정 [a] revisory 교정의, 정정의

[syn] modify, amend [ant] preserve, retain

The legislature tries to revise the law on immigration and asylum.

15 refute [rifjúːt]

v. 논박하다, 반박하다

to prove something is not correct or fair

[n] reputation 논박, 반박 [a] refutative 논박하는, 반증의

[syn] disprove, rebut, confute

The lawyer refuted the charges of the police in the judge's courtroom.

16 inflate [infléit]

v. 부풀게 하다, 팽창시키다

to fill or increase beyond what is normal

[n] inflation 팽창, 인플레이션 [a] inflated 부푼, 팽창한

[syn] swell, bloat, distend [ant] deflate

It is great fun to inflate balloons and then let the air out in a rush.

17 extinguish [ikstíŋgwiʃ]

v. (불·빛 등을) 끄다, 소멸시키다

to put out or destroy something

[n] extinguishment 소화, 절멸 [a] extinguishable 불을 끌 수 있는

[syn] eliminate, eradicate [ant] light, ignite, inflame

Sand is a much safer way to extinguish a dangerous chemical fire than water or foam.

18 sneak [sniːk]

v. 몰래 움직이다, 몰래 하다

to move or go secretly and quietly

[a] sneaky 몰래 하는, 비열한 [ad] sneakily 몰래, 비열하게

Jim snuck into the baseball game without a ticket yesterday.

19 rid [rid]

v. 없애다, 자유롭게 하다

to free or relieve, especially of something undesirable

[n] riddance 없애기, 제거

[syn] remove, disencumber, free

I will not be happy until I have rid the garden of these pests.

---

13 어린 아이는 악몽에서 깨어나 공포에 떨었다. 14 입법부는 이민법과 망명법을 개정하려고 하고 있다. 15 변호사는 법정에서 경찰의 혐의를 논박했다. 16 풍선을 불고 공기가 빠르게 빠져나오는 것을 보는 것은 재미있다. 17 화학 물질로 인한 위험한 화재를 끄는 데는 물이나 발포체 보다 모래가 훨씬 안전하다. 18 Jim은 어제 야구 표 없이 야구 경기장에 몰래 들어갔다. 19 정원의 해충을 다 없애기 전까지는 마음이 놓이지 않아.

20 **condemn** [kəndém]
v. 비난하다, 유죄 판결을 내리다

to say something is wrong and unacceptable

n condemnation 비난, 유죄 선고   a condemnatory 비난의, 유죄 선고의

syn blame, denounce, convict   ant approve, acquit, pardon

The professor was condemned for plagiarizing his student's thesis.

The murderer for killing two innocent bystanders was condemned to the death penalty.

---

21 **soak** [souk]
v. 적시다, 젖다, 잠기다
n. 담그기, 적시기

to make thoroughly wet

a soaked 흠뻑 젖은

syn drench, moisten, saturate   ant dry

The sudden, heavy rain soaked his shirt and pants.

Give the chopped potato a short soak in the cold water before you cook it.

---

22 **assimilate** [əsíməlèit]
v. 동화시키다, 일치시키다

to become a part of something, especially a country or group

n assimilation 동화, 융합   a assimilative 동화 작용의, 동화력 있는

syn absorb   ant dissimilate

The United States continuously assimilates ethnic groups and cultures from all over the world.

---

23 **cram** [kræm]
v. 억지로 밀어 넣다

to put things or people into a certain place

syn stuff, jam   ant empty, loose, unstuffy

I have a wardrobe crammed full of clothes but still nothing to wear.

---

24 **transact** [trænsǽkt]
v. 집행하다, 처리하다

to carry on or complete something

n transaction 처리, 업무   a transitional 업무의

syn deal, conduct

I have found that this is the best time to transact business at my bank.

---

25 **charter** [tʃɑ́:rtər]
v. 특허장을 주다, 설립을 인가하다, 전세 내다
n. 특허장, 전세

to hire or to grant a franchise

syn grant, borrow, lease

He had to charter a plane to get to his client meeting in time.

The government gave a new charter to the company to explore the New World.

---

20 그 교수는 자기 학생의 논문을 표절했다는 이유로 비난을 받았다. 두 명의 무고한 행인을 죽인 살인자는 사형을 선고받았다. 21 갑자기 내린 세찬 비로 그의 셔츠와 바지가 젖었다. 요리하기 전에 잘게 썬 감자를 잠깐 동안 찬물에 담그세요. 22 미국은 끊임없이 전 세계의 소수민족과 문화를 동화시키고 있다. 23 내 옷장은 옷으로 가득 차 있는데 입을 옷이 하나도 없어. 24 나는 지금이 은행업무를 보는 데 가장 적당한 시간이라는 것을 알게 되었다. 25 그는 고객이 제시간에 회의에 도착할 수 있도록 비행기를 전세 냈다. 정부는 그 회사가 신세계를 탐험할 수 있도록 새 허가서를 주었다.

Exercise

Word Check 각 단어의 뜻으로 알맞은 것을 찾아 연결하시오.

01 revise   ⓐ to swell something with gas or air
02 inflate   ⓑ a particular belief, policy or principle
03 doctrine   ⓒ existing everywhere at the same time
04 transact   ⓓ to conduct or handle, especially business
05 ubiquitous   ⓔ to change something in order to improve

Syn & Ant Check 주어진 단어의 동의어, 반의어를 골라 쓰시오.

decoration	expand	supervisor	stranger	public
indefinite	shiver	disprove	ignite	unstuffy

06 vague   =
07 tremble   =
08 ornament   =
09 monitor   =
10 refute   =

11 cram   ↔
12 acquaintance ↔
13 extinguish   ↔
14 confidential ↔
15 contract   ↔

Sentence Practice 문장을 읽고 빈칸에 알맞은 단어를 고르시오.

16 The _____ at the factory was due to the fluctuations in its power supply.
　ⓐ multitude　　　　ⓑ malfunction　　　　ⓒ monitor　　　　ⓓ contract

17 New York is a city that has _____ diverse communities into its enterprising framework.
　ⓐ transacted　　　　ⓑ refuted　　　　ⓒ trembled　　　　ⓓ assimilated

18 This project will be handled exclusively by our _____ in China.
　ⓐ prophet　　　　ⓑ ornament　　　　ⓒ counterpart　　　　ⓓ acquaintance

19 It is advisable to _____ the vegetables overnight to cut down on cooking time.
　ⓐ rid　　　　ⓑ soak　　　　ⓒ revise　　　　ⓓ extinguish

20 The entire world came together to _____ the dastardly act of terrorism.
　ⓐ condemn　　　　ⓑ cram　　　　ⓒ charter　　　　ⓓ inflate

🎧 **01 oath** [ouθ]
n. 맹세, 서약

a serious and formal promise

syn vow, word, pledge

The witness was under oath before he testified in the court.

---

02 retrospect [rétrəspèkt]
n. 회상, 회고

a look at the past

a retrospective 회고적인

syn recollection

In retrospect, the days I stayed in Rome are the golden days of my life.

---

03 specimen [spésəmən]
n. 견본, 표본

a sample of something used for analysis and examination

syn example, model, pattern

The doctor took a specimen of his blood to test for hepatitis.

---

04 dose [dous]
n. (약의 1회분) 복용량
v. 복용하다

an amount taken or experienced at one time, especially medicine

syn prescription, dosage

The bottle contains 80 adult doses of medication.

Do not dose these drugs for more than seven consecutive days.

---

05 consent [kənsént]
n. 동의, 허가
v. 동의하다, 승낙하다

agreement or permission

n consensus 일치, 합의   a consentient 일치한, 동의하는

syn assent, approval, accept   ant dissent, refusal, reject

All students need the consent of their parents to go on the field trip.

I cannot consent to this plan until I study it more carefully.

---

06 outlet [áutlet]
n. 배출구, 소매점

a passage to let something out

syn opening, exit, vent   ant closure

A brisk walk in the garden is usually a good outlet for my pent-up emotions.

As we are a leading clothing company we have outlets in several big cities like New York, LA and London.

---

01 증인은 법원에서 증언을 하기 전에 선서를 했다. 02 다시 생각해보니 내가 로마에서 지냈을 때가 내 인생에서 가장 소중했던 시절이었다. 03 의사는 간염을 진단하기 위해 그의 혈액 표본을 채취했다. 04 이 용기에는 성인이 80회 복용할 수 있는 만큼의 약이 들어 있습니다. 이 약을 7일 이상 계속 복용하지 마십시오. 05 모든 학생들은 현장학습을 가려면 부모님의 동의가 필요하다. 나는 그 계획을 세밀히 검토하기 전에는 동의할 수 없다. 06 공원에서의 가벼운 산책은 내 답답한 마음을 풀어주는 좋은 감정의 배출구이다. 저희는 선도적인 의류 회사로 New York, LA 그리고 London과 같은 대도시에 대리점을 가지고 있습니다.

07 fiscal [fískəl]
a. 국고의, 재정의, 회계의

relating to financial issues, especially public

[n] fiscality 재정 정책 [ad] fiscally 국고 수입상, 재정상

[syn] financial, monetary

The new fiscal policy of the government will focus on promoting the agricultural sector.

08 cordial [kɔ́:rdʒəl]
a. 진심의, 인정 있는, 공손한

warm and friendly but formal

[n] cordiality 진심, 충정 [a] cordially 진심으로, 정성껏

[syn] hearty, courteous, gracious, sincere [ant] insincere, hostile, unfriendly

The two rivals share a relationship that is cordial but not jovial.

09 imposing [impóuziŋ]
a. 인상적인, 훌륭한

large and impressive in appearance or manner

[ad] imposingly 인상적으로, 남의 눈을 끌어

[syn] magnificent, outstanding, grand [ant] unimposing

The Empire State Building is still an imposing landmark in New York City.

10 candid [kǽndid]
a. 솔직한, 노골적인

saying what one thinks frankly

[n] candidness 솔직함, 노골적임 [ad] candidly 솔직하게, 노골적으로

[syn] sincere, honest, forthright, outspoken [ant] deceitful, insincere,

To be candid with you, the reason you weren't hired is lack of work experience.

The candid newspaper article explained the governor's true feelings about the plan.

11 foreshadow [fɔ:rʃǽdou]
v. 예시하다, 전조가 된다

to suggest that something will happen in the future

[n] foreshadowing 예시, 전조

[syn] foretell, portend, prophesy

Some early religious writings foreshadowed many of the catastrophes and upheavals that rocked the modern world.

12 refrain [rifréin]
v. 억제하다, 그만두다, 삼가다

to stop oneself from doing something

[n] refrainment 자제, 삼가기

[syn] abstain, forbear, renounce [ant] continue

I was unable to refrain my mounting anger with my son's impudent behavior.

Please refrain from smoking cigarettes in the movie theater.

---

07 정부의 새로운 재정 정책은 농업부문을 증진하는 데 초점을 맞출 것이다. 08 두 라이벌은 서로 진실하긴 하지만 썩 유쾌하지만은 않은 관계를 유지하고 있다. 09 Empire State 빌딩은 여전히 New York 시를 상징하는 인상적인 건물이다. 10 솔직히 말씀 드리면, 당신이 고용되지 않은 이유는 경력 부족입니다. 그 신문 기사는 노골적으로 그 정책에 대해 주지사가 어떻게 느끼고 있는지를 진실되게 보여주었다. 11 일부 초기 종교 서적은 현대 세계를 뒤흔들어 놓은 많은 재앙과 대변동을 암시하고 있다. 12 나는 내 아들의 버릇없는 행동에 끓어오르는 화를 참을 수가 없었다. 영화관에서는 흡연을 삼가 주십시오.

13　dip [dip]
v. (살짝) 담그다, 내려가다
n. 살짝 담그기, 적시기

to put into liquid and quickly lift out again
[syn] souse, dunk, immerse

Jane loves to dip her cookie in warm milk before eating it.
Hindus believe taking a dip in the holy River Ganges will cleanse sin.

14　conceive [kənsíːv]
v. 생각하다, (생각 · 의견 등을) 품다

to form or develop an idea, etc.
[n] conception 개념, 생각　[a] conceptional 개념의　[a] conceivable 생각할 수 있는
[syn] consider, imagine, think

It is difficult for us to conceive of a time when there was no electricity.

15　assemble [əsémbl]
v. 모으다, 조립하다

to gather or put together
[n] assembly 모임, 집합　[a] assembled 모인, 결집된
[syn] convene, collect, construct　[ant] scatter, break, disassemble

The students assembled in the auditorium for the meeting.

16　wail [weil]
v. 울부짖다, 통곡하다

to make a long cry of grief or pain
[a] wailful 비탄에 잠긴, 울부짖는　[ad] wailingly 울부짖으며
[syn] moan, weep, howl

Once the sensor detects fumes or heat, the fire alarm starts wailing.
The baby was wailing non-stop but her helpless father did not know what to do with it.

17　warrant [wɔ́ːrənt]
v. 정당화하다, 보증하다
n. 권한, 보증, 영장

to prove that something is reasonable or right
[n] warranty 보증, 권한　[a] warrantable 정당한, 보증할 수 있는
[syn] justify, assure, guarantee

He warranted that there is no further charge for the service.
A warrant is issued only if there is a reasonable ground for belief of guilt.

18　distract [distrǽkt]
v. (주의 · 마음을) 흐트러뜨리다, 혼란시키다

to draw attention to something else
[n] distraction 주의 산만　[a] distracted 주의를 산만하게 하는
[syn] divert, deflect, confuse　[ant] focus, concentrate

The TV sound distracted the child's attention from his homework.

19　proliferate [prəlífərèit]
v. 급증하다, 증식[번식]하다

to increase rapidly
[n] proliferation 증식, 급증　[a] proliferative 증식[번식]하는, 급증하는
[syn] multiply, propagate　[ant] decrease, dwindle

The crimes against children have proliferated for the past ten years.

---

13 Jane은 쿠키를 따뜻한 우유에 찍어 먹는 것을 좋아한다. 힌두교 신자들은 신성한 Ganges 강에 몸을 담그면 죄가 씻긴다고 생각한다. 14 전기가 없던 시기를 상상하기 어렵다. 15 학생들은 회의를 하기 위해 강당에 모였다. 16 센서가 연기나 열기를 감지하면 화재 경보가 울리기 시작합니다. 아기가 쉬지 않고 울었지만 무력한 아기 아버지는 어떻게 해야 할지 알지 못했다. 17 그는 서비스를 이용하는 데 더 이상의 추가 비용은 없을 것이라고 보장했다. 영장은 죄를 지었다고 믿을 수 있는 합당한 근거가 있어야만 발부된다. 18 텔레비전 소리는 그가 숙제 하는 데 주의를 흐트러뜨렸다. 19 아동을 대상으로 하는 범죄가 지난 10년 동안 급증했다.

20 convert [kənvə́:rt]
v. 바꾸다, 전환하다
n. 개종자, 전향자

to change something into a different form
n conversion 전환, 변환 a convertible 바꿀 수 있는
syn alter, transform, switch ant keep, persist, stay

You should convert all of your Korean Won to Canadian Dollars before going to Vancouver.

I am considering becoming a convert of Jesus Christ.

21 intrigue [intríːg]
v. 흥미를 돋우다
n. 음모

to cause curiosity or interest
a intriguing 흥미를 자아내는
syn attract, fascinate, plot, conspiracy

I am intrigued by the man's capacity for consistent hard work.

Political intrigue during the war almost destroyed the government during those years.

22 consult [kənsʌ́lt]
v. 조언[의견]을 구하다, 참고로 하다

to seek advice or information
n consultation 상담, 자문 a consulting 자문의
syn confer, ask, inquire

The workers consulted the architect's plans before they dug the hole.

23 mold [mould]
v. (틀에 넣어) 만들다, (성격을) 형성하다
n. 틀, 형(型)

to shape something
syn form ant disassemble, dismantle

The man molded the boy's character through hard work and training.

You'll find the cupcake molds on the top shelf of the cupboard.

24 dictate [díkteit]
v. 명령하다, 지시하다
n. 명령, 지시

to give someone orders or instructions
a dictatorial 독재적인
syn command, prescribe, instruct, order ant follow, obey

He dictated that the new rules relating to security be implemented immediately.

The ruler issued a dictate for every citizen to obey.

25 versus [və́:rsəs]
prep. ~대, ~에 대하여

against or in contrast with
syn against, opposed to

It was the Browns versus the Cowboys during the football game on Sunday.

---

20 Vancouver로 출발하기 전에 당신이 가지고 있는 원화를 모두 캐나다 달러로 환전하셔야 합니다. 나는 기독교로 개종할까 생각 중이다. 21 시종일관 힘든 일을 해내는 그의 능력이 내 눈에 띄었다. 전쟁 중의 정치적인 음모가 전쟁을 하는 동안 중앙 정부를 거의 파괴했다. 22 노동자들은 구멍을 파기 전에 건축가의 설계도를 참고했다. 23 그 남자는 어려운 과제와 힘든 훈련을 통해 그 소년의 성격을 형성했다. 찬장 맨 위 선반에 컵 케이크 틀이 있어. 24 그는 보안에 관한 새로운 규정을 즉시 실행하라고 지시했다. 군주는 모든 시민에게 복종하라고 명령했다. 25 일요일 미식축구 경기는 Browns 대 Cowboys 팀의 경기였다.

Exercise

Word Check 각 단어의 뜻으로 알맞은 것을 찾아 연결하시오.

01 wail
02 dip
03 warrant
04 dictate
05 retrospect

ⓐ to put something in liquid
ⓑ thinking back of things in past
ⓒ to tell someone what they should do
ⓓ to make a long loud cry to express grief or pain
ⓔ a legal document for arresting someone, searching something, etc.

Syn & Ant Check 주어진 단어의 동의어, 반의어를 골라 쓰시오.

dissent	pledge	forthright	insincere	magnificent
convene	concentrate	persist	dwindle	against

06 candid =
07 assemble =
08 imposing =
09 versus =
10 oath =

11 consent ↔
12 convert ↔
13 proliferate ↔
14 distract ↔
15 cordial ↔

Sentence Practice 문장을 읽고 빈칸에 알맞은 단어를 고르시오.

16 Our greenhouse has rare _____ of plants from all over the world.

ⓐ oaths   ⓑ consent   ⓒ specimens   ⓓ outlet

17 Seismic data recorded near the volcano seems to _____ a massive eruption.

ⓐ wail   ⓑ proliferate   ⓒ foreshadow   ⓓ consult

18 Humans have always been _____ by the vastness of the universe and its many secrets.

ⓐ molded   ⓑ dictated   ⓒ conceived   ⓓ intrigued

19 The normal _____ for an adult is two teaspoons taken three times a day.

ⓐ dose   ⓑ retrospect   ⓒ warrant   ⓓ oath

20 Changes in the _____ policy have made loans available to farmers at easy rates.

ⓐ candid   ⓑ cordial   ⓒ fiscal   ⓓ imposing

01 **benefactor** [bénəfæ̀ktər]
n. 은혜를 베푸는 사람, 은인

someone who helps a person or organization, especially financially
n benefaction 자비, 은혜
syn helper, bestower, patron, sponsor   ant antagonist, opposer
Bill Gates is known around the world as a great benefactor.

02 **rage** [reidʒ]
n. 격노, 분노

uncontrolled anger
a raging 격노한, 격렬한   a rageful 격분한
syn madness, fury, wrath, resentment   ant calmness
The commander flew into a rage on finding that his orders had been disobeyed.

03 **catastrophe** [kətǽstrəfi]
n. 대참사, 큰 재앙, 파멸

a great and sudden disaster
a catastrophic 대이변의, 비극적인
syn calamity, fatality, ruin
Hurricane Katrina resulted in an unthinkable catastrophe in New Orleans.

04 **legislation** [lèdʒisléiʃən]
n. 법률 제정, 입법, 법률

the act or process of making laws
a legislative 입법상의   v legislate 법률을 제정하다
syn enactment, lawmaking
The new legislation lowers taxes on everyone this year.

05 **epoch** [épək]
n. (특정) 시대, 시기, 중요한 사건

an important period or event in history
a epochal 신기원의, 획기적인
syn era
Last year will be remembered as an epoch that marked the revival of the film industry in Korea.

06 **complexion** [kəmplékʃən]
n. 안색, (사태의) 외관, 상황

the natural appearance of the skin of the face
a complexioned 안색이 ~한   ad complexionally 외관[용모]상으로
Continual exposure to the sun has darkened her complexion and bleached her hair.

---

01 Bill Gates는 세계적으로 기부를 많이 하는 사람으로 알려져 있다. 02 사령관은 자신의 명령이 거역되었다는 것을 알고는 버럭 화를 냈다. 03 허리케인 Katrina는 New Orleans에 상상조차 할 수 없는 엄청난 재앙을 몰고 왔다. 04 올해 새로운 법령으로 모든 사람에게 부과되는 세금이 인하될 것이다. 05 지난 해는 한국에서 영화산업의 부활이라는 신기원을 이룬 한 해로 기억될 것이다. 06 계속된 햇빛 노출로 그녀의 얼굴이 검게 탔고, 머리카락이 탈색되었다.

07 glacier [gléiʃər]
n. 빙하

a large mass of ice that moves slowly

ⓐ glacial 얼음의, 빙하의   ⓥ glaciate 얼리다, 결빙시키다

syn iceberg

A glacier is melting because of rising temperatures.

08 bribe [braib]
n. 뇌물, 미끼
v. 뇌물을 주다, 매수하다

an illegal gift to persuade someone to do something

ⓝ bribery 뇌물 수수, 매수   ⓐ bribable 매수할 수 있는

syn inducement, allurement

The guard took a bribe from the strange visitor and let him in.

The man bribed the judge to make his punishment less severe.

09 pasture [pǽstʃər]
n. 목장, 목초지
v. 방목하다

land suitable for grazing animals

ⓝ pasturage 목초(지), 목장

syn hayfield, meadow, ranch

The farmer took his cows into the pasture to eat there.

10 vent [vent]
n. 통풍구, (감정 등의) 표출
v. (감정 등을) 발산하다

a small opening to allow something to be released

ⓐ ventless 구멍[통풍구]이 없는

syn ventilator, blowhole, outlet

The geologists discovered a new vent in the volcano.

He uses the punching bag in the gym whenever he needs to vent his emotions.

11 glimpse [glimps]
n. 힐끗 봄, 일견
v. 힐끗 보다

a brief look at someone or something

syn glance, peek   ant observation, scrutiny

I caught a glimpse of the distinguished politician as he stepped out of his car.

The fireman glimpsed at the fire and ran inside to save the child.

12 abrupt [əbrʌ́pt]
a. 갑작스러운, 뜻밖의, 무뚝뚝한

sudden and unexpected, possibly unpleasant

ⓝ abruptness 갑작스러움, 무뚝뚝   ad abruptly 갑자기, 불쑥

syn blunt   ant gradual, courteous, kind, polite

The demonstrators came to an abrupt halt on seeing police vehicles lined up ahead.

The reception staff was quite abrupt and rude and even didn't know what I asked about.

---

07 기온 상승으로 빙하가 녹고 있다. 08 경비원이 뇌물을 받고 낯선 사람을 안으로 들여보냈다. 그 남자는 죄를 경감시켜 달라고 판사를 매수했다. 09 농부는 그의 소들이 풀을 먹이려고 목초지로 데리고 갔다. 10 지리학자들은 그 화산의 새로운 분출구를 발견했다. 그는 그의 감정을 터뜨려야 할 때마다 체육관에 있는 샌드백을 두들긴다. 11 나는 저명한 정치가가 차에서 나올 때 그를 힐끗 쳐다보았다. 소방관은 화재를 보고 아이를 구하기 위해 안으로 달려갔다. 12 앞에 경찰차가 줄서 있는 것을 보자 시위자들이 갑자기 멈춰섰다. 리셉션 직원은 무뚝뚝하고 무례했으며 심지어 내가 물어본 것에 대해서도 알지 못했다.

13 **immense** [iméns]
a. 광대한, 막대한

very large or great
[n] immensity 광대, 무수 [ad] immensely 광대하게, 막대하게
[syn] huge, tremendous, enormous [ant] small, tiny
She was a little overawed by the **immense** responsibility given to her.

14 **nasty** [nǽsti]
a. 더러운, 불쾌한, 비열한

bad or unpleasant in any way
[n] nastiness 몹시 더러움, 불결함
[syn] foul, dirty, unpleasant [ant] clean, nice, delightful
She is well-known for making **nasty** remarks about her colleagues.

15 **upper** [ʌ́pər]
a. 더 위의, (지위 등이) 상위의

in a higher position
[syn] higher, superior [ant] lower, inferior
The apartments on the **upper** floors cost more money to rent.

16 **affluent** [ǽfluənt]
a. 풍족한, 부유한

having a lot of money
[n] affluence 풍부, 부유
[syn] wealthy, well-off, rich [ant] destitute, needy, penniless
The **affluent** area was flooded during the major hurricane several years ago.

17 **feudal** [fjúːdl]
a. 봉건(제도)의, 영지의

of or like the social system of medieval Europe
[n] feudality 봉건제, 봉건주의 [v] feudalize 봉건제도를 실시하다
The **feudal** landowners gave land to their serfs in exchange for their services as soldiers and farmers.

18 **erect** [irékt]
a. 직립한, 똑바로 선
v. 세우다, 건설하다

being a straight upright position
[n] erection 직립, 건설 [ad] erectly 직립하여, 수직으로
[syn] upright, vertical, perpendicular [ant] bent, horizontal
The man stood **erect** before the judge to listen to his punishment.
I think we should be able to **erect** this fence within a day.

19 **reimburse** [rìːimbə́ːrs]
v. 변상하다, (빚을) 갚다

to pay back for expense or loss incurred
[n] reimbursement 변제, 배상 [a] reimbursable 배상할 수 있는
[syn] repay, compensate
I'll **reimburse** you for this expense as soon as I get to the office.

---

13 그녀에게 주어진 막대한 책임에 그녀는 약간 겁이 났다. 14 그녀는 동료들의 험담을 하는 것으로 잘 알려져 있다. 15 아파트는 높은 층일수록 임대료가 높다. 16 몇 년 전에 대형태풍이 불어 부촌지역이 물에 잠겼었다. 17 봉건 영주는 농노들에게 농부나 군인으로 봉사하는 조건으로 토지를 제공했다. 18 그 남자는 판결을 듣기 위해 판사 앞에 똑바로 서 있었다. 나는 우리가 하루 안에 울타리를 세울 수 있다고 생각해. 19 제가 사무실에 도착하자마자 이 비용을 변상해 드리겠습니다.

20 foresee [fɔːrsíː]
v. 예견[예지]하다, 미리 보다

to know something before it happens

[n] **foreseeability** 예견 능력 [a] **foreseeable** 미리 알 수 있는

[syn] anticipate, forecast, predict, foretell

Experts **foresee** grave danger for humankind unless global warming is dealt with immediately.

---

21 grumble [grʌ́mbl]
v. 투덜거리다, 불평하다

to complain in a quiet but slightly angry way

[a] **grumbling** 투덜거리는, 불평하는 [ad] **grumblingly** 투덜거리며

[syn] mutter, grouch, growl

Try to overcome your difficulties instead of sitting around **grumbling** about them!

---

22 rejoice [ridʒɔ́is]
v. 기뻐하다, 좋아하다

to be glad or happy

rejoicing [n] 기쁨, 환호 [a] 기뻐하는, 좋아하는

[syn] exult, joy, delight [ant] lament, mourn

The soccer team members **rejoiced** because of the big victory.

---

23 reassure [rìːəʃúər]
v. 안심시키다, 자신감을 되찾게 하다

to ease someone's worry, pain, etc.

[n] **reassurance** 안심시킴, 안도 [a] **reassuring** 안심시키는, 위안을 주는

[syn] console, comfort [ant] unnerve, worry, vex

The policeman **reassured** the woman that they would find her daughter.

---

24 derive [diráiv]
v. 끌어내다, 얻다

to get something from someone or something

[n] **derivation** 기원, 유래 [a] **derivative** 끌어낸, 유도적인

[syn] deduce, gain, obtain

The design is **derived** from a famous painting by Rembrandt.

---

25 boycott [bɔ́ikɑt]
v. 불매 운동을 하다, 배척하다
n. 불매 운동

to refuse to do something as part of a protest

[syn] ostracize [ant] buy, patronize

The students **boycotted** the cafeteria until the school agreed not to use trans fats in any food.

An important part of the citizens' social movement was the **boycott** of the company's goods.

---

20 지구온난화에 즉시 대처하지 않으면 인류에 위험이 닥칠 거라고 전문가들은 예언하고 있다. 21 네 문제에 대해서 앉아서 투덜거리지만 말고 극복하려고 노력해봐! 22 축구 팀은 대승을 하여 매우 기뻐했다. 23 경찰관들은 그녀의 딸을 찾을 수 있는 거라면서 그녀를 안심시켰다. 24 그 디자인은 유명 화가인 Rembrandt의 그림에서 아이디어를 얻었다. 25 학교 측이 모든 요리에 트랜스 지방을 사용하지 않겠다고 할 때까지 학생들은 식당을 사용하지 않기로 했다. 회사의 제품을 불매 운동 하는 것이 시민 사회 운동의 중요한 역할이었다.

Exercise

Score ___ / 20

Word Check 각 단어의 뜻으로 알맞은 것을 찾아 연결하시오.

01 rejoice   ⓐ someone who gives money to help

02 bribe   ⓑ happening suddenly or unexpectedly

03 derive   ⓒ to feel pleasure and enjoyment about something

04 benefactor   ⓓ to obtain or take something from something or someone

05 abrupt   ⓔ to illegally give money or a gift to persuade to do something

Syn & Ant Check 주어진 단어의 동의어, 반의어를 골라 쓰시오.

wrath	scrutiny	era	tremendous		delightful
destitute	compensate		bent	mutter	unnerve

06 immense = _____

07 grumble = _____

08 rage = _____

09 reimburse = _____

10 epoch = _____

11 nasty ↔ _____

12 erect ↔ _____

13 reassure ↔ _____

14 affluent ↔ _____

15 glimpse ↔ _____

Sentence Practice 문장을 읽고 빈칸에 알맞은 단어를 고르시오.

16 The tsunami that hit Southeast Asia is a natural _____ that is hard to forget.

ⓐ rage   ⓑ glacier   ⓒ catastrophe   ⓓ pasture

17 This product is designed to protect your _____ by blocking out the harmful rays of the sun.

ⓐ vent   ⓑ glimpse   ⓒ benefactor   ⓓ complexion

18 There was a well-established hierarchy of power in the 10th Century _____ structure of England.

ⓐ feudal   ⓑ upper   ⓒ nasty   ⓓ abrupt

19 He's able to _____ troubles and find ways to prevent them from happening.

ⓐ rejoice   ⓑ reassure   ⓒ derive   ⓓ foresee

20 People threatened to _____ the elections if the anomalies in the voters' lists were not set right.

ⓐ grumble   ⓑ boycott   ⓒ bribe   ⓓ erect

01 fiber [fàibər]
n. 섬유

a natural or artificial thread used for making cloth
syn strand, filament
This fiber has the strength of cotton as well as the sheen of silk.

---

02 blemish [blémiʃ]
n. 흠, 티, 결점
v. ~에 흠을 내다

a small spot or scar
syn flaw, defect, stain, blot   ant perfection, flawlessness
Although she was badly hurt in the accident, there is no blemish on her face.
The rain blemished the wooden table in the restaurant.

---

03 demeanor [dimí:nər]
n. 행동, 태도, 처신

a person's behavior or attitude
v demean 처신하다, 행동하다
syn bearing, conduct, deportment, manner
The soldiers demonstrated excellent demeanor during their training.

---

04 mortgage [mɔ́:rgidʒ]
n. 저당, 저당권
v. 저당 잡히다

a legal agreement for taking out a loan using as security real property
syn security, hypothec
He wants to take out on a mortgage on his house to borrow money from a bank.
He refused to mortgage the land because the value of the land was evaluated much lower than he expected.

---

05 scorn [skɔ:rn]
n. 경멸, 모욕
v. 경멸하다, 멸시하다

the feeling that someone or something is worthless and unimportant
a scornful 경멸하는, 비웃는   ad scornfully 경멸하여, 깔보고
syn contempt, disdain   ant praise
The movie critic poured scorn on the last movie the director made.
The woman scorns anyone who disagrees with her ideas.

---

06 venture [véntʃər]
n. 모험, (투기적) 사업(기업)
v. 위험을 무릅쓰고 ~하다

a risky activity
syn adventure, peril, risk
The joint venture was a great success for the two men.
The brave explorers ventured into the dark Amazon jungle.

---

01 이 섬유는 비단의 광택과 면의 내구성을 모두 가지고 있다. 02 그녀는 교통사고로 심하게 다쳤지만 얼굴은 멀쩡했다. 비 때문에 레스토랑 안의 원목 식탁에 얼룩이 생겼다. 03 그 군인들은 훈련기간 동안 훌륭한 행동을 보여주었다. 04 은행에서 대출을 받으려고 그는 집을 저당 잡히려고 한다. 그는 토지의 가치가 생각보다 훨씬 적게 평가되어서 저당 잡는 것을 거부했다. 05 영화비평가는 그 감독이 만든 마지막 영화에 혹독한 비평을 했다. 그 여자는 자신의 견해에 반대하는 사람은 누구나 멸시한다. 06 합작사업은 두 남자에게 대성공이었다. 그 용감한 탐험가는 위험을 무릅쓰고 어두운 Amazon 정글로 들어갔다.

07 trail [treil]
n. 흔적, (발)자국, 오솔길
v. (질질) 끌다

a series of marks left by someone or something

syn trace, track, path, drag

The police are looking for the trail of the thief.

My little sister loves to walk around in mom's long dresses that trail behind her.

08 vibrant [váibrənt]
a. 활기찬, 흔들리는, 떨리는

lively, exciting and vigorous

n vibrancy 진동   ad vibrantly 진동하여

syn vivacious, active, shivering   ant lethargic

Jim, my best friend, makes his class vibrant all the time.

He mounted to the stage and began to make a speech with his vibrant voice.

09 aboriginal [æbərídʒənl]
a. 원시의, 토착의, 토착민의

relating to the people or animals having lived in a place from the earliest times

n aborigine 원주민, 토착민   ad aboriginally 원시 상태로

syn autochthonous, primeval, native

We are yet to understand and appreciate the value of traditional Australian aboriginal wisdom.

10 random [rǽndəm]
a. 임의의, 무작위의

having no definite plan, aim or order

ad randomly 임의로

syn haphazard, casual, accidental   ant ordered, systematic

An initial and random search of the crime scene revealed no clues about the killer.

11 obscure [əbskjúər]
a. 분명하지 않은, 애매한
v. 어둡게 [흐리게] 하다

unclear or not well-known

n obscureness 애매함, 희미함

syn vague, ambiguous, mist   ant clear, distinct

Philosophy is often dismissed as being an obscure branch of knowledge.

The heavy rain obscured our vision as we drove home.

12 embark [imbá:rk]
v. 승선[탑승]시키다, 착수하다

to go onto a ship or plane

n embarkation 승선, 탑승

syn board, commence, begin   ant disembark

The young couple embarked on their honeymoon to Hawaii.

The civic group will embark on an unprecedented campaign to protect human rights.

---

07 경찰은 도둑의 흔적을 찾고 있다. 내 여동생은 뒤로 질질 끌리는 엄마의 긴 드레스를 입고 돌아다니는 것을 좋아한다. 08 내 가장 친한 친구, Jim은 항상 그의 반을 활기차게 만든다. 그는 연단에 올라가 떨리는 목소리로 연설하기 시작했다. 09 우리는 아직 호주 토착민의 전통 지혜에 대한 가치를 이해할 수도 평가할 수도 없다. 10 초기 임의적인 범죄현장 조사에서 살인자에 대한 단서를 찾는 데 실패했다. 11 철학은 종종 분야가 불분명한 학문으로 치부된다. 운전하고 집으로 가고 있을 때 폭우가 우리의 시야를 흐리게 했다. 12 젊은 부부는 Hawaii로 신혼여행을 갔다. 그 시민 단체는 인권을 보호하기 위해 전례 없는 캠페인을 시작할 것이다.

13 enlighten [inláitn]
v. 계몽하다, 설명하다, 밝히다

to give more knowledge or understanding to someone

[n] enlightenment 계몽, 교화 [a] enlightened 계몽된, 개화된

[syn] illuminate, instruct, teach

The professor enlightened his students about the need for recycling.

14 deport [dipɔ́ːrt]
v. 국외로 추방하다, 이송[수송]하다

to force someone to leave a country or return to his country

[n] deportation 추방

[syn] exile, expel, banish

The man was deported after he committed a crime.

15 collide [kəláid]
v. 충돌하다, 부딪히다

to crash violently into something

[n] collision 충돌

[syn] clash, conflict [ant] avert, dodge

The street was closed temporarily when two vehicles collided at the intersection.

16 enchant [intʃǽnt]
v. 매혹하다, 황홀하게 하다, 마법을 걸다

to attract or delight someone

[n] enchantment 매혹, 매력 [a] enchanting 매혹적인

[syn] allure, fascinate, charm [ant] disenchant, disillusion

The woods around here are beautiful enough to enchant the most hardhearted person.

17 capitalize [kǽpətəlàiz]
v. 이용하다

to use something in order to gain an advantage

[syn] benefit, profit

The movie star capitalized on her fame and sold her own makeup.

18 defy [difái]
v. 반항하다, 도전하다

to openly resist or oppose

[n] defiance 도전, 완강한 반항 [a] defiant 반항적인, 도전적인

[syn] withstand, dare, challenge [ant] comply, obey

The students defied the new dress code by coming out in their most flamboyant clothes.

19 glitter [glítər]
v. 반짝반짝 빛나다

to shine brightly or sparkle

[a] glittering 반짝반짝 빛나는, 화려한 [ad] glitteringly 번쩍이며

[syn] twinkle, glimmer, glare

His eyes glittered with unshed tears as he recounted his harrowing experiences.

---

13 그 교수는 학생들에게 재활용의 필요성을 설명했다. 14 그 남자는 범죄를 저지른 후 국외로 추방당했다. 15 교차로에서 두 차량이 충돌해서 일시적으로 도로가 폐쇄되었다. 16 이 주위의 숲은 가장 냉혹한 사람도 매혹시킬 정도로 아름답다. 17 그 영화배우는 자신의 인기를 이용하여 자신의 화장품을 팔았다. 18 학생들은 가장 현란한 옷을 입고 나와서 새 복장 규정에 반발했다. 19 그가 고통스러웠던 경험을 얘기할 때 그의 눈이 고인 눈물로 반짝였다.

20 baffle [bǽfl]
v. 당황[난처]하게 하다, 좌절시키다

to make someone confused or puzzled

ⓐ baffling 좌절시키는, 당황하게 하는

syn perplex, bewilder, mystify   ant assist, encourage, help

The mysterious robbery baffled the police for several years.

21 evacuate [ivǽkjuèit]
v. 피난[대피]시키다, 비우다, 철수시키다

to move from a dangerous place to a safe place

ⓝ evacuation 비우기   ⓐ evacuative 철수의

syn remove, empty, displace   ant enter, occupy

The police are beginning to evacuate the residents living in the area close to the site of the forest fire.

22 bar [bɑːr]
v. 막다, 금하다, 빗장을 지르다

n. 빗장, 금지

to prevent someone from entering a certain place

syn barricade, blockade, exclude   ant admit

The newspaper reporters were barred from the president's meeting.

There is a bar on children below age 5 entering this room of the palace.

23 bid [bid]
v. (값을) 매기다, 입찰하다

n. 입찰, 입찰 가격

to offer to pay a particular price for something

ⓝ bidding 입찰

syn auction, tender

There were several people bidding against him for the painting and the price quickly rose to $3 million.

The woman entered a bid of $10 for the antique storybook.

24 quiver [kwívər]
v. 흔들리다, 떨다

n. 떨림, 진동

to shake slightly

ⓐ quivering 떨고 있는   ad quiveringly 덜덜 떨며

syn shudder, shiver, quake

The people standing at the square quivered from the cold and rain.

The small quiver demonstrated her anxiety in the situation.

25 gleam [gliːm]
v. 번쩍이다, 반짝 빛나다

n. 희미한 빛, 번쩍임

to shine, especially after being cleaned

ⓐ gleaming 반짝반짝 빛나는

syn glow, flash, sparkle

The furniture gleamed after my sister polished the wood.

He had a gleam in his eye as he told a story about a giant fish.

---

20 그 실체를 드러내지 않은 강도가 수년 동안 경찰을 당황케 했다. 21 경찰은 산불지역 인근에 거주하는 사람들을 피난시키기 시작했다. 22 신문 기자들은 대통령 회의에 참석하는 것이 금지되었다. 5세 이하의 어린이들은 궁전의 이 방에 들어오는 것을 금지한다. 23 그와 경쟁해 그 그림을 입찰하려고 하는 사람이 꽤 있었기 때문에 그림의 가격이 금방 3백만 달러로 올랐다. 그 여성은 오래된 동화책의 입찰가격을 10달러로 책정했다. 24 광장에 서 있는 사람들은 추위와 비에 떨었다. 그녀의 조그만 떨림이 그녀가 그 상황에서 긴장하고 있었다는 것을 보여주었다. 25 여동생이 가구를 닦자 가구가 빛났다. 그가 거대한 물고기에 대해 얘기를 할 때 눈에서 빛이 났다.

Exercise

Score /20

Word Check 각 단어의 뜻으로 알맞은 것을 찾아 연결하시오.

01 enlighten   ⓐ behavior or manner

02 gleam   ⓑ a dim or gentle light

03 demeanor   ⓒ to attract or please someone greatly

04 enchant   ⓓ to give intellectual insight to someone

05 aboriginal   ⓔ belonging to a certain place from early years

Syn & Ant Check 주어진 단어의 동의어, 반의어를 골라 쓰시오.

benefit	contempt	trace	distinct	avert
flawlessness	comply	sparkle	encourage	shudder

06 scorn = _____

07 capitalize = _____

08 trail = _____

09 quiver = _____

10 glitter = _____

11 blemish ↔ _____

12 obscure ↔ _____

13 baffle ↔ _____

14 collide ↔ _____

15 defy ↔ _____

Sentence Practice 문장을 읽고 빈칸에 알맞은 단어를 고르시오.

16 We retain the right to conduct _____ checks of employee identification badges for security reasons.

     ⓐ aboriginal   ⓑ random   ⓒ obscure   ⓓ vibrant

17 The government was forced to _____ the immigrants who had crossed the border illegally.

     ⓐ venture   ⓑ quiver   ⓒ capitalize   ⓓ deport

18 A record number of people _____ for ownership of the famous French painting.

     ⓐ bid   ⓑ baffle   ⓒ enlighten   ⓓ defy

19 The _____ on my house is for 25 years and must be paid back at $1,000 a month.

     ⓐ scorn   ⓑ mortgage   ⓒ trail   ⓓ fiber

20 Volunteers moved in to help _____ people from the flood-prone areas of the city.

     ⓐ gleam   ⓑ embark   ⓒ evacuate   ⓓ enchant

🎧 01 **compassion** [kəmpǽʃən]
n. 연민, 동정

a feeling of deep sympathy and sorrow for someone

ⓐ compassionate 인정 많은 ad compassionately 동정적으로

syn pity, commiseration ant disregard, indifference, unconcern

We have a lot of **compassion** for the people who lost homes in New Orleans.

02 **lawsuit** [lɔ́:sù:t]
n. 소송, 고소

a problem or disagreement brought to a court of law

syn suit, trial, litigation

My father filed a **lawsuit** against the owner of the apartment building because he did not fix the furnace.

03 **influx** [ínflʌks]
n. 유입, 쇄도

the arrival of a large number of people or things

syn incursion, inrush, inflow

The **influx** of unskilled workers from the Chinese countryside is creating problems in the cities.

04 **anatomy** [ənǽtəmi]
n. 해부학, 해부

the study of or the structure of living organisms

ⓐ anatomical 해부의 ad anatomically 해부학적으로

syn dissection

I enjoyed **anatomy** classes at medical school but was wary of dissection.

05 **grandeur** [grǽndʒər]
n. 웅장, 원대함

impressive beauty, power or size

ⓐ grand 웅대한, 성대한

syn majesty, splendor, eminence, magnificence

My class was amazed at the **grandeur** of the Rocky Mountains.

06 **sovereignty** [sʌ́vərənti]
n. 주권, 통치권, (권력 등의) 최고

supreme political power

ⓝ sovereign 주권자, 통치자

syn reign, supremacy, dominion

It is the Korean president's duty to protect the **sovereignty** of our country under all circumstances.

---

01 우리는 New Orleans의 집을 잃은 사람들에게 깊은 연민을 느낀다. 02 아버지는 난방을 고쳐주지 않았기 때문에 아파트 주인에게 소송을 제기했다. 03 중국 지방 출신의 미숙련 노동자들이 유입되어 도시에서 문제를 일으키고 있다. 04 나는 의과 대학에서 해부학 수업을 좋아했고 해부를 할 때 신중했다. 05 우리 반은 Rocky Mountains의 웅장함에 감탄했다. 06 어떤 상황에서도 나라의 주권을 지키는 것이 한국 대통령의 의무이다.

07 insane [inséin]
a. 제 정신이 아닌, 미친

mentally ill
[n] insanity 정신 이상, 광기　[ad] insanely 미쳐서, 정신 이상으로
[syn] crazy, lunatic　[ant] sane, sensible

The man went insane after experiencing the loss of his family and everything he owned.

08 spontaneous [spɑntéiniəs]
a. 자연적인, 자발적인

happening and arising naturally
[n] spontaneousness 자발성　[ad] spontaneously 자발적으로
[syn] self-generated, natural　[ant] deliberate, intended, forced

The actress received a spontaneous standing ovation from the audience for her performance.

09 resolute [rézəlù:t]
a. 굳게 결심한, 확고한

having a firm decision to do something
[n] resoluteness 결연함, 단호함　[ad] resolutely 굳은 결의로
[syn] steadfast, unwavering, determined　[ant] irresolute

The committee was resolute in its decision to continue with the project.

10 reluctant [rilʌ́ktənt]
a. 마음 내키지 않는, 마지못해 하는

unwilling to do something
[n] reluctance 싫음, 마지못해 함　[ad] reluctantly 마지못해, 싫어하며
[syn] unwilling, disinclined　[ant] willing, eager, enthusiastic

The man was a reluctant help to us because he wanted to be elsewhere.

11 pragmatic [prægmǽtik]
a. 실제[실용]적인, 실용주의의

relating to action rather than theory
[ad] pragmatically 실용적으로
[syn] utilitarian, practical　[ant] idealistic, impractical

These plans are pragmatic solutions rather than wishful thinking.

12 competent [kʌ́mpətənt]
a. 유능한, 적임의

having the abilities or skills necessary to do something
[n] competence 능력, 적성　[ad] competently 유능하게
[syn] qualified, capable, adequate　[ant] inadequate, incapable, incompetent
Tracy cannot be called a genius although she is certainly competent at her work.

13 mighty [máiti]
a. 강한, 힘센
n. 힘

strong and powerful
[syn] robust, forceful, vigorous　[ant] feeble, weak, puny
The mighty river flows through the country for thousands of miles.
He was among the mighty athletes in the group.

---

07 그 남자는 가족을 포함한 그가 가진 모든 것을 잃자 미쳐 버렸다. 08 그 여배우는 공연 후 관중들로부터 자연스레 우러나오는 기립 박수를 받았다. 09 위원회는 그 프로젝트를 계속해나갈 결의가 확고했다. 10 그 남자는 다른 곳에 있길 원했기 때문에 우리를 돕는 것을 내켜하지 않았다. 11 이 계획들은 부질없는 기대가 아니라 실용적인 해결책이다. 12 Tracy는 확실히 일에 관해서 유능하기는 하지만 천재라고 불릴 정도는 아니다. 13 그 힘차게 흐르는 강은 국토를 따라 수천 마일을 흐른다. 그는 그룹에서 힘이 센 운동선수 중의 하나이다.

14 temperate [témpərət]
a. 온건의, 온화한

not very violent or extreme in behavior

syn mild, clement, moderate   ant intemperate, extreme

Sandra's temperate mind is an asset to our group of rather excitable girls.

You must move to a more temperate region to help your son recover from pneumonia.

15 prominent [prámənənt]
a. 두드러진, 중요한

noticeable or important

n prominence 두드러짐, 현저함   ad prominently 두드러지게

syn eminent, remarkable, outstanding   ant inconspicuous, unimportant

My dad put my graduation picture in a prominent place.

The atmosphere has played a prominent role in maintaining the Earth at an even temperature.

16 withhold [wiðhóuld]
v. 보류하다, 억제하다

to keep back something

n withholdment 억제

syn restrain, repress, detain   ant reveal, release

The salesman withheld the problem from the customer until after the sale.

17 insert [insə́:rt]
v. 삽입하다, 끼워 넣다
n. 삽입물, 끼움

to put into something else

n insertion 삽입, 끼워 넣기   a inserted 끼워 넣은

syn embed, inlay, introduce   ant remove

My son inserted a coin into the pop machine, but nothing came out.

The shoe clerk placed the shoe inserts into the boots for me.

18 aspire [əspáiər]
v. 열망하다, 바라다

to seek eagerly

n aspiration 열망, 갈망   a aspiring 대망을 품은, 야심 있는

syn yearn, desire, crave, hope

Most people aspire to fame and power while I seek contentment.

19 snap [snæp]
v. 똑 부러지다
n. 획[딱] 소리나기

to break with a sudden, sharp sound

a snapping 딱 하고 소리내는

We enjoyed watching the bird snap twigs and sticks to build her nest.

Greta was startled when the window closed with a snap in the sudden gust of wind.

---

14 쉽게 흥분하는 우리 그룹에게 Sandra의 절제하는 마음은 하나의 자산이다. 네 아들을 폐렴에서 빨리 회복시키려면 좀 더 따뜻한 지방으로 이사를 가야 해. 15 나의 아버지는 내 졸업사진을 눈에 띄는 곳에 놓아두었다. 대기는 지구의 온도를 일정하게 유지하는 데 중요한 역할을 해왔다. 16 판매원은 그 물건을 판매하고 나서도 손님에게 그 문제를 알리지 않았다. 17 아들이 자판기에 돈을 넣었는데 아무것도 나오지 않았다. 구두 가게 점원이 나를 위해 부츠에 깔창을 넣어 주었다. 18 내가 만족을 추구하는 반면 대부분의 사람들은 명성과 권력을 열망한다. 19 나는 새들이 작은 나뭇가지를 부러뜨려 집을 짓는 모습을 보는 것을 즐겼다. Greta는 돌풍에 창문이 쾅 하고 닫히자 깜짝 놀랐다.

20 integrate [íntəgrèit]

v. 통합하다, 완성하다

to combine to make a whole

n integration 통합, 합병 a integrated 통합된

syn merge, unify, combine   ant disintegrate, separate

A 1954 Supreme Court ruling forced American schools across the country to racially integrate all classes.

21 intervene [ìntərvíːn]

v. 중재하다, 개입하다

to come between to modify

n intervention 중재, 조정 a intervenient 중재하는, 간섭하는

syn arbitrate, mediate, intercede

The police should intervene before the confrontation between the rival groups turns violent.

Some people say the U.S. government has unduly intervened in the conflict between Israel and Palestine.

22 disrupt [disrʌ́pt]

v. (제도 등을) 붕괴시키다, 혼란에 빠뜨리다

to put into confusion or disorder

n disruption 혼란, 붕괴 a disruptive 붕괴시키는

syn disturb, interrupt, disorganize   ant arrange, organize

The yelling protesters disrupted the speaker until the meeting ended.

23 intercept [ìntərsépt]

v. 가로채다, 가로막다, 차단하다

to stop or catch something or someone that is going someplace

n interceptor 방해자, 장해물 n interception 가로채기, 방해

syn stop, block, interrupt

The football player intercepted the ball and scored a touchdown.

24 assert [əsə́ːrt]

v. 단언하다, 주장하다

to speak firmly

n assertion 단언, 주장 a assertive 단정적인, 독단적인

syn affirm, declare, verify, aver   ant deny, negate

People tend to take advantage of Harry because he does not assert himself.

25 revitalize [rìːváitəlaiz]

v. 소생시키다, 활력을 불어넣다

to give a new life to someone or something

n revitalization 활성화

syn regenerate, rejuvenate

A sudden rain shower would revitalize the plants that are drooping in the heat.

---

20 1954년 대법원 판결에 따라 미국 학교의 모든 학급을 인종적으로 통합해야 했다. 21 경쟁 그룹의 대립이 격렬해지기 전에 경찰은 그들을 중재해야 한다. 일부는 미국 정부가 이스라엘과 팔레스타인 간의 분쟁에 지나치게 개입해왔다고 말한다. 22 집회가 끝날 때까지 고함을 지르는 시위자들이 연설자를 방해했다. 23 그 미식축구 선수는 공을 가로채고 터치다운을 기록했다. 24 사람들은 Harry가 자신의 권리를 주장하지 않기 때문에 그를 이용하곤 한다. 25 갑자기 내리는 소나기는 더위로 시들어가는 식물들을 다시 살릴 것이다.

Exercise

Score / 20

Word Check 각 단어의 뜻으로 알맞은 것을 찾아 연결하시오.

01 anatomy
02 aspire
03 pragmatic
04 intervene
05 insane

ⓐ of unsound mind
ⓑ concerned with practical matters
ⓒ to have a great desire to achieve something
ⓓ to get involved in a situation in order to change it
ⓔ the study of the structure of animals and humans bodies

Syn & Ant Check 주어진 단어의 동의어, 반의어를 골라 쓰시오.

disregard	deliberate	supremacy	unwilling	incapable
eminent	separate	organize	interrupt	regenerate

06 sovereignty =
07 reluctant =
08 prominent =
09 revitalize =
10 intercept =

11 compassion ↔
12 competent ↔
13 integrate ↔
14 spontaneous ↔
15 disrupt ↔

Sentence Practice 문장을 읽고 빈칸에 알맞은 단어를 고르시오.

16 It was fascinating to see the elephant _____ off the big branch so easily.
ⓐ snap ⓑ disrupt ⓒ intercept ⓓ intervene

17 All through the trial the defense attorney kept _____ his client's innocence.
ⓐ asserting ⓑ withholding ⓒ aspiring ⓓ revitalizing

18 _____ regions in the world do not experience extreme climatic conditions.
ⓐ Mighty ⓑ Temperate ⓒ Reluctant ⓓ Insane

19 The boom in the computer industry has led to the _____ of highly skilled workers into software hub areas like Silicon Valley and Bangalore.
ⓐ insert ⓑ influx ⓒ sovereignty ⓓ compassion

20 She is _____ and persistent in the face of all opposition.
ⓐ spontaneous ⓑ prominent ⓒ resolute ⓓ pragmatic

132 LEVEL 6

❖ against

anti : anti-communist 반공주의자, anticlimax 뜻밖의 결말, antipathy 혐오감
The minister has often spoken of his antipathy to foreigners in public.
그 장관은 공공연히 외국인에 대한 반감을 나타내는 발언을 한다.

counter : counterpart 대응하는 사람, counterfeit 위조, counteract 거스르다
The leader of Republican party decried his counterpart's opinion.
공화당 지도자는 상대편 지도자의 의견을 비난했다.

contro : controversy 논쟁, contrast 대조, controvertibly 논쟁할 수 있는
There has been a big controversy over the death penalty.
사형제도에 대해 큰 논쟁이 있어 왔다.

❖ for

pro : prospect (성공)가망성, pro-communist 친 공산주의자, proposal 제안
Due to the inflation many families have little prospect of buying their own houses.
통화팽창으로 많은 가정이 집을 마련할 가능성이 거의 없어졌다.

bene : benevolent 호의적인, benefactor 은인, beneficent 인정 많은
The marquis Beccaria was a beneficent patron to those who were starting their literary careers and was a good friend.
Beccaria 후작은 문학에 입문한 사람들에게 인정 많은 후원자이자 좋은 친구였다.

❖ together

syn : synchronize 동시에 진행하다, syncretic 통합적인, sympathy 공감
It's not easy to synchronize success with happiness in our lives.
우리 삶에서 성공과 행복을 동시에 이루기는 어렵다.

co : cooperate 협동하다, copilot 부기장, coexist 공존하다
Governments discussed how they would cooperate to fight international terrorism.
각 정부들은 국제적 테러와 맞서 어떻게 협력할지 토론했다.

con(m) : company 일행, contemporary 같은 시대사람, combine 결합하다
If you combine business with pleasure, success seems to be closer.
사업과 오락을 결합시킨다면, 성공에 한 걸음 더 가까이 다가갈 수 있을 것이다.

A 영어 풀이에 알맞은 단어를 보기에서 찾아 쓰시오.

dose	confidential	revitalize	catastrophe	boycott

01 kept secret or private from others _____

02 an act of refusing to buy or use something _____

03 the amount of medicine that one should take _____

04 to make someone or something active and energetic _____

05 an event causing great suffering, loss of life or damage _____

B 문장을 읽고 문맥에 적절한 단어를 고르시오.

06 We (snapped/sneaked) into the meeting to discover our opponents' game plan.

07 The government has (embarked/enlightened) on an ambitious plan to provide quality health care to all citizens.

08 Lately the newspapers have been full of stories about corrupt officials being caught accepting (bribes/bids).

09 It (intrigued/disrupted) us that such a difficult problem could have such a simple solution.

C 표시된 부분과 뜻이 가장 가까운 것을 고르시오.

10 His pragmatic approach to life is revealed in his love of simplicity and avoidance of all showiness.

ⓐ feudal   ⓑ cordial   ⓒ practical   ⓓ obscure

11 Authorities have agreed they will deport the criminal to Spain where he faces several charges.

ⓐ rid   ⓑ evacuate   ⓒ convert   ⓓ exile

12 Even as a newcomer Sam would not allow his colleagues to dictate ideas to him.

ⓐ assert   ⓑ command   ⓒ withhold   ⓓ consult

13 The latest government legislation on education will help put a lot of children back in school.

ⓐ doctrine   ⓑ oath   ⓒ lawsuit   ⓓ enactment

D 　표시된 부분의 반대말로 가장 알맞은 것을 고르시오.

13 **Affluent** societies forget that a large part of the world lives without basic necessities.
ⓐ destitute　　　　ⓑ immense　　　　ⓒ ubiquitous　　　　ⓓ nasty

15 Please **refrain** from using your mobile phones while transacting business in this office.
ⓐ warrant　　　　ⓑ continue　　　　ⓒ distract　　　　ⓓ boycott

16 Forensic experts thought it would be wiser to **withhold** some gruesome details of the murder.
ⓐ release　　　　ⓑ cram　　　　ⓒ capitalize　　　　ⓓ proliferate

17 **Random** testing is done on athletes to check for prohibited substances.
ⓐ obscure　　　　ⓑ reluctant　　　　ⓒ vague　　　　ⓓ systematic

E 주어진 단어를 알맞은 형태로 바꿔 빈칸에 쓰시오.

18 These _____ events were part of the transition between the Ice Age and a warmer period. (epoch)

19 Gandhi's untiring work for the less-privileged stemmed from his _____ nature. (compassion)

20 We are united in our _____ of mindless violence and financial exploitation. (condemn)

21 The ongoing sporting events are a source of _____ to students preparing for exams. (distract)

F 빈칸에 알맞은 단어를 보기에서 찾아 쓰시오. (필요한 경우 형태를 바꾸시오.)

integrate	reluctant	imposing	fiscal	mighty
tempreate	intervene	revise	assemble	nasty

22 호텔의 화려한 외관은 호화로운 실내 디자인과 어울렸다.
→ The _____ exterior of the hotel is matched by its opulent interiors.

23 지금이 아동 건강과 지역 사회 복지에 관련한 법률을 개정할 때가 됐다.
→ It is high time the laws relating to child health and community welfare were _____.

24 모든 주민들은 주간 모임을 위해서 클럽 회관으로 모이셔야 합니다.
→ All residents must _____ at the club house for the weekly meeting.

25 그 튼튼한 나무는 어젯밤 사나운 폭풍우 때문에 쓰러졌다.
→ The _____ tree was felled by the fury of last night's storm.

Accumulative test Day 1 ~ Day 20

A	B	C	D
120~101	100~81	80~61	60 이하

➤ 영어를 우리말로 옮기시오.

01 warrant _____

02 benefactor _____

03 baffle _____

04 insane _____

05 core _____

06 convert _____

07 doctrine _____

08 embark _____

09 condemn _____

10 imposing _____

11 integrate _____

12 refrain _____

13 trail _____

14 compassion _____

15 epoch _____

16 acquaintance _____

17 enchant _____

18 disrupt _____

19 tremble _____

20 feudal _____

21 circulate _____

22 consult _____

23 defy _____

24 vent _____

25 charter _____

26 sovereignty _____

27 mold _____

28 assimilate _____

29 foresee _____

30 outlet _____

31 affluent _____

32 obscure _____

33 distract _____

34 filter _____

35 malfunction _____

36 reassure _____

37 extinguish _____

38 gleam _____

39 deport _____

40 counterpart _____

41 reluctant _____

42 pragmatic _____

43 catastrophe _____

44 intrigue _____

45 cunning _____

46 collide _____

47 vibrant _____

48 lawsuit _____

49 ubiquitous _____

50 intervene _____

51 dose _____

52 complexion _____

53 erect _____

54 slope _____

55 dictate _____

56 consent _____

57 sneak _____

58 insert _____

59 conceive _____

60 glitter _____

우리말을 영어로 옮기시오.

61 진심의, 공손한 _____
62 조립하다 _____
63 광대한, 막대한 _____
64 막연한, 애매한 _____
65 견본, 표본 _____
66 빙하 _____
67 행동, 태도 _____
68 원시의, 토착의 _____
69 솔직한 _____
70 묘기, 곡예 _____
71 해부학, 해부 _____
72 목장, 목초지 _____
73 굳게 결심한 _____
74 흔들리다, 떨다 _____
75 유입, 쇄도 _____
76 다수, 군중 _____
77 논박하다 _____
78 유능한, 적임의 _____
79 계약 _____
80 저당, 저당권 _____
81 개정하다 _____
82 (살짝) 담그다 _____
83 울부짖다 _____
84 보류[억제]하다 _____
85 (값을) 매기다 _____
86 가로채다 _____
87 맹세, 서약 _____
88 피난시키다 _____
89 단언[주장]하다 _____
90 기뻐하다 _____

91 갑작스러운 _____
92 국고의, 재정의 _____
93 증식[번식]하다 _____
94 꾸밈, 장신구 _____
95 뇌물, 미끼 _____
96 자발적인 _____
97 끌어내다, 얻다 _____
98 계몽하다 _____
99 부풀게 하다 _____
100 모험 _____
101 힐끗 봄 _____
102 예언자, 선지자 _____
103 열망하다 _____
104 변상하다, 갚다 _____
105 흠, 티, 결점 _____
106 온건의, 온화한 _____
107 소작인 _____
108 ~에 대하여 _____
109 강한, 힘센 _____
110 이용하다 _____
111 두드러진, 중요한 _____
112 적시다, 잠기다 _____
113 똑 부러지다 _____
114 비밀의, 기밀의 _____
115 법률 제정 _____
116 집행하다 _____
117 경멸, 모욕 _____
118 투덜거리다 _____
119 전조가 되다 _____
120 회상, 회고 _____

Part 5

Day 21

01 dimension [diménʃən]
n. 치수, 넓이, 차원

a measure of length, width or height

ⓐ dimensional 치수의

syn size, measurement, extent, magnitude

Calculate the height and dimension of the regular triangle by applying the Pythagorean Theorem.

02 paradigm [pǽrədaim]
n. 사고의 체계, 모범, 전형

a model or pattern

ⓐ paradigmatic 모범의, 전형적인   ad paradigmatically 전형적으로

syn standard, paragon, example, type

Our institute is developing a new paradigm for English teaching and learning.

03 parasite [pǽrəsàit]
n. 기생충, 기생 식물

an organism that lives on another organism and obtains nourishment from it

ⓐ parasitic 기생의   ⓥ parasitize ~에 기생하다

syn bacteria   ant host

The leech is a parasite that feeds on the blood of its host.

04 conglomerate [kənglámərət]
n. 복합 기업체, 대기업체

a large business firm consisting of several companies

ⓐ conglomerative 복합기업 같은

syn group

There are rumors that the large steel conglomerate will be taken over by a foreign company.

05 vogue [voug]
n. 유행, 인기, 성행

the current fashion

ⓐ voguey 유행의, 유행하는

syn fashion, popularity, trend

I'm glad to see that colors in vogue this season are some of my favorite.

06 scrap [skræp]
n. 작은 조각, 파편
v. 버리다, 폐기하다

a small piece of something

syn fragment, particle, discard   ant preserve, restore

This useless scrap of paper has turned out to be an important clue in the case.

The company scrapped their old copier and bought a new one.

---

01 피타고라스의 정리를 이용하여 정삼각형의 높이와 넓이를 구하여라. 02 저희 협회는 영어 교수 학습의 새로운 패러다임을 전개하고 있습니다. 03 거머리는 숙주의 피를 먹는 기생 동물이다. 04 철강 대기업이 외국 회사에 인수된 것이라는 소문이 있다. 05 내가 좋아하는 색깔들이 이번 시즌에 유행하고 있어서 기분이 좋아. 06 이 쓸모 없는 종이조각이 그 사건의 중요한 단서가 되었다. 회사는 낡은 복사기를 폐기하고 새로운 것을 구입했다.

07 **pastoral** [pǽstərəl]
a. 전원 생활의, 시골의

relating to a peaceful or simple country life
[ad] pastorally 전원적으로, 목가적으로
[syn] rustic, rural, bucolic   [ant] urban

The artist painted a pleasant pastoral landscape for the couple.

08 **feeble** [fíːbl]
a. 연약한, 허약한

not having much physical strength
[ad] feebly 약하게, 무기력하게
[syn] frail, weak, impotent   [ant] healthy, powerful

It was clear that the feeble old man was ill and needed medical help.

09 **virtual** [və́ːrtʃuəl]
a. 사실상의, 실제의

almost or nearly true, but not really
[n] virtuality 실질, 실제   [ad] virtually 사실상, 실질적으로는
[syn] practical, realistic

The match was a virtual repeat of last year's finals when the home team won convincingly.

10 **neutral** [njúːtrəl]
a. 중립의, 공평한
n. 중립국, 중립 위치

not taking parts or supporting either side in a war or dispute
[n] neutrality 중립(상태)   [v] neutralize 중립화하다
[syn] unbiased, impartial   [ant] biased, partial

Many countries are not neutral on the issue of fair trade.
I put the car in neutral before it began to roll down the hill.

11 **vivid** [vívid]
a. 생생한, 생기 있는, 선명한

creating powerful feelings or lifelike images in the mind
[v] vivify 생명[생기]를 주다   [ad] vividly 생생하게, 활발하게
[syn] clear, animated, lively   [ant] dull, faint, pale

His teacher discovered that the child had a vivid imagination.

12 **irresistible** [ìrizístəbl]
a. 저항할 수 없는, 매혹적인

unable to oppose or fight against someone or something
[syn] resistless, attractive   [ant] resistible, unattractive

An irresistible desire for revenge surged through the man as he saw his enemy approach.
The luxuriant manes of male lions are a means of making them irresistible to females.

13 **compatible** [kəmpǽtəbl]
a. 양립할 수 있는, 호환성의

able to exist or be used together without causing problems
[n] compatibility 양립 가능성, 호환성   [ad] compatibly 양립할 수 있게, 모순 없이
[syn] congruous, harmonious   [ant] incompatible, inappropriate, incongruous

I cannot use this DVD as it is not compatible with my player.

---

07 예술가는 부부를 위해 쾌적한 시골의 풍경을 그렸다. 08 허약한 노인이 병을 앓고 있었고 의학적 도움을 필요로 했다는 것이 당연했다. 09 경기는 사실상 홈팀이 완승 했던 작년 결승전의 반복이나 다름이 없었다. 10 많은 나라들은 공정거래 문제에 있어서 중립적인 입장을 취하지 않는다. 나는 차가 언덕 아래로 굴러 내려가기 전에 기어를 중립에 두었다. 11 그의 선생님은 아이가 생생한 상상력을 가지고 있다는 것을 알게 되었다. 12 적이 다가오는 것을 보자 그에게 억누를 수 없는 복수의 욕망이 밀려왔다. 수사자들이 가지고 있는 풍성한 갈기가 암사자들을 유혹하는 방법이다. 13 이 DVD가 내 플레이어와 호환되지 않아 사용할 수 없어.

14 variable [vέəriəbl]
a. 변하기 쉬운, 변수
n. 변수

inclined to change often

n variability 변하기 쉬움, 가변성   v vary 바뀌다

syn inconstant, changeable, unstable   ant invariable, constant

The only variable factor in this production process is the cost of raw material.

The variable 'x' in this equation stands for the speed of light.

15 alter [ɔ́:ltər]
v. 바꾸다, 변경하다

to make something or someone different

n alteration 변경, 개조

syn vary, change, convert, modify   ant maintain, preserve, retain

You may have to alter this design if the client insists on it.

16 haul [hɔ:l]
v. 끌어당기다, 운반하다

to move by pulling or dragging

syn draw, convey, transport   ant push

The dump truck hauls sand from the construction site.

17 assure [əʃúər]
v. 보증[보장]하다, 확실하게 하다

to ensure something

n assurance 보증, 보장   a assured 보증 된, 확실한

syn guarantee, affirm, confirm

We assure you that your package will be delivered before 2 p.m. this afternoon.

18 discard [diská:rd]
v. 버리다, 포기하다
n. 포기, 버림받는 물건[사람]

to throw away or get rid of something

a discardable 포기할 수 있는

syn abandon, relinquish   ant retain, cherish, keep

Please discard old and unused articles so you have place for more important ones.

The discards from the deck are mostly small playing cards, not face cards like kings or queens.

19 agitate [ǽdʒətèit]
v. 선동하다, 흔들다

to excite people to change

n agitation 동요, 교란   a agitated 흥분한, 동요한

syn provoke, stimulate, rouse   ant calm, soothe, pacify

The men agitated for the rights of workers to form a union.

---

13 이 생산과정에서 한 가지 변수는 원자재 가격이다. 이 방정식에서 변수 'x'는 빛의 속도를 나타낸다. 15 고객이 요구하면 이 디자인을 바꿔야 할 것이다. 16 덤프트럭은 공사장으로부터 모래를 운반한다. 17 저희는 고객님의 상품이 오늘 오후 2시 이전까지 배달될 것이라고 보장합니다. 18 낡고 사용하지 않는 물건들은 버리고 더 중요한 것들을 위해 공간을 확보해 주십시오. 카드놀이에서 버려지는 대부분의 패들은 킹이나 퀸 아니라 점수가 낮은 카드이다. 19 그 사람들은 노동자들의 권리를 보호하기 위한 조합을 결성하려는 운동을 했다.

20 **erode** [iróud]

v. 부식시키다, 침식하다

to wear away or destroy something gradually

[n] erodibility 부식 가능성 [a] erodible 부식할 수 있는

[syn] disintegrate, deteriorate, corrode [ant] strengthen, reinforce

This picture shows how much soil has been eroded by deforestation.

21 **harass** [hərǽs]

v. 괴롭히다

to bother someone continually

[n] harassment 괴롭히기 [a] harassing 괴롭히는, 성가시게 구는

[syn] tease, vex, irritate, annoy [ant] delight, entertain, please

He's going to harass you in every way he can unless you stand up to his bullying.

22 **cripple** [krípl]

v. 불구가 되게 하다, 무력하게 만들다

n. 장애자, 불구자

to make someone disabled

[a] crippling 심한 손상[부상]을 입히는

[syn] deform, disable, incapacitate [ant] enable

The accident crippled the man in both legs for life.

My grandmother is an emotional cripple because of her experiences during the war.

23 **whirl** [hwəːrl]

v. 소용돌이치다, 빙빙 돌다

n. 회전, 소용돌이, 소란

to spin or rotate quickly in a circle

[a] whirly 소용돌이 치는, 빙빙 도는

[syn] whir, swirl, turn

See if you can make this top whirl for longer than I have.

My head was in a complete whirl and I had no idea what was going on.

24 **crave** [kreiv]

v. 열망하다, 간청하다

to desire something strongly

craving [n] 갈망 [a] 갈망[열망]하는 [ad] cravingly 갈망[간청]하듯이

[syn] solicit, implore

The boy craved love and attention from his parents more than anything else.

25 **disclose** [disklóuz]

v. 폭로하다, 드러내다

to make known or reveal

[n] disclosure 발각, 폭로

[syn] unveil, divulge, uncover [ant] conceal, hide

The teacher disclosed some of the contents of the test.

---

20 이 사진은 산림 벌채에 의해 얼마나 많은 토양이 파괴되는지 보여준다. 21 그의 괴롭힘에 맞서지 않는 한 그는 그가 할 수 있는 모든 방법으로 널 괴롭힐 것이다. 22 그 사고로 그 남자의 두 다리는 평생 불구가 되었다. 내 할머니는 전쟁 기간 동안에 겪은 경험으로 정신장애인이 되었다. 23 내가 이 뚜껑을 돌린 것보다 네가 더 오래 돌릴 수 있을지 지켜보자고. 내 머릿속이 너무나 복잡해서 무슨 일이 벌어지고 있는지 아무 생각이 없었어. 24 소년은 그 어떤 것보다도 부모님의 사랑과 관심을 원했다. 25 선생님은 테스트의 일부 내용을 공개했다.

Exercise

Word Check 각 단어의 뜻으로 알맞은 것을 찾아 연결하시오.

01 scrap　　　　　　　　ⓐ to long for something

02 agitate　　　　　　　ⓑ to decide not to use something

03 vogue　　　　　　　　ⓒ to stir up or shake something briskly

04 variable　　　　　　　ⓓ something that is likely to vary unpredictably

05 crave　　　　　　　　ⓔ a style of clothing or an appearance that is popular

Syn & Ant Check 주어진 단어의 동의어, 반의어를 골라 쓰시오.

urban	magnitude	powerful	practical	abandon
faint	conceal	corrode	disable	unattractive

06 dimension = _____　　　　11 pastoral ↔ _____

07 cripple = _____　　　　　 12 feeble ↔ _____

08 erode = _____　　　　　　13 vivid ↔ _____

09 virtual = _____　　　　　 14 irresistible ↔ _____

10 discard = _____　　　　　 15 disclose ↔ _____

Sentence Practice 문장을 읽고 빈칸에 알맞은 단어를 고르시오.

16 It's difficult to find components that are _____ with an old camera model.

　ⓐ feeble　　　　　　ⓑ virtual　　　　　　ⓒ compatible　　　　　ⓓ neutral

17 International sports events feature _____ referees to prevent biased or partisan decisions.

　ⓐ neutral　　　　　　ⓑ vivid　　　　　　　ⓒ feeble　　　　　　ⓓ virtual

18 That anonymous caller continued to _____ me until I registered a complaint.

　ⓐ crave　　　　　　　ⓑ cripple　　　　　　ⓒ whirl　　　　　　　ⓓ harass

19 The international retail _____ recently entered the European market in a big way.

　ⓐ parasite　　　　　　ⓑ conglomerate　　　ⓒ vogue　　　　　　　ⓓ dimension

20 She _____ me that my daughter will be in safe hands at the kindergarten.

　ⓐ hauls　　　　　　　ⓑ discards　　　　　　ⓒ alters　　　　　　　ⓓ assures

Day 22

01 ecstasy [ékstəsi]
n. 황홀경, 환희

a feeling of extreme happiness or joy

[a] ecstatic 희열에 넘친, 황홀한   [ad] ecstatically 도취하여, 무아지경으로

[syn] rapture, delight, bliss   [ant] depression, gloom, melancholy

The passengers looked on in ecstasy as the enormous whale swam near the boat.

02 antidote [ǽntidòut]
n. 해독제

a remedy to counteract something, especially poison

[a] antidotal 해독(제)의

[syn] counterpoison   [ant] poison, venom

The researcher found an antidote for the horrible poison.

03 jeopardy [dʒépərdi]
n. 위험

great danger or risk

[a] jeopardous 위험한   [v] jeopardize 위험에 빠뜨리다

[syn] endangerment, peril, hazard, insecurity   [ant] safety, security

The student's failure put his graduation in May in jeopardy.

04 sequence [síːkwəns]
n. 연속(물)

a series of something

[syn] succession, continuity

Fibonacci Numbers are a particular sequence of figures understood by students of advanced mathematics.

05 forgery [fɔ́ːrdʒəri]
n. 위조(물), 모조

the crime of illegally copying something or the object copied

[v] forge 위조하다

[syn] imitation, counterfeit, sham   [ant] original

The airport guard discovered that the man's passport was a very good forgery.

06 homicide [hámisàid]
n. 살인, 살인범

the crime of murder

[a] homicidal 살인(범)의   [ad] homicidally 살인(범)으로

[syn] killing, manslaughter, murderer

The local police think Mr. Parkinson's death was not a simple accident but rather a homicide.

---

01 승객들은 거대한 고래가 보트 근처에서 헤엄치자 도취되어 바라 보았다. 02 연구원은 치명적인 독 성분의 해독제를 찾아냈다. 03 낙제를 했기 때문에 학생의 5월에 있을 졸업이 위태로워 졌다. 04 Fibonacci 수열은 고등 수학반의 학생들만이 이해할 수 있는 숫자들의 특정한 연속이다. 05 공항 경비원들은 그 남자의 여권이 매우 정교하게 만들어진 위조 여권임을 알아냈다. 06 지역 경찰은 Parkinson 씨의 죽음이 단순한 사고가 아니라 타살에 의한 것이라고 생각하고 있다.

07 scheme [ski:m]

n. 계획, 설계
v. 계획하다, 음모를 꾸미다

a plan or a system, sometimes secret

[a] schemeless 계획이 없는, 무계획적인

[syn] project, design, plot

A government scheme was announced to root out real estate speculation.

He is constantly scheming to undermine his colleagues and get ahead of them.

08 disguise [disgáiz]

n. 변장, 가장
v. 변장시키다, 위장시키다

the act of changing the appearance in order to conceal identity

[a] disguised 변장한   [ad] disguisedly 변장하여

[syn] mask, dissemble, camouflage   [ant] revelation, expose, uncover

He left the country in disguise because the police were looking for him.

The teenager disguised herself as an older woman to get into the club.

09 sheer [ʃiər]

a. 순전한, 완전한
n. 비치는 얇은 천

not mixed with anything else

[n] sheerness 순전함   [ad] sheerly 순전히, 완전히

[syn] utter, unadulterated, complete, absolute

By sheer coincidence these practice questions were also asked on our exam.

My sister sewed a sheer over her dress for the dance.

10 weird [wiərd]

a. 기묘한, 초자연의

strange or supernatural

[ad] weirdly 초자연으로, 기묘하게

[syn] bizarre, uncanny, unusual   [ant] normal, regular, usual

My sister heard a weird noise in the garage last night.

11 wicked [wíkid]

a. 사악한, 나쁜

morally bad or wrong

[n] wickedness 사악   [ad] wickedly 사악하게

[syn] evil, immoral, depraved   [ant] moral, virtuous

In spite of being a victim of his wicked ways she never stopped trying to change him.

12 ferocious [fəróuʃəs]

a. 사나운, 잔인한

extremely fierce and violent

[n] ferocity 사나움, 야만   [ad] ferociously 사납게

[syn] savage, furious   [ant] mild, gentle, meek

Our ferocious guard dog is quite a tender and caring mother to her puppies.

---

07 부동산 투기를 근절시키기 위한 정부 계획안이 발표되었다. 그는 그의 동료들을 은밀히 해치고 그들보다 앞서 나가려는 계획을 끊임없이 세우고 있다. 08 경찰이 그를 찾고 있었기 때문에 그는 변장한 채로 그 나라를 떠났다. 10대 소녀는 클럽에 들어가려고 나이 들어 보이게 변장했다. 09 순전히 우연의 일치로 이 연습 문제가 우리의 시험에 나왔다. 내 여동생은 댄스파티를 위해 드레스에 얇은 천을 꿰맸다. 10 어젯밤 내 여동생은 차고에서 나는 이상한 소리를 들었다. 11 그녀는 그의 나쁜 행동의 피해자임에도 그를 바꾸려는 노력을 멈추지 않았다. 12 우리의 사나운 경비견은 자기 새끼들에게는 매우 다정하고 세심한 어미개이다.

13 attentive [əténtiv]
a. 경청하는, 주의 깊은

carefully watching and listening to someone

n attention 주의, 경청   v attend 주의해서 듣다, 경청하다

syn mindful, heedful, careful   ant unconcerned, inattentive

She has always been a diligent and attentive student in my class.

---

14 wither [wíðər]
v. 시들다

to become dried up or fade

a withering 시들게 하는   ad witheringly 시들게 하여

syn wilt, shrivel   ant revive, bloom, grow

The plants withered under the hot summer sun without any rain.

---

15 evaporate [ivǽpərèit]
v. 증발하다

to change into vapor or disappear like vapor

n evaporation 증발   a evaporative 증발의, 증발을 일으키는

syn vaporize, fume   ant dampen, drench, wet

The water in the small pond evaporated during the day.

---

16 detest [ditést]
v. 매우 싫어하다, 혐오하다

to hate something

n detestation 혐오, 증오   a detestable 몹시 미운, 증오하는

syn abhor, loathe, despise   ant adore, cherish

My boss detests workers who arrive late to work every day.

---

17 abduct [æbdʌ́kt]
v. 납치[유괴]하다

to take someone away by force

n abductor 유괴자   n abduction 유괴

syn kidnap   ant free, release, ransom

The two men abducted the little child and demanded money for his safe return.

---

18 hinder [híndər]
v. 방해하다, 가로막다

to prevent from progressing or accomplishing

n hindrance 방해, 장애   ad hinderingly 방해하여, 장애가 되게

syn obstruct, block, hamper, impede   ant encourage, facilitate

The storm hindered the planes from taking off on time this morning.

---

19 overestimate [òuvəréstəmèit]
v. 과대평가하다

to think too highly of something or someone

n overestimation 과대 평가

syn exaggerate, overvalue, overrate   ant underestimate, underrate

It is said that we must never overestimate our capabilities or underrate those of our rivals.

---

13 우리 반에서 그녀는 항상 부지런하고 세심한 학생이다. 14 비가 한 방울도 내리지 않자 식물들은 뜨거운 여름 태양 아래서 시들었다. 15 작은 연못에 있던 물은 낮 동안 증발하였다. 16 나의 사장님은 매일 회사에 지각하는 직원들을 매우 싫어한다. 17 두 사나이는 어린 아이를 납치한 뒤 그를 안전하게 돌려보내는 대가로 돈을 요구했다. 18 오늘 아침에 폭풍으로 인해 비행기가 제시간에 이륙하지 못했다. 19 우리의 능력을 과대평가하거나 라이벌의 능력을 과소평가하면 절대 안 된다고 한다.

20 impeach [impíːtʃ]
v. (공무원 등을) 탄핵하다

to charge someone with committing a crime against the state

n impeachment 탄핵, 고소 a impeachable 탄핵해야 할, 고소할 수 있는

syn denounce, indict, accuse ant free, acquit, absolve

The government impeached a high official during the legislature.

21 appraise [əpréiz]
v. 평가하다, 감정하다

to judge the value of something, often an official amount

n appraisal 평가, 감정 a appraising 평가하는

syn assess, evaluate, estimate, valuate

The painting will be appraised at the art gallery in the morning.
The land foreclosure team will appraise the property before it is put up for auction.

22 liberate [líbərèit]
v. 자유롭게 하다, 해방하다

to free someone from a difficult situation

n liberation 해방, 석방 a liberal 자유주의의, 자유로운

syn release, emancipate ant imprison, confine, enslave

The soldiers liberated the people from the dictator's oppression.
Many valiant lives were lost in the bid to liberate the city from the marauding raiders.

23 dazzle [dǽzl]
v. 눈부시게 하다, 놀라게 하다

to make unable to see by using a bright light

a dazzling 눈부신, 현혹시키는

syn blind, daze, amaze

The deer was dazzled by the headlights on our car and stood still in the middle of the road.

24 garnish [gáːrniʃ]
v. 장식하다, 꾸미다
n. (요리의) 고명, 장식, 장식물

to decorate something or someone

n garnishment 장식

syn embellish, adorn, ornament

The chef garnished the main dish with green vegetables.
The fruit garnish tasted very sweet with the dessert.

25 dispose [dispóuz]
v. 처리[처분]하다

to arrange things in a certain order

n disposal 처분, 처치 a disposable 처분할 수 있는

syn arrange, settle

Sam disposed of the bottles by taking them to the recycling bin.
Please dispose of these crates by loading them into the west warehouse.

---

20 정부는 주의회에서 고위 공무원들을 탄핵했다. 21 아침에 그 그림은 화랑에서 감정할 것이다. 토지 유질 처분 팀은 그 대지를 경매에 붙이기 전에 감정평가할 것이다. 22 군인들은 독재자의 탄압에서 사람들을 해방시켰다. 약탈을 일삼는 침입자들로부터 도시를 구하기 위해 용감한 많은 사람들이 목숨을 잃었다. 23 사슴은 우리 차의 헤드라이트 때문에 놀라 도로의 한가운데 가만히 서 있었다. 24 주방장은 녹황색 채소들로 주 요리를 장식했다. 디저트에 곁들인 과일은 매우 달콤했다. 25 Sam은 병을 재활용품 통에 넣어 처분했다. 이 나무틀을 서쪽 창고에 넣어서 처리해 주세요.

Exercise

Score / 20

Word Check | 각 단어의 뜻으로 알맞은 것을 찾아 연결하시오.

01	attentive		ⓐ	the illegal killing of someone
02	appraise		ⓑ	to change a liquid into vapor
03	antidote		ⓒ	paying attention to something or someone
04	evaporate		ⓓ	to estimate the value or price of something
05	homicide		ⓔ	a drug or substance that stops the effect of a poison

Syn & Ant Check | 주어진 단어의 동의어, 반의어를 골라 쓰시오.

original	succession	bizarre	gentle	adore
kidnap	confine	exaggerate	embellish	security

06 weird   = _____

07 overestimate = _____

08 abduct   = _____

09 garnish   = _____

10 sequence   = _____

11 forgery ↔ _____

12 jeopardy ↔ _____

13 detest ↔ _____

14 ferocious ↔ _____

15 liberate ↔ _____

Sentence Practice | 문장을 읽고 빈칸에 알맞은 단어를 고르시오.

16 Hunters use torches both to _____ small prey as well as keep large predators away.

   ⓐ dazzle   ⓑ abduct   ⓒ hinder   ⓓ overestimate

17 Taking advantage of people's ignorance or naivety is a _____ thing to do.

   ⓐ sheer   ⓑ weird   ⓒ attentive   ⓓ wicked

18 My sister is in a state of _____ after meeting her favorite pop star in person.

   ⓐ ecstasy   ⓑ homicide   ⓒ antidote   ⓓ forgery

19 Congress _____ the president for his alleged ties to organized crime.

   ⓐ detested   ⓑ disposed   ⓒ impeached   ⓓ liberated

20 The master criminal always used clever _____ to hide his identity and escape.

   ⓐ sequences   ⓑ disguises   ⓒ jeopardy   ⓓ forgeries

Day 23

01 impulse [ímpʌls]
n. 충동, 자극, 추진(력)

a sudden desire to do something
ⓐ impulsive 충동적인, 추진력이 있는
syn urge, motivation, drive

I'm so fat because I can't control my constant impulses to eat all the time.

02 friction [fríkʃən]
n. 마찰(력), 불화

the rubbing of one surface against another
ⓐ frictional 마찰(성)의　ⓥ frictionize 마찰을 일으키다
syn rubbing, attrition, confliction, clash

The friction between the hooked and looped surfaces of a Velcro strip helps to fasten them together.
The disagreement was a source of friction between the two teachers for many months.

03 obstacle [ábstəkl]
n. 장애(물)

something that makes it difficult to succeed for someone
syn hindrance, impediment, obstruction　ant help, aid, assist

The woman had to overcome the obstacle of being the first Korean astronaut.

04 sector [séktər]
n. 구역, 분야

a part of an area or a system
syn section, division, zone

The soldiers searched a different sector for the missing men.
Increased construction activity has ensured the cement sector's boom over the last quarter.

05 liquor [líkər]
n. 알코올 음료, 술

an alcoholic drink
ⓐ liquorly 독한 술의

The men drank too much liquor and became very noisy.

06 mania [méiniə]
n. 열광, 열중, ~광

intense desire or interest in something, sometimes a mental disorder
ⓝ maniac 미치광이, 광적인 애호가　ⓐ maniacal 광적인, 정신 이상의
syn passion, frenzy

Automobile companies are competing to exploit the mania for powerful and stylish cars.

01 항상 먹으려고 하는 나의 끊임없는 충동을 조절할 수 없기 때문에 나는 매우 뚱뚱하다. 02 벨크로 테이프의 갈고리 모양과 고리 모양 표면의 마찰이 그 둘을 서로 단단히 고정해 준다. 수개월 동안 의견 차이로 두 선생님 사이에 불화가 있었다. 03 그 여인은 한국 최초의 우주인이 되기 위해서 장애물을 극복해야만 했다. 04 군인들은 실종된 남자들을 찾기 위해 다른 지역을 수색했다. 건설 경기 성장으로 시멘트 분야가 호황을 누리고 있다. 05 남자들은 술을 많이 마시고는 굉장히 소란스러워졌다. 06 자동차 회사들은 자동차 매니아들에게 힘이 좋고 멋진 차를 선전하기 위해 경쟁하고 있다.

07 monument [mǽnjumənt]
n. 기념비[물]

a structure to remind people of an important person or event
ⓐ monumental 기념비의
syn memorial, remembrance, reminder

The Crazy Horse Memorial in the Black hills of South Dakota is a mountain monument to the Indian war hero named Crazy Horse.

08 suffrage [sʌ́fridʒ]
n. 투표권, 선거권

the right to vote
ⓝ suffragette 여성 참정권론자

At first, only a few people fought for women's suffrage in the United States.

09 regime [reiʒíːm]
n. 정치 제도, 정권

a political system or an administration
syn government, authorities

There has been strong condemnation of the brutal methods employed to bring this regime to power.

10 roar [rɔːr]
n. (맹수의) 포효, 고함소리
v. 으르렁거리다, 고함치다

a loud, deep, rumbling sound
ⓐ roaring 울부짖는, 고함치는
syn howl, cry, thunder, shout　ant silence, whisper

Above the roar of the crowd, she couldn't hear her son's screaming.
Wildlife experts say that male bears roar to convey distinct messages to rivals and mates.

11 surge [səːrdʒ]
n. 쇄도, 급 상승
v. 파도가 일다. 쇄도하다

a sudden strong increase
syn rush, deluge, flow, swell

A large surge of refugees arrived at the shelter after the hurricane.
We exited the street on seeing the crowds surge towards us in a carnival procession.

12 mortal [mɔ́ːrtl]
a. 죽을 운명의, 치명적인, 인간의
n. 죽게 마련인 것, 인간

destined to die
ⓝ mortality 죽음을 피할 수 없는 운명, 인간
syn fatal, deadly, lethal　ant immortal

We humans must realize that we are mortal and live our lives accordingly.
The character in the story had powers greater than an ordinary mortal.

---

07 South Dakota의 Black Hills에 있는 크레이지 호스 메모리얼은 성난 말이라고 불리는 인디언 전쟁 영웅을 기리는 기념비이다. 08 처음에는 미국에서 소수의 사람들만이 여성의 투표권을 위해 투쟁했다. 09 정권을 잡으려고 쓰인 잔인한 방법에 대해 강력한 비난이 있어 왔다. 10 군중의 아우성 때문에 그녀는 아들이 외치는 소리를 듣지 못했다. 야생동물 전문가들은 수컷 곰들이 적과 동료에게 서로 다른 메시지를 전달하기 위해 포효한다고 말한다. 11 허리케인이 물러간 후 엄청난 수의 이재민들이 보호소에 도착했다. 우리는 축제 행렬 속에서 우리쪽으로 밀려오는 군중들을 보고는 거리를 빠져 나왔다. 12 우리 인간은 죽음을 피할 수 없고 그에 순응해 살아가야 한다는 것을 깨달아야 한다. 그 이야기에 등장하는 인물은 보통 사람들이 가진 힘보다 더 강한 힘을 지녔다.

13 **hideous** [hídiəs]
a. 끔찍한, 소름끼치는

extremely ugly or unpleasant

syn grisly, appalling, horrific   ant attractive, pleasing

I could not believe that the hideous picture won an award at the arts fair.

14 **fragile** [frǽdʒəl]
a. 부서지기 쉬운, 약한

easily broken or damaged

n fragility 깨지기 쉬움

syn delicate, frail, breakable, brittle   ant strong, unbreakable

This room in the palace has some of the most fragile and graceful vases of the Ming Dynasty.

15 **fluid** [flúːid]
a. 유동적인, 변하기 쉬운
n. 유체, 액체

changing or moving like a liquid or gas

syn liquid, unstable, variable   ant unchangeable, solid

The plans for the new science class are still fluid.

The oily fluid spilled onto the new garage floor.

16 **recall** [rikɔ́ːl]
v. 상기하다, 생각해내다

to remember or bring back

a recallable 회상할 수 있는

syn recollect, evoke   ant forget

Sarah has the ability to recall what she has read.

17 **overthrow** [òuvərθróu]
v. (정부, 제도 등을) 전복시키다, 폐지하다

to remove a government by power

syn overturn, overpower, vanquish

The entire country came together to overthrow the general and establish democratic rule.

18 **shatter** [ʃǽtər]
v. 산산이 부수다, 파괴하다

to break into pieces suddenly

a shattering 파괴적인 a shattered 산산이 부서진

syn smash, burst, crack, ruin

The accident shattered his dream of competing in the next race.

19 **perceive** [pərsíːv]
v. 인식하다, 지각하다

to recognize or become aware of something

n perception 지각, 인식 a perceptive 지각력이 있는, 지각의

syn comprehend, notice, realize

Although it is cold, we don't perceive it as a reason not to go camping.

---

13 나는 그 소름끼치는 그림이 예술전에서 수상을 했다는 사실을 믿을 수 없었다. 14 궁전의 이 방에는 명조 시대의 우아하고 섬세한 꽃병이 몇 개 전시되어 있다. 15 새 과학 수업에 대한 계획은 여전히 유동적이다. 유성액체가 새로 지은 창고 바닥에 엎질러졌다. 16 Sarah에게는 읽은 것을 회상할 수 있는 능력이 있다. 17 온 국민이 장관을 타도하고 민주주의 재정을 설립하기 위해 단결했다. 18 그 사고로 다음 경기에 출전하려던 그의 꿈이 산산이 부서졌다. 19 날씨가 춥긴 하지만, 우리는 이것을 캠핑을 가지 못하는 이유로 생각하지 않아.

20 oppress [əprés]
v. 압박하다, 억압하다

to treat people in an unfair or cruel way

[n] oppression 압박, 압제 [a] oppressive 압제적인

[syn] suppress [ant] uphold, encourage

The dictator oppressed the people of his country for thirty years.

The fear that I may have misjudged my colleagues continues to oppress my mind.

21 linger [líŋgər]
v. 꾸물거리다, 남아 있다

to stay or remain, sometimes in a leisurely manner

[a] lingering 질질 끄는, 망설이는 [ad] lingeringly 질질 끌면서, 망설이면서

[syn] tarry, persist, remain [ant] end

The smell of smoke lingered for hours after the fire was extinguished.

22 imitate [ímətèit]
v. 모방하다

to mimic or copy someone or something

[n] imitation 모조품, 모방 [a] imitative 모방의, 모사의

[syn] mock, simulate

The comedian imitated an actor from a famous movie.

23 summon [sʌ́mən]
v. (증인 등을) 소환하다, 소집하다

to call or notify someone to appear

[n] summons 소환, 소집

[syn] assemble, convene

The doctor was summoned to the hospital for an emergency.

The manager plans to summon us all to the conference room for an important meeting.

24 suspend [səspénd]
v. 매달다, 미루다, 중지하다

to hang up something

[n] suspension 매달리기, 미결 [a] suspensive 미결정의

[syn] postpone, discontinue, restrain, halt [ant] continue, proceed

A large number of lanterns were suspended on poles to illuminate the pathway.

The company suspended the shipment of computers until the order was corrected.

25 merely [míərli]
ad. 단지, 다만

only or no more than

[a] mere 단순한, 단지 ~한

[syn] only, solely, simply

This is not an order, but is merely a suggestion for the committee.

---

20 독재자는 30년 동안 국민들을 억압했다. 내가 동료를 잘못 판단했을지도 모른다는 두려움이 계속해서 내 마음을 짓눌렀다. 21 불이 꺼지고 몇 시간이 지나도 연기 냄새는 남아 있었다. 22 코메디언은 유명한 영화의 배우를 흉내냈다. 23 의사는 응급상황 때문에 병원에 호출되었다. 매니저는 중요한 회의를 위해 우리 모두를 회의실로 소집할 예정이다. 24 길을 비추는 많은 랜턴들이 기둥에 달려 있다. 회사는 주문이 정정될 때까지 컴퓨터 방송을 연기했다. 25 이것은 명령이 아니라 단지 위원회를 위한 제안일 뿐입니다.

Exercise

Word Check 각 단어의 뜻으로 알맞은 것을 찾아 연결하시오.

01 liquor   ⓐ a strong alcoholic drink

02 fragile   ⓑ likely to be broken easily

03 shatter   ⓒ to increase unexpectedly

04 summon   ⓓ to destroy something completely

05 surge   ⓔ to order someone to appear in a specific place

Syn & Ant Check 주어진 단어의 동의어, 반의어를 골라 쓰시오.

assist	memorial	howl	fatal	pleasing
unchangeable	forget	notice	end	solely

06 perceive = _____

07 monument = _____

08 merely = _____

09 mortal = _____

10 roar = _____

11 obstacle ↔ _____

12 linger ↔ _____

13 recall ↔ _____

14 hideous ↔ _____

15 fluid ↔ _____

Sentence Practice 문장을 읽고 빈칸에 알맞은 단어를 고르시오.

16 Individuals who do things on a(n) _____ are likely to regret them later.

   ⓐ friction   ⓑ obstacle   ⓒ impulse   ⓓ monument

17 Primates commonly _____ many kinds of human behaviors and actions.

   ⓐ recall   ⓑ summon   ⓒ surge   ⓓ imitate

18 It was only in the early part of the 20th Century that women were granted _____.

   ⓐ suffrage   ⓑ sector   ⓒ liquor   ⓓ regime

19 All citizens' rights and privileges are automatically _____ during a state of emergency.

   ⓐ perceived   ⓑ suspended   ⓒ roared   ⓓ shattered

20 The general is planning to _____ the elected government in an army coup tomorrow.

   ⓐ overthrow   ⓑ linger   ⓒ oppress   ⓓ summon

Day 24

01 incentive [inséntiv]
n. 자극, 동기, 장려금

a stimulus or motive to do something

ⓥ incentivize (보상금을 주어) 장려하다

syn spur, stimulation, encouragement   ant deterrent

The promise of a chocolate cake was enough incentive for my brother to finish all his chores.

02 motif [moutí:f]
n. 주제, 동기

a recurring idea or subject in a book, film, etc.

syn theme, motive

The motif of the play was easy to understand because of the title.

03 riot [ráiət]
n. 폭동, 반란
v. 폭동을 일으키다

a violent or wild disturbance by a large group of people

syn uprising, tumult, turmoil

The police had difficulty controlling the huge riot by the angry workers.
The people rioted in the streets because of the terrible living conditions.

04 revenue [révənjù:]
n. 세입, 총 수입

money earned or received by a company or government

syn income, earnings   ant expenditure

The company experienced a growth in revenue during the last three months.

05 plea [pli:]
n. 간청, 진술, 변론

an excuse or appeal

ⓥ plead 간청하다   ⓐ pleading 간청하는

syn appeal, request, justification

Peter responded instantly to our plea for extra funds and manpower.

06 revolt [rivóult]
n. 반란, 폭동
v. 반란[폭동]을 일으키다

a strong action against someone or something, often violent

ⓐ revolting 반항하는

syn uprising, revolution, insurrection, rebellion

The young man led a revolt against the evil ruler.
The people revolted after the king placed more taxes on them.

---

01 초콜릿 케이크를 주겠다고 한 약속이 동생에게 집안일을 끝내게 하는 충분한 동기가 되었다. 02 제목 덕분에 연극의 주제를 쉽게 이해할 수 있었다. 03 경찰이 화가 난 노동자들이 일으킨 거대한 폭동을 진압하는 데 어려움이 겪었다. 사람들은 지독한 생활 환경 때문에 거리에서 폭동을 일으켰다. 04 회사의 수익이 지난 3개월 동안 증가했다. 05 Peter는 우리의 추가 자금과 인력 요청에 즉시 응답했다. 06 그 청년은 사악한 통치자에 대항하여 폭동을 일으켰다. 왕이 더 많은 세금을 부과하자 사람들은 폭동을 일으켰다.

07 **surplus** [sə́:rplʌs]
n. 나머지, 잉여금
a. 나머지의, 과잉의

an amount of something that is more than is required or used
[syn] residue, extra, remainder, redundant [ant] shortage, insufficient

The company expects to increase a trade surplus of goods at the end of the year.

Please store the surplus food carefully so that we can either use it later or give it away.

08 **superficial** [sù:pərfíʃəl]
a. 표면의, 피상적인

relating to the surface of something
[n] superficies 표면, 외면 [n] superficiality 피상
[syn] external, apparent, surface [ant] deep, profound, inside

The lake teems with myriad forms of life under its superficial layer of ice.

This book offers a very superficial view of the topic and is not worth consulting.

09 **marvelous** [má:rvələs]
a. 놀라운, 믿기 어려운

extraordinary or splendid
[n] marvel 놀라운 일, 경이 [ad] marvelously 놀라울 만큼, 믿을 수 없을 만큼
[syn] fabulous, astonishing, amazing [ant] terrible, commonplace, ordinary

Our hotel room gave us a marvelous view of the placid and pristine lake below.

10 **synthetic** [sinθétik]
a. 인조의, 종합의, 합성의

artificial or not natural
[syn] man-made [ant] analytic, natural

We are proud to say that our products contain no synthetic colors or flavoring.

The company's scientists have created a synthetic vitamin tablet.

11 **stationary** [stéiʃənèri]
a. 움직이지 않는, 고정된

not moving and unchanging
[syn] fixed, stable, immobile [ant] moving, shifting

Residents grew suspicious of the stationary van on the street and called the police to investigate.

12 **subtle** [sʌ́tl]
a. 미묘한, 민감한

not easily noticed
[syn] delicate, elusive, impalpable [ant] obvious, distinct

The beautiful flowers had a subtle smell that seemed familiar to me.

13 **swift** [swift]
a. 빠른, 신속한

very fast
[n] swiftness 신속, 빠름 [ad] swiftly 재빨리, 즉각적으로
[syn] speedy, expeditious, fleet, rapid [ant] delayed, slow, sluggish

The school made a swift decision about their new science program.

---

07 회사는 올해 말 무역 흑자가 증가할 것이라고 전망하고 있다. 남은 음식을 잘 저장해서 나중에 우리가 사용하거나 다른 이에게 주도록 하자. 08 언 호수의 표면 아래에는 수많은 생물들로 가득하다. 그 주제에 대해 매우 피상적인 관점을 제공하고 있어 이 책은 참고할 가치가 없다. 09 우리의 호텔 방에서 잔잔하고 맑은 호수의 멋진 풍경을 볼 수 있었다. 10 저희 회사 제품에 화학 조미료와 인공 색소가 첨가되지 않았다는 것을 발표하게 되어 자랑스럽습니다. 회사의 과학자들은 종합 비타민 알약을 개발하였다. 11 거주자들은 길가에 정지된 밴을 의심하고 경찰에게 수사를 요청했다. 12 아름다운 꽃에서 내게 익숙한 미묘한 향기가 났다. 13 학교는 새로운 과학 프로그램을 위해 신속한 결정을 내렸다.

14 mutter [mʌ́tər]
v. 중얼거리다
n. 중얼거림, 불평

to speak unclearly

syn mumble, murmur   ant articulate

He muttered about the interesting number on the blackboard in class, today.

The boys heard a mutter from behind them in the dark room.

15 pierce [piərs]
v. 관통하다, 꿰뚫다

to make a hole in or through with a sharp object

ⓐ pierced 구멍이 뚫린   ⓐ piercing 꿰뚫는, 사무치는

syn penetrate

The creature's shrill sounds pierced my ears like a sharp knife.

Vera wants to pierce her ears so that she can wear earrings.

16 implant [implǽnt]
v. 심다, 꽂아 넣다, 깊이 새기다

to put or fix firmly, sometimes by an operation

ⓝ implantation 이식, 심어넣기

syn insert, root

Surgeons hope to implant a metal rod into Rick to provide support for his broken thigh bone.

The teacher implanted basic principles of mathematics in her young students.

17 lurk [lə:rk]
v. 숨다, 숨어 기다리다

to stay hidden as one ready to attack

ⓐ lurking 숨은, 잠복한

I grew tense at the sight of a stranger lurking in the shadow of the tree.

18 stroll [stroul]
v. 한가롭게 거닐다, 떠돌다
n. 산책

to walk in a slow, relaxed way

ⓐ strolling 유랑하는, 순회 공연하는

syn ramble, roam, amble

The man strolled through the forest and sang a happy tune.

Autumn is the best time to take a stroll through the streets.

19 recite [risàit]
v. 암송하다, 낭송하다

to give an account or say from memory

ⓝ recitation 설명, 이야기   ⓝ recital 암송, 낭송, 리사이틀

syn declaim

The children recited the letters of the English alphabet.

---

14 오늘 그는 수업중에 칠판에 적힌 흥미로운 숫자를 중얼거렸다. 소년들은 어두운 방에서 그들 뒤에서 중얼거리는 소리를 들었다. 15 동물들의 날카로운 소리가 내 귀를 예리한 칼로 찢는 것처럼 들렸다. Vera는 귀를 뚫어 귀걸이를 하고 싶었다. 16 외과 의사들은 Rick의 부러진 허벅지 뼈를 지탱하는 금속 나사못을 박기를 원하고 있다. 선생님은 어린 학생들에게 수학의 기본 법칙을 주입시켰다. 17 낯선 사람이 나무 그늘에 숨어 기다리는 것을 보고 내 가슴이 조마조마했다. 18 남자는 한가로이 숲을 거닐며 행복한 곡을 노래했다. 가을은 거리를 따라 산책하기에 가장 좋은 계절이다. 19 아이들은 영어 알파벳을 복창했다.

20 **stalk** [stɔ́ːk]
v. (사냥감 등에) 몰래 접근하다, 가만히 뒤를 밟다

to follow someone quietly as prey

ⓝ stalker 집요하게 남을 따라다니는 사람, 활보하는 사람

ⓢⓨⓝ pursue, haunt

We managed to capture footage of the cheetah cub as it stalked its prey.

21 **overlap** [òuvərlǽp]
v. 겹치다, 포개다

to cover part of something

ⓢⓨⓝ overlay, cover

Animals in the wild are known to fight for supremacy when their territories overlap.

22 **infer** [infə́ːr]
v. 추측하다, 추론하다

to conclude by reasoning from something known or assumed

ⓝ inference 추리, 추론, 추측 ⓐ inferable 추론할 수 있는

ⓢⓨⓝ assume, deduce, guess

The policeman inferred that the man had stolen the book from the bookstore.

23 **inflict** [inflíkt]
v. (벌을) 과하다, 고통을 가하다

to make someone suffer harm or damage

ⓝ infliction 고통, (고통 따위를) 가하기 ⓐ inflictive 고통을 주는, 고통의

ⓢⓨⓝ impose

The storm inflicted millions of dollars of damage on the state's agriculture.

24 **purge** [pəːrdʒ]
v. 정화하다, (더러움 등을) 제거하다
n. 정화, 제거

to cleanse or empty, especially of bad things

ⓝ purgation 정화 ⓐ purgation 깨끗하게 하는

ⓢⓨⓝ rid, cleanse, purify ⓐⓝⓣ defile

Castor oil is frequently used to purge the body of its toxins.

The nation experienced a terrible purge of intellectuals when the dictator became president.

25 **suppress** [səprés]
v. 억압하다, 진압하다, 금지하다

to stop or prevent someone from continuing, sometimes by force

ⓝ suppression 억압, 진압 ⓐ suppressive 억압하는, 은폐하는

ⓢⓨⓝ overpower, subdue, repress, quash

The government suppressed the truth about the plane's accident while it searched for the dangerous cargo.

---

20 우리는 치타 새끼가 먹이를 뒤쫓을 때 그 장면을 포착할 수 있었다. 21 야생 동물들은 자신들의 영토가 다른 동물과 겹치면 주권을 가지기 위해 싸우는 것으로 알려져 있다. 22 경찰관은 그 남자가 서점에서 책을 훔쳤다고 생각했다. 23 폭풍이 그 주의 농업에 수백만 달러의 손해를 입혔다. 24 아주까리 기름은 우리 몸의 독소를 제거하는 데 자주 사용된다. 독재자가 대통령이 되자 그 나라의 지식인들은 무차별 숙청되었다. 25 정부는 위험한 화물을 조사했을 뿐 비행기 사고의 진실을 덮어 두었다.

Exercise

Score / 20

Word Check 각 단어의 뜻으로 알맞은 것을 찾아 연결하시오.

01	marvelous	ⓐ	moving very fast
02	swift	ⓑ	wondering or astonishing
03	motif	ⓒ	to say something unclearly in a low voice
04	inflict	ⓓ	to make someone suffer something unpleasant
05	mutter	ⓔ	the idea or subject repeating in the book, film, etc.

Syn & Ant Check 주어진 단어의 동의어, 반의어를 골라 쓰시오.

deterrent	tumult	residue	profound	natural
shifting	ramble	declaim	defile	overpower

06	surplus	=		11	incentive	↔
07	riot	=		12	stationary	↔
08	stroll	=		13	synthetic	↔
09	suppress	=		14	superficial	↔
10	recite	=		15	purge	↔

Sentence Practice 문장을 읽고 빈칸에 알맞은 단어를 고르시오.

16 Our _____ from manufacturing operations have tripled in the past three years.

    ⓐ pleas   ⓑ surpluses   ⓒ riots   ⓓ revenues

17 The people took to the streets in open _____ against the repressive regime.

    ⓐ revolt   ⓑ incentive   ⓒ plea   ⓓ motif

18 The nuances of his performance are too _____ to be appreciated by a lay person.

    ⓐ synthetic   ⓑ stationary   ⓒ marvelous   ⓓ subtle

19 From the pile of newspapers outside the front door it was easy to _____ that the Robinsons were not home.

    ⓐ overlap   ⓑ infer   ⓒ implant   ⓓ stroll

20 The paper clip makes it possible to put documents together without _____ them.

    ⓐ lurking   ⓑ reciting   ⓒ piercing   ⓓ inflicting

🎧 01 **provision** [prəvíʒən]

n. 공급, 제공, (법) 조항

the act of providing something

syn supplying

The person in the next office is responsible for the provision of those services.

---

02 **mode** [moud]

n. 방법, 양식, 형태

a way of behaving, living or doing something

syn manner, mechanism, method, style

Despite his immense wealth Warren Buffet has adopted a frugal mode of life.

---

03 **shrine** [ʃrain]

n. 전당, 성지, 성당

a place related to a holy or famous person that people visit

syn altar, church, sanctuary

The dead movie star's home has become the man's shrine.

---

04 **moan** [moun]

n. 신음, 신음 소리
v. 신음하다, 한탄하다

a low, mournful sound of sorrow or pain

ⓐ moanful 구슬픈, 슬퍼하는

syn groan, grumble, lament

The ward was filled with the moans of wounded soldiers waiting for medical help.

The audience moaned because the movie was very poorly made.

---

05 **incline** [inklàin]

n. 경사, 기울기
v. (~하는) 경향이 있다, 기울다

a surface or land that slopes

ⓐ inclined 경사진, ~하는 경향이 있는

syn slope, gradient, slant, tilt

Our house is at the top of an incline and gives us a great view of the neighborhood.

The actor is not inclined to attend the award ceremony tonight.

---

06 **personnel** [pə̀ːrsənél]

n. (조직, 직장 등의) 총인원, 전 직원

people who work for a company

syn workers, staff, employees, workforce

Store personnel are asked to gather at the entrance to receive special instructions.

---

01 옆 사무실 직원이 그와 같은 서비스를 제공하는 업무를 맡고 있습니다. 02 Warren Buffet의 엄청난 재산이 있음에도 불구하고 검소한 삶의 방식을 받아들였다. 03 사망한 영화배우의 집은 사람들의 명소가 되었다. 04 수용소는 의료 손길을 기다리고 있는 부상을 당한 군인들의 신음소리로 가득했다. 어설프게 만들어진 영화를 두고 관객들이 불평했다. 05 우리집이 비탈길 위에 있어서 근처의 멋진 경관을 볼 수 있어. 그 배우는 오늘밤 시상식에 참가하고 싶지 않았다. 06 상점 직원들은 특별 교육을 받기 위해 입구 쪽으로 모이라고 요청 받았다.

07 murmur [mɔ́ːrmər]

n. 중얼거림, (옷·나뭇잎 등이) 스치는 소리

v. 중얼거리다

something that is said in a low and unclear tone

a murmurous 중얼거리는, 사각거리는

syn mumble, mutter   ant articulate

The man spoke in a deep murmur that no one could understand.

The stranger kept murmuring the same two words until he fell asleep.

08 theology [θiːɑ́lədʒi]

n. 신학

the study of God and religion

a theological 신학의

syn divinity

One needs to undergo years of intensive training study in theology before becoming a priest.

09 robust [roubʌ́st]

a. 튼튼한, 건강한

very strong and healthy

n robustness 건장함   ad robustly 억세게, 건장하게

syn sound, vigorous   ant feeble, frail

Despite his thin and lean figure he is a robust little fellow who can run 10 kilometers easily and lift heavy weights.

10 redundant [ridʌ́ndənt]

a. 여분의, 과다한, (표현이) 장황한

not necessary because something is more than needed or desired

n redundancy 여분, 과잉   ad redundantly 장황하게, 과다하게

syn extra, surplus, wordy   ant essential, necessary

The teacher said that he wrote too many redundant words in his article.

11 prudent [prúːdnt]

a. 신중한, 세심한, 분별 있는

careful and sensible

ad prudently 사려 깊게, 분별 있게

syn cautious, discreet   ant imprudent, careless

You can count on Dan to give you tips on prudent financial investment.

12 infinite [ínfənət]

a. 무한한, 끝없는

without specified limits

ad infinitely 무한히, 무수히

syn countless, measureless, immense   ant small, limited

The speaker had infinite patience with the man asking strange questions.

---

07 남자가 너무 심하게 중얼거려서 아무도 알아들을 수 없었다. 낯선 사람은 잠에 들 때까지 두 단어를 계속 중얼거렸다. 08 성직자가 되기 전에는 수년 동안 신학을 집중적으로 훈련 학습하는 과정을 견뎌야 한다. 09 비록 몸은 마르지만 그는 10km정도는 무리없이 뛰고 무거운 역기를 드는 작고 건장한 녀석이다. 10 선생님은 그의 기사에 불필요한 단어를 너무 많이 사용되었다고 말했다. 11 현명한 투자를 위해 당신에게 주는 Dan의 비결을 신뢰해도 됩니다. 12 연설자는 그 남자의 이상한 질문에 무한한 인내력을 보였다.

13 **rigid** [rídʒid]
a. 경직된, 단단한, 완고한

stiff or difficult to change

[syn] inflexible, firm, determined   [ant] flexible, elastic, lax

Sometimes it is the younger generation that is more rigid and conservative about issues than the older one.

14 **symmetrical** [simétrikəl]
a. 대칭적인, 균형이 잡힌

having an exact similarity between two parts

[n] symmetry 대칭, 균형

[syn] balanced   [ant] unbalanced, unsymmetrical

The diameter of a circle divides it into two symmetrical parts.

15 **submissive** [səbmísiv]
a. 복종하는, 순종적인

always willing to obey someone

[n] submission 복종, 유순   [ad] submissively 복종하게, 유순하게

[syn] compliant, amenable, obedient   [ant] disobedient, obstinate

Tanya has good friends who do not exploit her naturally submissive and obliging nature.

16 **subtract** [səbtrǽkt]
v. 공제하다, 빼다

to take one number or an amount from another

[n] subtraction 빼기, 감하기   [a] subtractive 감하는, 공제하는

[syn] deduct   [ant] add

I use small objects like marbles to teach young children how to subtract one number from another.

17 **propel** [prəpél]
v. 추진하다, 나아가게 하다

to push something forward or make something happen

[n] propeller 추진기, (비행기의) 프로펠러, 추진자

[syn] impel, drive

A mixture of solid and liquid fuel propels the rocket through the atmosphere and into space.

18 **muse** [mjuːz]
v. 묵상[명상]하다, 숙고하다

to think or meditate about something

[syn] ponder, reflect

My hectic schedule leaves me with little time to muse over my life or my work.

19 **reap** [riːp]
v. (농작물을) 수확하다, (성과 등을) 거두다

to cut or gather grain, corn, etc.

[syn] collect, harvest, gain

The students reaped the rewards of all their hard work on the mathematics project.

---

13 어떤 문제에 있어서는 때때로 젊은 세대들이 구세대들 보다 더 완고하고 보수적이다. 14 지름은 원을 두 개의 대칭적인 부분으로 나눈다. 15 Tanya에게는 그녀의 순종적이고 친절한 성격을 악용하지 않는 좋은 친구들이 있다. 16 나는 작은 공깃돌 같은 물건들을 이용하여 하나의 숫자에서 다른 숫자를 빼는 방법을 아이들에게 가르친다. 17 고체와 액체의 혼합 연료가 로켓이 대기를 통과해 우주로 나아가게 한다. 18 바쁜 스케줄 때문에 나의 삶과 일에 대해 명상할 시간이 거의 없다. 19 학생들은 수학 프로젝트에 열심히 한 결과로 상을 받았다.

20 **poke** [pouk]
v. 찌르다, 쑤시다
n. 찌르기, 쑤시기

to push a pointed object at or into something

[syn] jab, stab, stick

The children poked their heads into the room to see if any presents were under the Christmas tree.
The child accidentally received a poke in the eye from someone's elbow during the fight.

21 **startle** [stá:rtl]
v. 깜짝 놀라게 하다

to surprise or frighten someone or something slightly

[a] startling 깜짝 놀라게 하는

[syn] shock, astonish, scare

The sudden light startled the children in the dark movie theater.

22 **eradicate** [irǽdəkèit]
v. 근절하다, 뿌리뽑다

to remove or destroy something completely

[n] eradication 근절, 박멸 [a] eradicative 근절시키는

[syn] uproot, exterminate, eliminate [ant] create, generate

Eradicating disease throughout Africa is the goal of the group "Doctors Without Borders."

23 **outlaw** [áutlɔ̀:]
v. 무법자로 선언하다, 비합법화하다
n. 무법자, 법의 보호를 박탈당한 사람

to make something illegal

[n] outlawry 비합법화, 무법

[syn] proscribe, illegalize [ant] legalize, legitimate

The government outlawed smoking in public buildings several years ago.
Citizens are being asked to help the FBI in the search for the outlaw.

24 **rewind** [ri:wáind]
v. 되감다, 다시 감다
n. 되감기

to wind again

[syn] reverse [ant] fast forward

I'd like you to rewind the VCR to the beginning so I can watch the movie's first scenes again.
My brother pushed the rewind button on the video player after we watched the video.

25 **commemorate** [kəmémərèit]
v. 기념하다

to remember something with a ceremony, etc.

[n] commemoration 기념, 축하

[syn] memorialize

These celebrations commemorate the victory of Korean forces over Japanese invaders.

---

20 아이들은 크리스마스트리 아래에 선물이 있는지 보려고 방 안으로 머리를 내밀었다. 싸움 도중에 실수로 누군가가 팔꿈치로 아이의 눈을 찔렀다. 21 갑자기 비친 빛 때문에 어두운 극장 안에 있던 아이들이 깜짝 놀랐다. 22 아프리카의 질병을 근절시키는 것이 "Doctors Without Borders" 그룹의 목표이다. 23 정부는 수년 전 공공 건물에서의 흡연을 비합법화 했다. 시민들은 상습범을 찾는 데 FBI를 도와달라는 요청을 받았다. 24 나는 VCR을 맨 처음으로 돌려서 첫 장면을 다시 보고 싶다. 우리가 비디오를 본 후에 내 남동생은 비디오의 되감기 버튼을 눌렀다. 25 이 의식은 일본 침략자들로부터 이루어낸 한국 군대의 승리를 기념한다.

Exercise

Word Check 각 단어의 뜻으로 알맞은 것을 찾아 연결하시오.

01 muse
02 moan
03 commemorate
04 theology
05 submissive

ⓐ to consider something carefully
ⓑ to honor something by a celebration
ⓒ the field of study of religion and religious belief
ⓓ to make a low and mournful sound of grief or pain
ⓔ inclined to do what one is told to do by someone

Syn & Ant Check 주어진 단어의 동의어, 반의어를 골라 쓰시오.

supplying	mumble	harvest	astonish	necessary
careless	flexible	add	reverse	unbalanced

06 startle   = _____
07 reap   = _____
08 provision   = _____
09 rewind   = _____
10 murmur   = _____

11 redundant   ↔ _____
12 rigid   ↔ _____
13 symmetrical ↔ _____
14 prudent   ↔ _____
15 subtract   ↔ _____

Sentence Practice 문장을 읽고 빈칸에 알맞은 단어를 고르시오.

16 Poor health continues to trouble a world that still cannot _____ smallpox.
ⓐ eradicate   ⓑ propel   ⓒ subtract   ⓓ muse

17 We are yet to discover the _____ secrets of our planet and the wonders of life on it.
ⓐ rigid   ⓑ infinite   ⓒ robust   ⓓ prudent

18 Ancient Sparta was famous for its frugal and austere _____ of life.
ⓐ shrine   ⓑ mode   ⓒ moan   ⓓ incline

19 All _____ are asked to report to the conference room for an important meeting.
ⓐ personnel   ⓑ murmurs   ⓒ provision   ⓓ rewinds

20 Although poaching has been internationally _____ it continues to flourish in secret.
ⓐ poked   ⓑ startled   ⓒ outlawed   ⓓ reaped

✛ single

mono : **mono**poly 독점, **mono**valent 1가 염색체, **mono**gamy 일부일처제
In some countries Cigarette production is a government monopoly.
몇몇 나라에서 국가가 담배 생산을 독점한다.

uni : **uni**que 유일한, **uni**form 균일한, **uni**on 결합
No one has same genetic information, and every individual is unique.
누구도 동일한 유전자 정보를 가진 사람은 없으며 개개인은 모두 독특하다.

sol : **sol**itary 외로운, **sol**oistic 독창자의, **sol**e 혼자서, 단독으로
Thoreau led a solitary life in the woods and *Walden, or life in the woods* is his famous book.
Thoreau는 숲 속에서 고독한 삶을 살았고 'Walden, or life in the woods'는 그의 유명한 작품이다.

✛ many

multi : **multi**ply 증가시키다, **multi**tude 다수, **multi**ple 다수의
The inflammation of the intestines germs multiply rapidly in hot weather.
장염균은 더운 날씨에 빠르게 증식한다.

poly : **poly**gon 다각형, **poly**acid 다중산, **poly**gamy 일부다처제
In a regular polygon the sum of interior angles increases regularly.
정다각형에서 내각의 합은 일정하게 증가한다.

✛ dec(a)(10), cen(100)

decimal 십진법의, **dec**agon 10각형, **Dec**ember 12월, 그리스 10번째 달
century 100년, **cen**tillion 10의 303승
The decimal numeral system has ten as its base.
십진법 수 체계는 숫자 10을 기본으로 한다.

품사를 변화시키는 Prefix

en- : 명사, 형용사, 동사를 동사로 만드는 동사형 접두사
· 명사 → 동사 **en**danger 위험에 빠트리다, **en**trance 끌어 넣다
· 형용사 → 동사 **en**able 가능하게 하다, **en**large 증가시키다, **en**dear 사랑받게 하다
· 동사 → 동사 **en**lighten 계몽하다, **en**fold ~를 접다

be- : 명사를 동사로 만드는 동사형 접두사
befriend ~의 친구가 되다, **be**little 얕보다, **be**fit ~에 적합하다

Review test Day 21 ~ Day 25

A 영어 풀이에 알맞은 단어를 보기에서 찾아 쓰시오.

neutral	overestimate	mania	stalk	redundant

01 not necessary _____

02 a strong desire for something _____

03 to judge something more than its value _____

04 to follow or approach someone secretly _____

05 taking neither side in an argument or war _____

B 문장을 읽고 문맥에 적절한 단어를 고르시오.

06 Experts have already arrived and will soon (appraise/overestimate) the current financial situation.

07 The ends of the paper should (garnish/overlap) to ensure that the gift is properly wrapped.

08 We will (alter/dispose) this item to meet the client's specifications.

09 Agreeing to negotiations is more (prudent/rigid) than confronting the workers' union at this time.

C ▨▨▨▨ 표시된 부분과 뜻이 가장 가까운 것을 고르시오.

10 Beth fought the impulse to run off the stage and stayed on to complete her talk.

ⓐ paradigm   ⓑ fraction   ⓒ urge   ⓓ mode

11 This plane is propelled by powerful engines that have advanced technological features.

ⓐ whirled   ⓑ impelled   ⓒ assured   ⓓ shattered

12 It is too early to disclose the details of the accord being drawn up between the two countries.

ⓐ divulge   ⓑ overthrow   ⓒ impeach   ⓓ summon

13 The mercy plea will now be forwarded to the president for his approval.

ⓐ appeal   ⓑ scheme   ⓒ monument   ⓓ regime

D 표시된 부분의 반대말로 가장 알맞은 것을 고르시오.

14 Despite occasional disagreements the Franks are quite a compatible couple.

ⓐ neutral   ⓑ sheer   ⓒ inappropriate   ⓓ synthetic

15 The subtle shades used in this painting add to its softness and appeal.

ⓐ superficial   ⓑ feeble   ⓒ redundant   ⓓ obvious

16 We have a long way to go before we eradicate sickness and attain high health standards worldwide.

ⓐ generate   ⓑ reap   ⓒ purge   ⓓ imitate

17 Her music is so sublime that it produces a sense of ecstasy in the listeners.

ⓐ vogue   ⓑ melancholy   ⓒ mania   ⓓ obstacle

E 주어진 단어를 알맞은 형태로 바꿔 빈칸에 쓰시오.

18 The refugees fled from the camp to escape the _____ of the authorities. (harass)

19 The man's _____ was sold for the same price as an original painting. (imitate)

20 I find shopping online is _____ preferable to going shopping. (infinite)

21 _____ is defined as the process by which water turns into vapor. (evaporate)

F 빈칸에 알맞은 단어를 보기에서 찾아 쓰시오. (필요한 경우 형태를 바꾸시오.)

suffrage	theology	garnish	ferocious	startle
monument	recall	shrine	vivid	commemorate

22 영국의 York 시는 중세 시대의 아름다운 기념비가 많은 곳으로 잘 알려져 있다.

→ The English city of York is known for its large number of beautiful _____ from the medieval era.

23 David는 옷을 입는 특이한 취향과 괴상한 유머로 친구들을 계속해서 놀라게 한다.

→David continues to _____ friends with his weird sense of humor and odd taste in clothes.

24 이 성지가 소박하고 우아했기 때문에 내 기억 속에 생생하게 남아 있을 것이다.

→ This _____ will always remain _____ in my memory for its simplicity and grace.

25 우리는 전쟁에서 목숨을 잃은 용감한 군인들을 기리기 위해 모였습니다.

→ We are gathered to _____ the valiant soldiers who lost their lives in the war.

Accumulative test Day 1 ~ Day 25

A	B	C	D
120~101	100~81	80~61	60 이하

➤ 영어를 우리말로 옮기시오.

01 assure

02 detest

03 random

04 purge

05 monument

06 abduct

07 revolt

08 impeach

09 startle

10 roar

11 inflict

12 whirl

13 personnel

14 eradicate

15 liquor

16 outlaw

17 riot

18 conglomerate

19 scheme

20 suspend

21 attentive

22 redundant

23 irresistible

24 oppress

25 commemorate

26 overthrow

27 symmetrical

28 stationary

29 propel

30 recite

31 surplus

32 animate

33 agitate

34 overestimate

35 compatible

36 regime

37 parasite

38 monitor

39 evaporate

40 appraise

41 cripple

42 nasty

43 linger

44 sheer

45 scrap

46 jeopardy

47 theology

48 plea

49 friction

50 liberate

51 virtual

52 variable

53 wicked

54 lurk

55 summon

56 shatter

57 suppress

58 marvelous

59 provision

60 fluid

61 사나운, 잔인한		91 추진(력), 충동	
62 세입, 총 수입		92 살인, 살인범	
63 처리[처분]하다		93 자극, 장려금	
64 쇄도[급증]하다		94 죽을 운명의	
65 위조(물), 모조		95 소름끼치는	
66 피상적인		96 묵상[명상]하다	
67 생각해내다		97 간청[열망]하다	
68 시들다		98 가로막다	
69 변장시키다		99 연속(물)	
70 부서지기 쉬운		100 치수, 넓이	
71 분별 있는		101 튼튼한, 건장한	
72 구역, 분야		102 불매 운동	
73 변경하다, 바꾸다		103 폭로하다	
74 한가롭게 거닐다		104 미묘한, 민감한	
75 인조의, 종합의		105 전원 생활의	
76 공제하다, 빼다		106 기묘한	
77 모범, 실례		107 무한한, 끝없는	
78 인식[지각]하다		108 되감다	
79 끌어당기다		109 섬유	
80 투표권, 선거권		110 연약한, 허약한	
81 모방하다		111 포기하다, 버리다	
82 중얼거리다		112 단지, 다만	
83 빠른, 신속한		113 겹치다, 포개다	
84 찌르다, 쑤시다		114 부식시키다	
85 생생한, 선명한		115 중립의, 공평한	
86 추측[추론]하다		116 수확하다	
87 눈 부시게 하다		117 경멸, 모욕	
88 경직된, 단단한		118 복종하는	
89 괴롭히다		119 장식하다	
90 해독제		120 황홀경, 환희	

Appendices 부록

INDEX

filthy	13	groan	84	infuse	51
fiscal	114	gross	33	inhabit	98
flee	29	grumble	121	initiate	94
fling	25			inquire	25
fluctuate	20			insane	129
fluid	152			insert	130

liquor	150
litter	84
lurk	157

M

magnetic	77
magnificent	13
magnify	99
malfunction	108
mania	150
margin	54
marvelous	156
mediate	79
merchandise	32
merely	153
merge	84
metropolis	64
mighty	129
minimize	47
mischievous	28
mislead	56
moan	160
mob	91
mode	160
modify	15
mold	116
monarch	91
monitor	109
monument	151
morale	81
mortal	151
mortgage	123
motif	155
mount	57
multitude	108
mumble	82
murmur	161
muse	162

| mutate | 34 |
| mutter | 157 |

N

namely	84
nasty	120
neutral	141
norm	27
nourish	29
numb	92

O

oath	113
obese	13
obscure	124
obsess	56
obstacle	150
omit	98
oppress	153
optimal	50
ornament	109
outburst	23
outlaw	163
outlet	113
outlive	79
outskirts	87
overestimate	147
overlap	158
override	35
oversee	25
overthrow	152

P

paradigm	140
paradox	12
paralyze	47
parasite	140

partial	24
particle	96
paste	57
pastoral	141
pasture	119
pat	23
pathetic	50
peasant	91
peep	76
penetrate	29
perceive	152
perplex	66
perseverance	87
personnel	160
petition	55
pierce	157
plausible	55
plea	155
plead	14
pledge	98
poke	163
polish	67
ponder	62
pragmatic	129
precaution	60
precede	46
predator	96
predominant	88
prehistoric	24
preoccupied	77
prescribe	62
proficient	49
profound	18
proliferate	115
prolong	94
prominent	130
prone	50
propaganda	12
propel	162

sturdy	45	timber	22	variable	142
submissive	162	tissue	44	vent	119
subtle	156	torture	93	venture	123
subtract	162	toss	79	venue	54
suck	56	toxic	49	versus	116
sufficient	45	trail	124	vibrant	124
suffocate	83	trait	77	vigorous	33
suffrage	151	tranquil	45	virtual	141
summon	153	transact	111	vivid	141
superficial	156	transmit	82	vocal	33
suppress	158	transparent	45	vogue	140
supreme	65	tremble	110	vulnerable	65
surge	151	tremor	17		
surpass	19	trifling	61		
surplus	156	trigger	99		
suspend	153	trim	61		
swell	35	tumble	29		
swift	156	turmoil	64		
symmetrical	162	tyrant	22		
synthetic	156				

W

wail	115
wander	19
warrant	115
weary	92
weird	146
whirl	143
wicked	146
withdraw	83
wither	147
withhold	130
withstand	20

T

tablet	59
tacit	33
tactic	87
tailor	30
tame	60
teem	19
temperament	81
temperate	130
terminate	57
testify	35
textile	54
theology	161
thesis	18
thrive	61
throb	27
thrust	66

U

ubiquitous	109
unanimous	50
undertake	78
untimely	82
uphold	35
upper	120
upright	50
urge	83
utensil	44
utmost	91
utter	77

V

vacuum	17
vague	109
vain	28
vanish	89

Z

zeal	87

ANSWERS

Day 1 | Exercise   p.16

Word Check

01 ⓔ	04 ⓑ
02 ⓐ	05 ⓓ
03 ⓒ	

Syn & Ant Check

06 nasty	11 obey
07 connotative	12 regularity
08 profit	13 deny
09 unearth	14 endow
10 alter	15 ordinary

Sentence Practice

16 ⓓ	19 ⓐ
17 ⓓ	20 ⓑ
18 ⓒ	

Day 2 | Exercise   p.21

Word check

01 ⓔ	04 ⓐ
02 ⓑ	05 ⓓ
03 ⓒ	

Syn & Ant Check

06 sufficient	11 lower
07 comprehension	12 promote
08 trembling	13 primary
09 stray	14 lack
10 exceed	15 surrender

Sentence Practice

16 ⓑ	19 ⓓ

17 ⓐ	20 ⓓ
18 ⓑ	

Day 3 | Exercise   p.26

Word check

01 ⓔ	04 ⓐ
02 ⓓ	05 ⓒ
03 ⓑ	

Syn & Ant Check

06 eruption	11 catch
07 apply	12 enhance
08 arduous	13 disengage
09 entreat	14 earthly
10 victim	15 veteran

Sentence Practice

16 ⓐ	19 ⓐ
17 ⓒ	20 ⓓ
18 ⓓ	

Day 4 | Exercise   p.31

Word check

01 ⓓ	04 ⓒ
02 ⓔ	05 ⓐ
03 ⓑ	

Syn & Ant Check

06 fling	11 add
07 imminent	12 well-behaved
08 criterion	13 bravery
09 concur	14 modest
10 lament	15 starve

Sentence Practice

16 ⓓ	19 ⓐ
17 ⓑ	20 ⓒ
18 ⓓ	

Day 5 | Exercise p.36

Word check

01 ⓔ	04 ⓑ
02 ⓒ	05 ⓐ
03 ⓓ	

Syn & Ant Check

06 brief	11 advantage
07 primary	12 reasonable
08 accomplish	13 refined
09 robust	14 prudent
10 combination	15 oppose

Sentence Practice

16 ⓓ	19 ⓐ
17 ⓓ	20 ⓒ
18 ⓒ	

Review Test Day 1 ~ Day 5 p.38

A

01 casualty	04 paradox
02 eloquent	05 withstand
03 advocate	

B

06 testify	08 encounter
07 coincide	09 replicating

C

10 ⓓ	12 ⓐ
11 ⓒ	13 ⓐ

D

14 ⓑ	16 ⓐ
15 ⓓ	17 ⓒ

E

18 partiality	20 normal
19 absurdity	21 adequacy

F

22 Prehistoric, excavated

23 agenda

24 vigorous

25 recruits

Accumulative Test Day 1 ~ Day 5 p.40

01 직면하다	61 paradox
02 지구 밖의, 외계인	62 agenda
03 빼다, 공제하다	63 vain
04 옹호[지지]하다	64 sake
05 분류하다	65 conjunction
06 일치, 조화	66 juvenile
07 기준, 표준	67 casualty
08 낙담시키다	68 tumble
09 딜레마, 진퇴 양난	69 bleak
10 능가하다	70 scope
11 설득력 있는, 웅변의	71 absurd
12 친밀한, 개인적인	72 excavate
13 지위를 낮추다	73 grind
14 달성하다, 이루다	74 authentic
15 (능력, 힘을) 쓰다	75 partial
16 가공하지 않은	76 corpse
17 겁, 비겁	77 drift

18 불결한, 더러운
19 평가하다
20 목재
21 억제[제지]하다
22 제2위의, 부차적인
23 올리다, 향상시키다
24 만나다, 직면하다
25 추방시키다
26 장대한, 훌륭한
27 증명하다
28 증대시키다
29 (집합적) 상품
30 풍부하다, 많다
31 진공(상태)
32 세게 던지다, 퍼붓다
33 돌연변이하다
34 변동하다
35 간결한, 간명한
36 도움이 되다
37 부풀다, 증가하다
38 (기뻐서) 방긋 웃다
39 신병, 신참자
40 충만하다, 가득 차다
41 내던지다
42 개정[수정]하다
43 왕국, 범위, 영역
44 비난[한탄]하다
45 비만의
46 힘든, 고된
47 적당한, 충분한
48 우위에 서다
49 변경[수정]하다
50 묻다, 조사하다
51 원기 왕성한, 힘찬
52 쌓다, 모으다
53 반항하다, 반역자
54 무모한, 부주의한

78 ratio
79 accelerate
80 compass
81 impending
82 shuffle
83 propaganda
84 thesis
85 garment
86 scribble
87 concur
88 impair
89 apprehension
90 replicate
91 creed
92 mischievous
93 deprive
94 profound
95 wander
96 throb
97 withstand
98 eerie
99 sanctuary
100 sneer
101 chaos
102 tyrant
103 penetrate
104 slaughter
105 outburst
106 implicit
107 foremost
108 tacit
109 confide
110 prehistoric
111 affirm
112 pat
113 uphold
114 tremor

55 담그다, 몰두시키다
56 비정상적인, 이상한
57 결점, 단점
58 묘사[표현]하다
59 정지하다
60 달아나다, 도망치다

115 entangle
116 oversee
117 gross
118 nourish
119 glaze
120 roam

Day 6 | Exercise   p. 48

Word check
01 ⓑ
02 ⓓ
03 ⓒ

04 ⓔ
05 ⓐ

Syn & Ant Check
06 placid
07 equipment
08 enliven
09 adequate
10 distinguish

11 feeble
12 rise
13 succeed
14 frown
15 maximize

Sentence Practice
16 ⓑ
17 ⓒ
18 ⓓ

19 ⓐ
20 ⓓ

Day 7 | Exercise   p. 53

Word check
01 ⓓ
02 ⓔ
03 ⓑ

04 ⓒ
05 ⓐ

Syn & Ant Check
06 truthful
07 battle

11 calm
12 release

08 authorize
09 inspire
10 piteous

13 nonpoisonous
14 corrupt
15 disclose

Sentence Practice

16 ⓐ
17 ⓐ
18 ⓑ

19 ⓒ
20 ⓑ

08 domesticated
09 among
10 weariness

13 increase
14 ambiguous
15 meager

Sentence Practice

16 ⓐ
17 ⓓ
18 ⓓ

19 ⓐ
20 ⓓ

Day 8 | Exercise   p.58

Word check

01 ⓒ
02 ⓓ
03 ⓐ

04 ⓔ
05 ⓑ

Syn & Ant Check

06 response
07 blank
08 adhere
09 apprehensible
10 predict

11 increase
12 pacify
13 commence
14 front
15 descend

Sentence Practice

16 ⓑ
17 ⓓ
18 ⓐ

19 ⓑ
20 ⓐ

Day 10 | Exercise   p.68

Word check

01 ⓐ
02 ⓒ
03 ⓔ

04 ⓑ
05 ⓓ

Syn & Ant Check

06 susceptible
07 worsen
08 pretentiousness
09 maintain
10 quotation

11 unconvincing
12 muddle
13 rush
14 inferior
15 burning

Sentence Practice

16 ⓑ
17 ⓓ
18 ⓐ

19 ⓒ
20 ⓑ

Day 9 | Exercise   p.63

Word check

01 ⓑ
02 ⓔ
03 ⓐ

04 ⓓ
05 ⓒ

Syn & Ant Check

06 neat
07 demonstration

11 entirety
12 congregate

Review Test Day 6 ~ Day 10   p.70

A

01 unanimous
02 blunder
03 paralyze

04 deteriorate
05 petition

B

06 exclaim
07 perplexed

08 obsessed
09 abundant

C

10 ⓓ	12 ⓒ
11 ⓑ	13 ⓐ

D

14 ⓐ	16 ⓓ
15 ⓑ	17 ⓒ

E

18 deformity	20 astounding
19 vulnerability	21 feasibility

F

22 accustomed	24 seal
23 feedback	25 aristocracy, seized

Accumulative Test Day 1 ~ Day 10 p.72

01 능숙한, 숙달한	61 tissue
02 (한 벌의) 기구, 장치	62 accustomed
03 당황케[혼란케] 하다	63 thrive
04 이해할 수 있는	64 trifling
05 일부, 조금	65 tame
06 명백히 하다	66 righteous
07 오르다	67 heredity
08 피로, 피곤	68 epilogue
09 튼튼한, 견고한	69 enrage
10 흩뿌리다	70 sermon
11 대회, 집회	71 tailor
12 상처[공격] 받기 쉬운	72 avalanche
13 깜짝 놀라게 하다	73 turmoil
14 악화시키다	74 sufficient
15 활주하다	75 shed
16 경향이 있는	76 ponder
17 불구로 만들다	77 puberty
18 동의[일치]하다	78 compelling
19 조심, 예방 조치	79 fuzzy
20 투명한	80 fraud
21 꽉 잡다, 이해하다	81 render
22 오도하다, 속이다	82 secrete
23 습격하다	83 tranquil
24 싸우다, 다투다	84 draft
25 노려보다	85 rear
26 몹시 추운, 냉랭한	86 lessen
27 야단법석하다	87 conceal
28 물러나다, 철회하다	88 prescribe
29 세심한, 양심적인	89 kinship
30 슬럼프, 폭락	90 graze
31 직물	91 toxic
32 풍부한, 많은	92 feasible
33 ~의 사이에, 한복판에	93 foretell
34 빨다, 흡수하다	94 upright
35 잠자는, 휴면 중인	95 altitude
36 의견을 달리하다	96 optimal
37 그럴듯한, 정말 같은	97 aristocracy
38 최고의, 최대의	98 steer
39 모임 장소	99 beam
40 만장일치의	100 utensil
41 영웅적 행위, 위업	101 stir
42 습관적인, 관습의	102 decrease
43 큰 실수	103 margin
44 숭배[경외]하다	104 trim
45 마비시키다	105 affectation
46 휴정[휴교, 휴회]하다	106 retain
47 간청하다	107 ruthless
48 떨다, 흔들거리다	108 discern
49 급파[발송]하다	109 petition
50 사로잡다, 괴롭히다	110 alley
51 최저[최소]로 하다	111 interpret
52 중심 도시	112 tablet
53 불어넣다, 고취하다	113 relay
54 끝내다, 종결시키다	114 seal
55 명백한	115 formulate
56 유행하는, 만연하는	116 thrust

57 편집[수집]하다
58 붙이다
59 권한[권능]을 부여하다
60 비행(술), 항공(술)

117 precede
118 polish
119 pathetic
120 exclaim

Sentence Practice
16 ⓒ
17 ⓐ
18 ⓑ
19 ⓐ
20 ⓓ

Day 11 | Exercise   p.80

Word check

01 ⓔ
02 ⓒ
03 ⓑ
04 ⓓ
05 ⓐ

Syn & Ant Check

06 enemy
07 interfere
08 furnish
09 standard
10 assure
11 dissuade
12 integrate
13 incomplete
14 advantage
15 abandon

Sentence Practice

16 ⓐ
17 ⓐ
18 ⓓ
19 ⓓ
20 ⓒ

Day 13 | Exercise   p.90

Word check

01 ⓔ
02 ⓒ
03 ⓐ
04 ⓑ
05 ⓓ

Syn & Ant Check

06 counterpart
07 passion
08 sacred
09 disperse
10 banish
11 minor
12 appear
13 ransom
14 denounce
15 impatience

Sentence Practice

16 ⓓ
17 ⓐ
18 ⓓ
19 ⓐ
20 ⓒ

Day 12 | Exercise   p.85

Word check

01 ⓓ
02 ⓒ
03 ⓐ
04 ⓑ
05 ⓔ

Syn & Ant Check

06 stifle
07 medium
08 rove
09 enhance
10 struggle
11 exterior
12 receive
13 articulate
14 forgive
15 dutifulness

Day 14 | Exercise   p.95

Word check

01 ⓔ
02 ⓐ
03 ⓒ
04 ⓑ
05 ⓓ

Syn & Ant Check

06 maximum
07 sovereign
08 paralyzed
09 avert
10 provoke
11 disapprove
12 energetic
13 detach
14 conclude
15 defense

Sentence Practice

16 ⓑ   19 ⓓ
17 ⓐ   20 ⓑ
18 ⓐ

Day 15 | Exercise   p.100

Word check

01 ⓑ   04 ⓔ
02 ⓒ   05 ⓓ
03 ⓐ

Syn & Ant Check

06 dwell   11 disagreement
07 carnivore   12 release
08 expand   13 profane
09 segregate   14 jeer
10 vow   15 include

Sentence Practice

16 ⓓ   19 ⓐ
17 ⓐ   20 ⓒ
18 ⓑ

Review Test   Day 11 ~ Day 15   p.102

A

01 numb   04 magnify
02 divine   05 criterion
03 strive

B

06 intimidate   08 entrust
07 seduce   09 dispels

C

10 ⓓ   12 ⓐ
11 ⓒ   13 ⓒ

D

14 ⓒ   16 ⓓ
15 ⓑ   17 ⓓ

E

18 predatory   20 intuitional
19 persevere   21 conspired

F

22 merged   24 relish
23 morale   25 pledge, avenge

Accumulative Test   Day 1 ~ Day 15   p.104

01 겁주다, 협박하다   61 attribute
02 유괴[납치]하다   62 tactic
03 그만두다, 철회하다   63 predator
04 연장하다   64 conspiracy
05 정당화하다   65 vocal
06 복제, 사본   66 engender
07 도래, 출현   67 foe
08 자석의, 매력이 있는   68 concord
09 싸우다, 투쟁하다   69 mumble
10 흐르지 않다, 침체하다   70 zeal
11 10진법의, 소수의   71 intuition
12 맡기다, 위임하다   72 drawback
13 구제자, 구제, 구원   73 pledge
14 설치하다, 갖추다   74 soar
15 인색한   75 snatch
16 방패로 막다, 보호하다   76 predominant
17 신성한, 성스러운   77 escort
18 특성, 특징   78 excursion
19 속이다, ~ 시키다   79 magnify
20 (가볍거나 만성적인)병   80 eligible
21 습격, 맹공격   81 relish
22 차별대우하다   82 rigorous
23 분할분, 월부   83 deem

24 조정[중재]하다	84 vanish
25 간청[탄원]하다	85 arouse
26 감각을 잃은, 마비된	86 immune
27 길을 잃다, 방황하다	87 peep
28 원자의	88 spur
29 부추기다, 유혹하다	89 grasp
30 완전한, 철저한	90 inhabit
31 재촉[격려]하다	91 suffocate
32 멸망, 비운	92 outskirts
33 보다 더 오래 살다	93 weary
34 군중, 폭도, 무리	94 coverage
35 위선(적 행위)	95 preoccupied
36 의견을 달리하다	96 convey
37 뒤집다, 반대로 하다	97 blaze
38 동의하다	98 morale
39 애매한, 확실치 않은	99 antibiotic
40 갈채, 환호	100 strive
41 확인하다, 알아내다	101 perseverance
42 반응, 피드백	102 temperament
43 복수를 하다	103 litter
44 약삭빠른, 빈틈없는	104 exile
45 자극[격려]하다	105 undertake
46 (가볍게) 던지다	106 proportion
47 군주	107 torture
48 신음하다, 신음 소리	108 utmost
49 침입하다	109 omit
50 (의무 등이) 면제된	110 divert
51 직무태만, 의무 불이행	111 salute
52 (사건 등을) 일으키다	112 intermediate
53 찬사, 칭찬	113 imprint
54 분리[차별]하다	114 spank
55 달라붙다, 매달리다	115 particle
56 신의, 신성한	116 namely
57 때 아닌, 시기 상조의	117 transmit
58 질식시키다	118 grant
59 합병하다	119 dispel
60 풍부하게 하다	120 criterion

Day 16 | Exercise p.112

Word check

01 ⓔ	04 ⓓ
02 ⓐ	05 ⓒ
03 ⓑ	

Syn & Ant Check

06 indefinite	11 unstuffy
07 shiver	12 stranger
08 decoration	13 ignite
09 supervisor	14 public
10 disprove	15 expand

Sentence Practice

16 ⓑ	19 ⓑ
17 ⓓ	20 ⓐ
18 ⓒ	

Day 17 | Exercise p.117

Word check

01 ⓓ	04 ⓒ
02 ⓐ	05 ⓑ
03 ⓔ	

Syn & Ant Check

06 forthright	11 dissent
07 convene	12 persist
08 magnificent	13 dwindle
09 against	14 concentrate
10 pledge	15 insincere

Sentence Practice

16 ⓒ	19 ⓐ
17 ⓒ	20 ⓒ
18 ⓓ	

Day 18 | Exercise p.122

Word check

01 ⓒ 04 ⓐ
02 ⓔ 05 ⓑ
03 ⓓ

Syn & Ant Check

06 tremendous 11 delightful
07 mutter 12 bent
08 wrath 13 unnerve
09 compensate 14 destitute
10 era 15 scrutiny

Sentence Practice

16 ⓒ 19 ⓓ
17 ⓓ 20 ⓑ
18 ⓐ

Day 20 | Exercise p.132

Word check

01 ⓔ 04 ⓓ
02 ⓒ 05 ⓐ
03 ⓑ

Syn & Ant Check

06 supremacy 11 disregard
07 unwilling 12 incapable
08 eminent 13 separate
09 regenerate 14 deliberate
10 interrupt 15 organize

Sentence Practice

16 ⓐ 19 ⓑ
17 ⓐ 20 ⓒ
18 ⓑ

Day 19 | Exercise p.127

Word check

01 ⓓ 04 ⓒ
02 ⓑ 05 ⓔ
03 ⓐ

Syn & Ant Check

06 contempt 11 flawlessness
07 benefit 12 distinct
08 trace 13 encourage
09 shudder 14 avert
10 sparkle 15 comply

Sentence Practice

16 ⓑ 19 ⓑ
17 ⓓ 20 ⓒ
18 ⓐ

Review Test Day 16 ~ Day 20 p.134

A

01 confidential 04 revitalize
02 boycott 05 catastrophe
03 dose

B

06 sneaked 08 bribes
07 embarked 09 intrigued

C

10 ⓒ 12 ⓑ
11 ⓓ 13 ⓓ

D

14 ⓐ 16 ⓐ
15 ⓑ 17 ⓓ

E

18 epochal   20 condemnation

19 compassionate   21 distraction

F

22 imposing   24 assemble

23 revised   25 mighty

Accumulative Test Day 1 ~ Day 20 p.136

01 보증하다   61 cordial
02 은혜를 베푸는 사람   62 assemble
03 당황[난처]하게 하다   63 immense
04 제 정신이 아닌, 미친 64 vague
05 핵심, 중요 부분, 속   65 specimen
06 바꾸다, 전환하다   66 glacier
07 (종교의) 교의   67 demeanor
08 승선[탑승]시키다   68 aboriginal
09 비난하다   69 candid
10 인상적인, 훌륭한   70 stunt
11 통합하다   71 anatomy
12 억제하다, 그만두다   72 pasture
13 흔적, (발)자국   73 resolute
14 연민, 동정   74 quiver
15 (특정) 시대, 시기   75 influx
16 아는 사람[사이]   76 multitude
17 매혹하다   77 refute
18 혼란에 빠뜨리다   78 competent
19 떨리다, 떨다   79 contract
20 봉건(제도)의   80 mortgage
21 순환하다, 돌다   81 revise
22 조언[의견]을 구하다   82 dip
23 반항하다   83 wail
24 구멍, 통풍구   84 withhold
25 특허장을 주다   85 bid
26 주권, 통치권   86 intercept

27 (틀에 넣어) 만들다   87 oath
28 동화시키다   88 evacuate
29 예견[예지]하다   89 assert
30 (액체 등의) 배출구   90 rejoice
31 풍족한, 부유한   91 abrupt
32 분명하지 않은, 애매한 92 fiscal
33 (주의를) 흐트러뜨리다 93 proliferate
34 여과기   94 ornament
35 고장, 오작동   95 bribe
36 안심시키다   96 spontaneous
37 끄다, 소멸시키다   97 derive
38 번쩍이다   98 enlighten
39 국외로 추방하다   99 inflate
40 대응하는 사람[것]   100 venture
41 마음 내키지 않는   101 glimpse
42 실제[실용]적인   102 prophet
43 대참사, 큰 재앙   103 aspire
44 흥미를 돋우다   104 reimburse
45 교활한, 간사한   105 blemish
46 충돌하다, 부딪히다   106 temperate
47 흔들리는, 진동하는   107 peasant
48 소송, 고소   108 versus
49 어디에나 존재하는   109 mighty
50 중재하다, 개입하다   110 capitalize
51 (약의 1회분) 복용량 111 prominent
52 안색, 외관   112 soak
53 직립한, 똑바로 선   113 snap
54 기울기, 비탈   114 confidential
55 명령[지시]하다   115 legislation
56 동의, 허가   116 transact
57 몰래 움직이다   117 scorn
58 삽입하다, 끼워 넣다   118 grumble
59 (생각 · 의견 등을) 품다 119 foreshadow
60 반짝반짝 빛나다   120 retrospect

Day 21 | Exercise p.144

Word check

01 ⓑ   04 ⓓ
02 ⓒ   05 ⓐ
03 ⓔ

Syn & Ant Check

06 magnitude   11 urban
07 disable   12 powerful
08 corrode   13 faint
09 practical   14 unattractive
10 abandon   15 conceal

Sentence Practice

16 ⓒ   19 ⓑ
17 ⓐ   20 ⓓ
18 ⓓ

Day 23 | Exercise p.154

Word check

01 ⓐ   04 ⓔ
02 ⓑ   05 ⓒ
03 ⓓ

Syn & Ant Check

06 notice   11 assist
07 memorial   12 end
08 solely   13 forget
09 fatal   14 pleasing
10 howl   15 unchangeable

Sentence Practice

16 ⓒ   19 ⓑ
17 ⓓ   20 ⓐ
18 ⓐ

Day 22 | Exercise p.149

Word check

01 ⓒ   04 ⓑ
02 ⓓ   05 ⓐ
03 ⓔ

Syn & Ant Check

06 bizarre   11 original
07 exaggerate   12 security
08 kidnap   13 adore
09 embellish   14 gentle
10 succession   15 confine

Sentence Practice

16 ⓐ   19 ⓒ
17 ⓓ   20 ⓑ
18 ⓐ

Day 24 | Exercise p.159

Word check

01 ⓑ   04 ⓓ
02 ⓐ   05 ⓒ
03 ⓔ

Syn & Ant Check

06 residue   11 deterrent
07 tumult   12 shifting
08 ramble   13 natural
09 overpower   14 profound
10 declaim   15 defile

Sentence Practice

16 ⓓ   19 ⓑ
17 ⓐ   20 ⓒ
18 ⓓ

Day 25 | Exercise   p.164

Word check
01 ⓐ   04 ⓒ
02 ⓓ   05 ⓔ
03 ⓑ

Syn & Ant Check
06 astonish   11 necessary
07 harvest   12 flexible
08 supplying   13 unbalanced
09 reverse   14 careless
10 mumble   15 add

Sentence Practice
16 ⓐ   19 ⓐ
17 ⓑ   20 ⓒ
18 ⓑ

Review Test   Day 21 ~ Day 25   p.166

A
01 redundant   04 stalk
02 mania   05 neutral
03 overestimate

B
06 appraise   08 alter
07 overlap   09 prudent

C
10 ⓒ   12 ⓐ
11 ⓑ   13 ⓐ

D
14 ⓒ   16 ⓐ
15 ⓓ   17 ⓑ

E
18 harassment   20 infinitely
19 imitation   21 Evaporation

F
22 monuments   24 shrine, vivid
23 startle   25 commemorate

Accumulative Test   Day 1 ~ Day 25   p.168

01 확실하게 하다   61 ferocious
02 매우 싫어하다   62 revenue
03 임의의, 무작위의   63 dispose
04 정화하다   64 surge
05 기념비[물]   65 forgery
06 납치[유괴]하다   66 superficial
07 반란, 폭동   67 recall
08 탄핵하다   68 wither
09 깜짝 놀라게 하다   69 disguise
10 포효   70 fragile
11 (벌을) 과하다   71 prudent
12 소용돌이치다   72 sector
13 총인원, 전직원   73 alter
14 근절하다, 뿌리뽑다   74 stroll
15 알코올 음료, 술   75 synthetic
16 비합법화하다   76 subtract
17 폭동, 반란   77 paradigm
18 복합 기업체   78 perceive
19 계획, 설계   79 haul
20 매달다, 미루다   80 suffrage
21 경청하는, 주의 깊은   81 imitate
22 여분의, 과다한   82 mutter
23 저항할 수 없는   83 swift
24 압박[억압]하다   84 poke
25 기념하다   85 vivid
26 전복시키다, 폐지하다   86 infer

27 대칭적인, 균형이 잡힌	87 dazzle
28 움직이지 않는	88 rigid
29 추진하다	89 harass
30 암송[낭송]하다	90 antidote
31 나머지, 여분	91 impulse
32 생명이 있는	92 homicide
33 흔들다, 휘젓다	93 incentive
34 과대평가하다	94 mortal
35 양립할 수 있는	95 hideous
36 정치제도, 정권	96 muse
37 기생충[균]	97 crave
38 감시자	98 hinder
39 증발하다	99 sequence
40 평가[감정]하다	100 dimension
41 불구가 되게 하다	101 robust
42 더러운, 불쾌한	102 boycott
43 꾸물거리다, 남아 있다	103 disclose
44 순전한, 완전한	104 subtle
45 작은 조각, 파편	105 pastoral
46 위험	106 weird
47 신학	107 infinite
48 간청, 탄원, 진술	108 rewind
49 마찰(력)	109 fiber
50 자유롭게 하다	110 feeble
51 사실상의, 실제의	111 discard
52 변수	112 merely
53 사악한, 나쁜	113 overlap
54 숨다, 숨어 기다리다	114 erode
55 소환[소집]하다	115 neutral
56 산산이 부수다	116 reap
57 억압[진압]하다	117 scorn
58 놀라운, 믿기 어려운	118 submissive
59 공급, 제공	119 garnish
60 유동적인, 변하기 쉬운	120 ecstasy

MEMO

MEMO

수준별 맞춤

Vocabulary 시리즈

**초등필수
영단어**
1-2, 3-4, 5-6 학년용

**This Is
Vocabulary**
입문, 초급, 중급, 고급,
수능완성, 어원편, 뉴텝스

**The
VOCA+**
완전 개정판 1~7

Grammar 시리즈

OK Grammar
Level 1~4

**초등필수
영문법+쓰기**
1, 2

**Grammar
공감**
Level 1~3

**Grammar
101**
Level 1~3

**도전 만점
중등 내신
서술형 1~4**

**Grammar
Bridge**
Level 1~3
개정판

그래머 캡처
1~2

The Grammar
with Workbook
Starter
Level 1~3

**This Is
Grammar**
초급 1·2
중급 1·2
고급 1·2

넥서스 영어 교재 시리즈

Reading 시리즈

**Reading
공감**
Level 1~3

**Reading
101**
Level 1~3

**THIS IS
READING**
1~4
전면 개정판

**Smart Reading
Basic**
Level 1~2
Smart Reading
Level 1~2

**구사일생
BOOK 1~2**

**구문독해 204
BOOK 1~2**

특단
어법어휘 모의고사
구문독해
독해유형

Listening 시리즈 / NEW TEPS 시리즈

**Listening
공감**
Level 1~3

**After School
Listening**
Level 1~3

The Listening
Level 1~4

**도전! 만점
중학 영어듣기
모의고사**
Level 1~3

**만점 적중
수능 듣기
모의고사**
20회 / 35회

**NEW TEPS
실전 300+
실전 400+
실전 500+**